WATERSHED MANAGEMENT
An Encyclopaedia

WATERSHED MANAGEMENT

An Encyclopaedia

R.S. KUROTHE
A.K. VISHWAKARMA
GOPAL KUMAR
BRAJENDRA

BIOTECH
2012
BIOTECH BOOKS®

ISBN 978-81-7622-247-1

Published by: **BIOTECH BOOKS®**
4762-63/23, Ansari Road, Darya Ganj,
New Delhi - 110 002
Phone: +91-011-23262132
E-mail: biotechbooks@yahoo.co.in

Printed at: **Chawla Offset Printers**
Delhi - 110 052

PRINTED IN INDIA

Preface

Watershed management is a subject that not only deals with agriculture development of a place but is a very comprehensive and complex subject that includes, engineering aspects, social science, agronomy, soil science, horticulture, forestry, animal sciences and other relevant subjects in such a synchronized way that a holistic approach is evolved which when applied in the field will result in overall development of the watershed in a participatory mode. When such a large number of subjects are involved a very large number of terms from these vast subjects are frequently used during execution of watershed in fields. Selective prominent terminologies from a vast amount of information on watershed management are collected and presented in this book. A large number of field functionaries are involved in execution of watershed such as state government departments, NGOs, students, scientists, forest departments and other agencies; they often need these terms for their practical purposes to interpret various terms by their correct meanings. A large number of books are available covering core theoretical aspects of watershed management, but this book is written with a view to meet the requirement of vast majority of people working in watershed for their day to day requirements in watershed management.

Authors

A

A horizon: It refers to the surface horizon of a mineral soil characterized by maximum biological activity or eluviations (removal of materials dissolved or suspended in water) or both.

Abatement: The process of minimizing pollution through recycling or waste management/treatment.

ABC soil: A soil having an A, B, and a C horizon in the profile.

Abiotic factors: Relating to non-living factors. Physical, chemical and other non-living components of the environment such as light, temperature, moisture, nutrients and other edaphic factors.

Abiotic stress: The stress caused by environmental factors such as drought or extreme heat or cold, not by biological factors.

Abrasion: Mechanical wearing down of earth's surface by material carried by water, ice or wind.

Absolute error: The difference between a measured value and the true or accepted value.

Absolute humidity: On volume basis it is the ratio of quantity of water in a particular volume of air. The most common units are grams per cubic meter.

Absolute transpiration: The rate of water that is transpired from a plant surface and is expressed as the average transpiration per hour, it can be determined experimentally and is expressed in mm/hour or mm/ day.

Absolute water requirement: This is the quantity of water in ha-cm per crop season absorbed by the crop together with the evaporation from the crop producing land. It includes the water used by evapo-transpiration and retained in plant body.

Absolute zero: The zero point on the absolute temperature scale; -273.15°C or 0° K; theoretically, the temperature at which molecular motion ceases.

Absorption: It is the process by which a substance is taken into and included within another substance (absorbed) *e.g.* absorption of water by a soil, absorption of nutrient by plant roots or through the leaf surface, taking in water dissolved minerals and other nutrients across cell membranes, entry of herbicide from the surface into the plant system.

AC soil: Soil with only A and C horizons without clearly developed B horizon.

Accelerated erosion: Erosion of soil at a rate higher than under natural conditions due to destruction of vegetative cover or some activity of man or animal like mining, overgrazing, excessive tree destruction, erosion inducing agricultural activities etc. Accelerated erosion takes place by the action of water, wind, gravity and glaciers.

Access tube- Small-diameter tube (typically about 50 mm) inserted through the soil root zone to provide passage of a neutron probe to determine the water content of soil at various depths.

Accreditation: Refers to procedure by which an authoritative body gives a formal recognition that a body or person is competent to carry out a specific task. The term is now used for monitoring organically-grown farm produce as well as organic fertilizers. The functions of such accreditation agencies include prescribing packages of practices for organic production in their respective schedule, laying down the production procedure, certification of produce etc. For example IFOAM (International Foundation of Organic Agriculture Movement) is an accreditation agency for organic farming and organically-produced farm produce.

Accretion: The accumulation of sediment by deposition often occurring along a shoreline or in a river delta.

Accumulation: The uptake of substances against a concentration gradient and hence an energy-requiring process, resulting in build-up or increase of one or more constituents in the soil/plant at a given position as a result of translocation. The build-up may be a residue due to the translocation of material out of the horizon or may be due to an addition of material. Usually refers to soluble substances and clay particles.

Accuracy assessment: Comparison of a classification with ground-truth data to evaluate how well the classification represents the real world.

Accuracy: How closely a measured value agrees with the correct value.

Acid drainage: Any drainage from mine workings, waste or tailings, with a low (acidic) pH.

Acid rain: Rain with a pH less than 5.6. Rain water containing excessive concentration of acidic compounds, primarily $N0_3^-$, $S0_4$ and H^+. This is common phenomenon in areas with high atmospheric pollution through industrial activity and vehicular exhaust.

Acid soil: A soil with a pH value less than 7.0 hence having more hydrogen (H^+) ions than hydroxyl (OH^-) ions in the soil solution. Acid soils range from slightly acid (pH 6.1-6.5) to extremely acid (pH below 4.5). Micronutrient availability, except in case of Mo is usually higher in acid soils than in alkaline soils. Very acid soils can be amended with calcitic or dolomitic limestone and calcium-rich industrial by-products such as sugar factory press mud, paper mill sludge etc.

Acid sulphate soil: These are soils that have within a 50 cm depth a pH below 3.5 to 4.0 that is directly or indirectly caused by sulphuric acid formed by the oxidation of pyrite (FeS_2) or of other reduced sulphur compounds. Potentially acid sulphate soils occur in tidal swamps. Apart from high salinity, their productivity is restricted due to factors such as iron and aluminium toxicities, deficiency of phosphorus etc. Found primarily in coastal, deltaic and estuarine areas of the humid tropics. Sometimes also called cat clays.

Acid-forming fertilizer: Refers to a fertilizer that leaves behind an acidic effect in the soil (reduces soil pH). Mostly such fertilizers which lack a metallic cation are acid forming. Their continuous use makes a soil acidic (lowers pH) and reduces soil quality and hence productivity. The excess acidity can be neutralized by lime application. This is generally of practical importance in case of nitrogenous fertilizers. Example: ammonium sulphate, ammonium chloride, anhydrous ammonia and urea.

Acidity of a base: The number of hydrogen atoms with which one molecule of a base reacts when it combines, *e.g.* NaOH is monoacid base; $Ca(OH)_2$ is a diacid base and $Cr(OH)_3$ is a triacid base.

Acidity potential: The amount of exchangeable hydrogen ion that can be rendered free or active in the soil solution by cation exchange. Usually expressed in milli equivalents per unit mass of soil.

Acidity: A measure of the capacity of a solution to neutralize bases

Acidoid: Inorganic and organic colloidal substances in soil. They behave as anions and are capable of adsorbing or reacting with cations.

Acre: It is a unit of measurement of land area, which is equivalent to 43,560 square feet or equivalent to 4,840 sq. yards or 0.4047 of a hectare. It is the traditional unit of measurement of land.

Acre foot of water: It is the amount of water that would cover an acre of land (43,560 square feet) to a depth of one foot, assuming no seepage, evaporation and run- off losses.

Acre inch: The volume of water necessary to cover one-acre (43,560 sq. feet) surface to a depth of one inch.

Acreage: The area of a piece of land measured in acres.

Activated carbon filter: A filter made of activated carbon that removes, taste, odour, added compounds and anions.

Activated sewage sludge: Refers to biologically active sewage sludge which has been obtained by repeated exposure of sewage to atmospheric oxygen, thus facilitating the growth of aerobic bacteria and other unicellular micro-organisms and in the process has been improved for use on land. Typical nutrient content of activated sewage sludge is 5.8% N, 3.2% P_2O_5 and 0.6% K_2O. It also contains lesser and variable amounts of secondary and micronutrients and toxic heavy metals.

Actual crop evapo-transpiration: The rate of evapo-transpiration equal to or less than potential evapo-transpiration as affected by the level of the available soil water, salinity, field size, or other causes expressed in mm/day.

Adaptability of crop: It is the crop's ability to survive and reproduce in diverse environments.

Adaptability: The ability to adapt to different environments by modifications in physiological responses.

Adaptation: The process of becoming suited to new or different environmental conditions or for particular functions. Example: the adaptation of *Rhizobium* to acidic or saline soil conditions.

Adiabatic lapse rate: It is the rate at which temperature changes as air rise or falls is called adiabatic lapse rate. The rate is constant for dry air and value near surface is 6.5°C per kilometer rise.

Adiabatic: A process in which heat does not enter or leave a system.

Adoption (technology): It is a process through which people start using a new technology. Adoption process includes five sequential steps *ie* awareness, assessment, acceptance, learning and usage. Adoption is considered full when appropriate and effective use of the technology is frequently demonstrated by user

Adsorption complex: Collection of various organic and inorganic substances in soil those are capable of adsorbing ions and molecules.

Adsorption isotherm: A graph of the quantity of a given chemical species bound to an adsorption complex, at fixed temperature, as a function of the concentration of the species in a solution that is in equilibrium with the complex. Called an isotherm only because adsorption experiments are done at constant temperature.

Adsorption: Process by which atoms, molecules, or ions are taken up and retained on the surfaces of solids by chemical or physical binding. Solid colloids adsorb large amounts of water. Gathering of herbicide molecules on the surface of soil colloidal particles (clay).

Advance curve: The curve to depict relationship between distances travelled by a advancing front of water and time in surface irrigation methods.

Advance phase (irrigation): It is the part of the total irrigation time during which water advances in over land flow surface from the upper end of the field to the lower end of the field.

Advance time: It is time taken by water to travel the length of an irrigation furrow/border/basin.

Advective energy: The energy developed as a result of horizontal heterogeneity in climatic parameters or the energy brought in an area through horizontal movement of winds.

Adventitious prop roots: Roots formed at the higher nodes above the soil surface.

Adventitious roots: Roots developing from the part of a plant other than roots, which are formed from nodes of the plant.

Adventitious: Structures arising from places other than the usual, for example, roots growing from leaves or buds develop at locations other than in leaf axils or shoot apices. Organs arising in unusual positions, as buds from roots.

Aeolian deposits: Fine sediments transported and deposited by wind; they include loess, dunes, desert sand and some volcanic ash.

Aeolian: Sediments transported and deposited by wind such as loess or desert sand.

Aeration (soil): The process by which air and other gases in the soil are renewed. The rate of soil aeration depends largely on the size and number of soil pores and on the amount of water in the soil to permit rapid aeration.

Aeration porosity: The proportion of the bulk volume of the soil that is filled with air when the moisture tension is at some specified value. The tension is usually specified in the range 40 to 100 cm of water.

Aerial photograph: A photograph of earth's surface taken with air borne equipment. Same as aerial photo or air photograph.

Aerobe: Group of organisms that grows best in the presence of free oxygen (under well-aerated conditions). Aerobic culture refers to microbes which are cultured in air (with the supply of oxygen). Example: *Rhizobium, Azotobacter*.

Aerobic: Any biological process that occurs in the presence of oxygen; also applies to organisms that require oxygen to survive.

Aerodynamically rough surface: A surface whose roughness elements are sufficiently large that the turbulent boundary layer reaches the surface.

Aerodynamically smooth surface: A surface whose roughness elements are sufficiently small to be entirely embedded in the laminar sub layer.

Aesthetics: Appeal or beauty of plants, animals, natural or improved areas etc. to viewers and their appreciation for the same.

Afforestation: Artificial establishment of forest trees by sowing or planting on land which was previously or recently not under forest.

Aggradation: Building up of a valley by deposition of sediment at the bed. A long term or geologic trend in sedimentation.

Aggregate: Soil particles held in a single cluster such as a clod, crumb, block or prism.

Aggregation: The cementing or binding together of several soil particles into a secondary unit, aggregate or granule. Soil aggregates are arranged to form soil peds, units of soil structure, classified by size, shape (platy, prismatic, columnar, angular, sub angular, blocky, granular) and grade (single-grain, massive, weak, moderate, strong). Water-stable aggregates are particularly important to soil structure.

Agric horizon: A mineral soil horizon in which clay, silt and humus derived from an overlying cultivated and fertilized layer have accumulated. The wormholes and illuvial clay, silt, and humus occupy at least 5% of the horizon by volume. The illuvial clay and humus occur as horizontal lamellae or fibers, or as coatings on ped surfaces or in wormholes.

Agri-chemical: Chemicals (fertilizers and pesticides) used in agricultural production.

Agricultural drainage: It is removal of excess water known as free or gravitational water from the surface or below the surface of farm land to create favourable condition for proper growth and development of the plant.

Agricultural drought: A condition where soil moisture and rainfall are inadequate during the growing season to support healthy crop growth to maturity and causes severe moisture stress and wilting to plants.

Agricultural ecosystem or agro-ecosystem: A complex system composed of the crops or animals in an area together with overall environment and as modified by management practices.

Agricultural ecotype: An ecotype adapted to certain agricultural practice(s).

Agricultural forest: Forests containing mixtures of tree crops, meadows, domestic animals, living fences (hedge and wind breaks), other perennial plants that produce food, fibre and chemicals.

Agricultural lime: A soil amendment consisting principally of calcium carbonate but including magnesium carbonate and is used to furnish calcium and magnesium as elements for the growth of plants and to neutralize soil acidity. Their usage is referred to as liming.

Agricultural meteorology: It is the applied branch of meteorology, which deals with the relationship between climates, weather and life and growth of the cultivated plants and animals.

Agricultural pollution: Liquid and solid wastes produced in farming such as run-off from pesticides, fertilizers, erosion due to cultivation, crop residues and animal manures as well as carcasses etc.

Agricultural production system: The whole structured set of plants, animals, and activities involved in agricultural production.

Agricultural statistics: A systematic and scientific method of collecting, organizing, summarizing, presenting and analyzing data generated from agricultural experiments as well as drawing valid conclusions and making reasonable decision on the basis of such analysis.

Agricultural system: A system with agricultural outputs and containing all the major components. Agricultural systems are organized to produce food and to meet other household goals through the management of available resources- whether owned, rented or jointly managed – within the existing social, economic and institutional environment. These encompass different farming systems, from smallholder farm-held to large scale systems publicly or privately managed.

Agricultural waste: Waste matter produced on a farm.

Agriculture: A human activity, primarily aimed at the production of food, fibre, fuel etc. by optimum use of terrestrial resources. It includes practice of cultivation, farming, tillage and horticulture; plant and animal production. Fundamental basis for agriculture is the miraculous process of photosynthesis, the many useful products synthesized by it and the fact that plants and animals (including humans) by and large have a common list of essential nutrients. Nature has endowed the soils with these nutrients, which support much of agricultural activity. The science of agriculture and its application includes many branches such as agronomy, plant breeding, soil science, horticulture etc. In addition, being an applied science, it interacts with most of the physical and biological sciences. Agriculture is now predominantly dependent on external nutrient additions to supplement soil fertility.

Agri-silviculture: It is the conscious and deliberate use of land for the concurrent production of agricultural and forest crops.

Agro-climate: Compilation of the average and extreme weather of an area as it affects agricultural cropping in that area.

Agroclimatic regions: The classification and grouping of different physical areas within the country based on climatic and edaphic factors into broadly homogeneous zones.

Agro-climatology: The study of those aspects of climate which influences agriculture development and crop production.

Agro-ecological zones: A land resource mapping unit, defined in terms of climate, land form and soils, and/or land cover, and having a specific range of potentials and constraints for land use. Agro-ecological zones are defined and delineated by FAO based on the average annual length of growing period for crops, which depends on, inter alia, precipitation and temperature. The length of growing period for these zones are: humid, greater than 270 days, moist subhumid, 180 to 269 days; dry subhumid, 120 to 179 days; semiarid, 60 to 119 days; arid, 0 to 59 days.

Agro-ecology: The study of the relationship of agricultural crops and environment.

Agro-ecosystem: The collection of physical, environmental, economic and social factors that affect a cropping enterprise.

Agro-forestry system: A land-use system in which woody perennials (trees, shrubs, palms, bamboos) are used on the same land management unit as agricultural crops (woody or not), animals or both, either in some form of spatial arrangement or temporal sequence. In agroforestry systems there are both ecological and economic interactions between the different components. 'Agroforestry' is a generic term for different types of systems, for example, agrosilvicultural system, silvipastoral system.

Agromet station: An agricultural meteorological station that provides either meteorological or biological data otherwise supplies data in establishing relation between weather and life of plants and animals.

Agro-meteorology: A science dealing with influence of climatologically conditions which have direct relation or relevance to agriculture.

Agronomic efficiency: Unit of crop produced per unit of applied input (nutrient). Example: kg grain/kg of a nutrient (macro or micro) added. Agronomic efficiency has a direct bearing on better utilization of applied nutrients, the profitability of their usage and minimization of nutrient losses.

Agronomical measures: Practice of growing vegetation on mild sloppy land to cover them and to control the erosion from there. Agronomical measures include contouring, strip cropping and tillage practices to control the soil erosion. The use of these measures is entirely dependent upon the soil types, land slope and rainfall characteristic. It plays second line of defence after mechanical or engineering measures. It is more economical, long lasting and effective.

Agronomy: Field of science that studies phenomena related to agriculture. The word has been derived from the Greek word 'agros' meaning fields and 'nomos' meaning management. It is a specialized branch of agriculture that deals with principles and practices of crop production and soil management.

Agropastoral system: A land-use system in which crops and livestock (but not trees) are the only components.

Agrosilvicultural system: An agroforestry system for the concurrent production of agricultural crops (including woody perennial crops) and forest crops.

Agro-silvi-pastoral system: A system in which land is managed for the concurrent production of agricultural and forest crops and for the rearing of domesticated animals. This system is, in fact a combination of agri-silviculture and the silvi-pastoral system.

Agrostology: A branch of science which deals with the study of grasses, their classification, management and utilization.

Air monitoring: Continuous assessment of atmospheric contamination.

Air pollution: Presence of contaminants in the air in concentrations interfering with normal dispersive ability of air and harmful to human health and safety.

Alfalfa valve: A screw type valve installed on an irrigation pipe to regulate supply of irrigation water.

Alfisols: Soils having grey to brown surface horizons, medium to high supply of bases and B horizons having accumulation of illuvial clay. These soils are formed under forest or savannah vegetation in climates having moisture deficit.

Alkali soil: A soil that contains sufficient sodium to interfere with the growth of most crop plants. Soils which have exchangeable sodium percentage (ESP) above 15, electrical conductivity below 4 dS/m and usually pH above 8.5. Also called sodic soils (high in sodium). Deficiencies of nitrogen and of zinc are most important. All alkali soils are alkaline but not vice versa, as a soil can have an alkaline reaction but have an ESP below 15. Gypsum application and green manuring are important components of the reclamation technology of these soils.

Alkaline (or basic) fertilizer: A fertilizer which leaves behind an alkaline reaction in the soil (raises soil pH). Example: calcium nitrate, sodium nitrate. Opposite of acid forming fertilizer.

Alkalization: Process by which exchangeable sodium of soil is increased.

Alley cropping: A conservation-oriented farming system in which arable (field) crops are grown in alleys formed by trees or shrubs, mainly to hasten soil fertility restoration, enhancing soil productivity and conserving the soil. This system is commonly practiced in tropical and subtropical rainfed areas.

Alluvial fan: A sloping fan like sediment deposition made by the stream when it leaves the uplands and enters the plains.

Alluvial soil: Soil formed from alluvium or water transported and recently deposited material exhibiting no horizon formation indicated by absence of B horizon, the soils belong to a zonal great soil group.

Alluvial terrace: Former flood plain which either has no longer floods or rarely floods due to deepening or enlargement of the stream channel.

Alluvial: Made of soil and sand left by rivers or floods. Pertaining to alluvium; a clayey, silty, sandy, or gravely material deposited by a stream or other bodies of running water.

Alluviation: The process of building up of sediments by a stream at places where stream velocity is decreased. It is the resultant of accumulation of gravel deposits, sand, silt or clay, at places in rivers, lakes, or estuaries. The coarsest particles settle first and the finest particles settle last.

Alluvion: It is a term which describes the increase in the plain area of land due to sediment (alluvium) which is deposited by a river forming sedimentary clastic rocks.

Alluvium: A term for clay, silt, sand, gravel, pebble or other detrital materials deposited by water. It includes gravel, sand, silt, clay and their mixtures. Alluvium is generally unconsolidated.

Alpine: Portion of mountains above tree growth or timberline.

Alternate agriculture: A concept of farming based on the exclusion of mineral fertilizers and synthetic pesticides but including mainly organic manures, waste recycling and biological agents, as in organic farming, in contrast to modern agriculture in which optimum use of mineral fertilizers and pesticides is sought to be made.

Alternate drying and wetting (rice): Refers to the frequent draining and reflooding (aerobic and anaerobic cycle) in rice fields.

Alternative farming: Farming not in the current, conventional manner; for example, not using fertilizers and pesticides, or by using intermediate technology and renewable energy.

Alternative hypothesis (H1): Is a hypothesis that has been suggested because it is believed to be false or because it is to be used as a starting point for assigning to organize arguments.

Altimeter: An instrument which indicates the vertical distance above a specified datum plane.

Altitude: Refers to the vertical measurement of a level, a point or an object considered, from mean sea-level.

Ambient monitoring: A monitoring performed to determine existing environmental conditions or contaminant levels in the environment, against which future conditions can be compared.

Amelioration (land): Refers to the process of enhancing agricultural value of a land by adopting suitable measures, such as drainage, tillage, liming, manuring, terracing etc.

Amendment, physical: Any substance (such as sand, calcined clay, peat, or sawdust) added to soil for the purpose of altering physical conditions.

Amendment, soil: Substance added to soil to improve its suitability for plant growt, like lime, gypsum, industrial waste, saw dust, paddy husk, groundnut shell etc. It alters the physical and chemical properties of the soil to an extent. Fertilizers are a special group of soil amendments, but the term is commonly used for materials other than fertilizers.

Ammonification: Biochemical process that releases ammonia from nitrogen containing organic matter.

Ammonium fixation: Adsorption or absorption of ammonium ions by mineral or organic fractions in soil, making them less water soluble and relatively unexchangeable through usual cation exchange process.

Anaerobic (soils): These are soils that are deficient in free oxygen and where reducing processes predominate. This condition generally occurs in poorly drained or waterlogged soils.

Anaerobic: Any process that can occur without oxygen; also applies to organisms that can survive without oxygen

Analog data: Can possess any value - it is continuously and infinitely variable.

Analysis of variance (ANOVA): A statistical procedure that allows subdivision of the total variation among experimental units into known sources of variation and provides a measure for each source.

Analysis: A close look at something to find out more about it; can involve looking closely at the individual parts of something and describing them

Analysis: In reference to fertilizers, it designates the percentage composition of the product expressed in terms which the existing trade practice and law require and permit.

Analytical model: A model in which all functional relationships can be expressed in closed form and the parameters fixed, so that the equations can be solved by classical methods of analytical mathematics.

Anemometer: An instrument used for the measurement of velocity of wind.

Aneroid barometer: Instrument used for measuring atmospheric pressure. Its main advantage over a mercury barometer is its portability.

Angle of incidence: Angle at which the Sun's rays strike the Earth's surface. If the Sun is positioned directly over head or 90° from the horizon, the incoming insolation strikes the surface of the Earth at right angles and is most intense.

Angle of repose: Angle between the maximum slope a soil (assumes naturally) and the horizontal. Maximum angle at which soil remains stable naturally.

Angstrom: A unit of length equal to 10^{-8} cm.

Animal unit month: Measure of forage or feed required to maintain one animal unit for 30 days.

Animal unit: Livestock number equivalent to one mature cow (approximately 1000 lbs or 455 kg live weight), roughly one cow, one horse, one mule, five sheep, five swine, and six goats.

Animal waste: Waste generated during the raising and utilization of animals on and off the farm. These include cattle shed waste, digested slurry, poultry litter, sheep and goat droppings, by-products of slaughter house and animal carcasses (blood, waste meat, bones, horns, hooves, and leather and hair wastes). These are often utilised for producing organic fertilizers, farmyard manure, compost etc.

Anion exchange: The replacement of one anion by another on positively charged soil surfaces or other anion exchange media such as resins. Example: exchange of $H_2PO_4^-$ with F^-, NO_3^- with Cl^-. Anions can enter and exit the soil solution through anion exchange while still remaining in the soil. Anion exchange is of lesser significance than cation exchange in soil fertility management and plant nutrition.

Anion-exchange capacity: It is the sum total of exchangeable anions that a soil can adsorb, expressed as mili equivalents/100 g of soil or as centimoles of negative charge per kilogram of soil.

Annual flood: Highest peak discharge in a water year.

Annual plant: A plant that completes its life in one year or less.

Antecedent soil moisture: Moisture content of soil prior to irrigation or at beginning of a run-off event.

Anthropogenic: Any process caused or produced as a result of human activity.

Anti-transpirant: A material which reduces transpiration from plant leaves, when applied to them in the form of water spray like aqueous spray of kaolin, cetyl alcohol etc.

A_p: Horizon surface layer of soil disturbed by cultivation or pasturing.

Apedal: These soils are either single grained (incoherent) or massive (coherent). Peds are not apparent when the soil is moderately moist.

Apparent nutrient recovery (ANR): A conventional measure of the proportion of applied nutrient recovered in the crop biomass. If a crop absorbs 10 kg P/ha without P application and 16 kg P/ha when 30 kg P/ha is applied, then the apparent recovery of P is 20% {(16-10) x100/30}.

Apparent specific gravity: A term formerly used to designate the ratio of the mass per unit bulk volume of soil and water and is worked out by following formula: AS = Bulk density of soil/density of water.

Apparent thermal inertia (ATI): An approximation of thermal inertia calculated as one minus albedo divided by the difference between day-time and night-time radiant temperatures.

Application rate: Rate at which water is applied per unit area; usually in millimeter per hour, or weight or volume of a fertilizer, soil amendment, or pesticide applied per unit area.

Applied research: Research in which results can be used immediately by the farmer and can be applied to the peculiar problems of a country or a region.

Appropriate technology: Refers to a technology that is suitable or proper in the context of a particular community, region, or country. It must be economically viable, technologically feasible and should fit in the socio-economic fabric of the local communities.

Approved fertilizer/fertilizer grade: A fertilizer/fertilizer grade which is recognised through fertilizer legislation and listed in the fertilizer legislation documents of a country. Example: fertilizers which are listed in the Fertilizer Control Order (FCO) and approved for production or sale in India.

Apron (soil engineering): A floor or lining constructed to protect soil surface from erosion below chutes, spillways or dams.

Aquaculture: The farming of aquatic organisms including fish, molluscs, crustaceans and aquatic plants with some sort of intervention in the rearing process to enhance production, such as regular stocking, feeding, protection from predators, etc. Farming also implies individual or corporate ownership of the stock being cultivated.

Aquasilvicultural system: An agroforestry system that combines trees with the raising of aquatic animals.

Aquatic plants: Plants with true roots, stems and leaves, growing near or inside water bodies, excluding algae.

Aquatic: Refers to plant that grows in water. There are three types of aquatic plants (*a*) submergent grows beneath the surface of water, such as waterweed and green algae; (*b*) emergent; grows above the surface of water, such as cattails and water lilies; (*c*) floaters:

floats on water such as water-hyacinth and water lettuce.

Aquerts: Vertisols that are saturated with water for periods long enough to limit their use for most crops other than pasture and woodland unless they are artificially drained. Aquerts have in one or more horizons between 40 and 50 cm from the surface, aquic conditions for some time or most.

Aquic: These soils have stagnant water on the soil surface and/or can be saturated in some part of the upper 0.5 m of the profile, more or less continuously for 2 to 3 months. In this condition, the soil is free of dissolved oxygen. Gley (bluey-grey) colours are often an indication of prolonged saturation.

Aquifer (unconfined): An aquifer whose upper water surface (water table) is at atmospheric pressure, and thus is able to rise and fall.

Aquifer recharge area: Surface area that provides water for an aquifer.

Aquifer: A saturated, permeable geologic unit of sediment or rock that is capable of yielding water in sufficient quantity and transmits significant quantities of water to wells and springs under hydraulic gradients in sufficient quantity to constitute a usable supply.

Arable crops: These are crops which require tillage operations for cultivation.

Arable farming: Farming system that involves the cultivation of crops requiring tillage.

Arable land: Land which is suitable for ploughing. The term also applies to land which is actually ploughed and cultivated under the crops.

Arboretum: A collection of plants, trees, shrubs grown for demonstration, recreation etc.

Arch dam: Curved masonry or concrete dam, convex upstream that depends on arch action for stability.

Area curve (channel hydraulics): It is the plotting between stage or elevation and associated water surface area.

Arid climate: A extremely dry climate with an annual average precipitation usually less than 250 mm and generally rainfall is well short of evapo-transpiration demand of the atmosphere.

Arid lands: Area where precipitation is insufficient for crop production.

Arid zone: A zone of very low rainfall with most of the deserts.

Arid: A term applied to a region or climate in which precipitation is too low to support crop production.

Aridic: A soil moisture regime that limits plant growth during much of the growing season.

Aridisols: Mineral soils found in arid or dry areas that have an arid moisture regime, an ochric epipedon, and other pedogenic horizons, but no oxic horizon (An Order in the USDA soil taxonomy). These are desert soils with weak ochric, posses $CaCO_3$, gypsem and other soluble salts.

Arithmetic mean: The average obtained by summing the value of a series of data and dividing by the number of items in the series $\overline{X} = \frac{\Sigma X}{n}$.

Artesian (Flowing) aquifer: Aquifer, in which water is held under pressure by confining layers, forcing water to rise in wells above the top of the aquifer.

Artesian basin: Basin in which aquifer is enclosed between impermeable strata. Boring in the aquifer causes the water to rise due to its own pressure (artesian well).

Artesian water- Ground water that is able to rise above the level at which it is first encountered. Sometimes flow out at ground level.

Artificial recharge: A process where water is put back into ground-water storage from surface-water supplies such as irrigation, or induced infiltration from streams or wells.

Assessment: It is a written report about the importance, size or value of something; for example, an environmental assessment may describe the value of arctic char after a study of the char, the fishermen, the method of fishing and the effect on the environment

Assimilative capacity (Soil): Refers to natural ability of soil and water to use and decompose potential pollutants without harmful effects to the environment.

Assimilative capacity (Water body): the amount of pollutants that a water body may absorb while continuing to meet water quality standards

Atmospheric pressure: The pressure exerted by the atmosphere as a consequence of the weight of the air lying directly above the unit of area in question. At sea-level, the average atmospheric pressure is 1013.25 millibars.

Atmospheric Stability: Relative stability of parcels of air relative to the atmosphere that surrounds them. Three conditions are generally described: stable, unstable, and neutral.

Attenuate: Reduction in significance or concentration

Auger A tool for boring holes into the soil. A soil auger is used to withdraw a small soil sample for observation.

Augmentation cropping: It means growing of a crop to supplement the yield/monetary returns accruing from the main crop. For example, growing of forage brassica to augment the fodder yield of berseem in first cut.

Autecology (forestry): Study of the individual or members of a species collectively with respect to environment.

Auxiliary spillway: A dam spillway which serves to carry run-off in excess of that carried by the principal spillway.

Available forage: Forage which is accessible for consumption by farm animals.

Available moisture: It is the moisture range or limit present in the soil that is available to the plants which lies between field capacity (FC) and wilting point (WP) of the soil.

Available nitrogen: The proportion of N present in the rooting zone of soils, which is directly available to plants. It is mainly in the form of NO_3^- present in soil solution and the dissolved and adsorbed NH_4.

Available nutrient: A portion of any nutrient in the soil that can be readily absorbed and assimilated by growing plants.

Available or desirably available water: Portion of water in soil which could be readily absorbed by plant roots. Water which is held in the soil between field moisture capacity and permanent wilting point or against pressure between 1/3 and 15 bars.

Available phosphoric acid: It is that part of phosphorus which is soluble in water or in a weak dilute acid, such as 2% citric acid.

Average intake rate: Rate of entry of water into the soil obtained by dividing the total depth of water infilterated by the total time, from start to finish, of water application; expressed in mm/hr.

Axis of the telescope: It is a line joining the optical center of the object glass to the center of the eye piece.

Azonal soils: Soils without distinct genetic horizons. (1949 Soil classification system)

B

Back diffusion: Accumulation of certain ions at the root surface against the concentration gradient because the root is unable to absorb them at a sufficiently rapid rate.

Back furrow: A raised ridge of soil formed when the furrow slice overlaps another slice, this ridge is slightly higher than the other ridges.

Backfilling: The return of wastes or other material underground for disposal.

Back-fire: A fire control practice in forestry. A controlled fire is started ahead of an advancing fire in order to destroy inflammable or dry material so as to control the advancing forest fire.

Background level: amount of a substance which occurs naturally in the environment.

Bacteria: Microscopic one-celled organisms which live almost everywhere and perform a variety of functions.

While decomposing organic matter in water, bacteria can greatly reduce the amount of oxygen in the water.

Bad land: A miscellaneous type of land, poor in vegetation and cut up with gullies and humps resulting from severe erosion of soft geological materials.

Balanced fertilizer: A soil additive containing suitable proportions of each necessary mineral element to grow a plant or a crop.

Balanced rations: Rations for livestock, with proper balance between digestible protein and total digestible nutrients and between concentrates and bulky roughage. In addition, the' minerals and vitamins should also be in adequate quantities.

Band application: An application to a continuous restricted band along a crop row rather than over the entire area, mostly done in case of total killer or non selective herbicides.

Bar: A unit of pressure. SI measure of pressure composed of 1000 millibar. Equal to around 14.2 lbs/sq. inch.

Barogram: The continuous record of atmospheric pressure made by a barograph.

Barograph: A self-recording barometer in which continuous trace of the atmospheric pressure is made on barograms.

Barometer: An instrument used for measuring the atmospheric pressure.

Barometric levelling: It is the method of levelling in which the altitudes of points are determined by means of a barometer, which measures atmospheric pressure.

Barrage: A large structure erected across a river store water, usually for irrigation.

Barren: An area without vegetation.

Basal dose: Refers to the quanlity of manures or fertilizer applied in the field just before the crop is sown or planted or transplanted.

Basal tillers: Tillers produced from basal nodes near the soil surface; the term 'basal' is used to differentiate the tillers produced on the upper nodes from those developing at the base.

Basal treatment: Applied to encircle the stem of a plant above and at the ground such that foliage contact is minimal. A term used mostly to describe treatment of woody plants.

Basalt: It is a dark coloured igneous rock formed by solidification of lava and has relatively low per cent (45-55) of silica. Basalt may vary in colour from dark grey to black, which on weathering may become softer and show a greenish or rusty brown tinge on the joints or cracks. The rock is very compact and shining black crystals of augite and patches of bottle green olivine can often be seen with naked eye or through a lens.

Base (period): Period in days during which irrigation is supplied to a crop.

Base crop: Refers to a crop which is planted at its optimum sole crop population in an intercropping situation and the second crop is planted in between rows of the main or base crop.

Base data analysis: The computation and synthesis of available data for delineating homogeneous areas and for determining research priorities and strategies.

Base exchange capacity: The maximum capacity to which the soil can adsorb exchangeable cations other than hydrogen and aluminium.

Base flow: Discharge in a stream from ground water run-off.

Base lines: It is main and longest line, which passes approximately through the centre of the field. All the other measurements to show the details of the work are taken with respect to this line.

Base map: Map showing basic data, which may be supplemented with other information.

Base saturation: The extent to which the exchange sites of a complex soil is saturated with exchangeable cations other than hydrogen and expressed as a percentage of the cation-exchange capacity.

Baseline data: An initial set of observations or measurements used for comparison; a starting point.

Basic fertilizer: After application to and reaction with soil, decreases residual acidity and increases soil pH.

Basic intake rate: Rate at which water will enter into the soil. After initial wetting of the soil the intake rate becomes essentially constant; which is equal to saturated hydraulic conductivity; mm/hr.

Basic research: Research that deals with fundamental principles of organisms.

Basin irrigation: Water is applied in basins formed around stumps of trees. The basin may be square, rectangular or circular shape. This method is suitable for orchids and other high value crops where the size of the plot to be irrigated is very small.

Basin lister: A double plough which leaves the field in a series of alternate ridges and furrows. The operation helps in detention storage of rain water.

Basin listing: Tillage operation that forms lister furrows at regular intervals to create small basins to retain store rain or applied water.

Basin: Area drained by a river, lower part of a floodplain landscape, usually saucer-shaped.

Baule unit: A unit of growth factors. It is defined as the amount of a certain growth factor necessary to produce a yield that is 50% of the difference between the maximum possible yield and the yield before that growth factor or unit added.

BC soil: Soil with B and C horizons with little or no A horizon.

Bed load: Sediment which moves on or near the stream bed by sliding, rolling or bounding.

Bed or border method (Sara and flat beds or check basin): In this method the field is leveled and divided into small beds surrounded by bunds of 15 to 30 cm high. Small irrigation channels are provided between two adjacent rows of beds. The length of the bed varies from 30 meters for loamy soils to 90 meters for clayey soils. The width is so adjusted as to permit the water to flow evenly and wet the land uniformly.

Bed rock: Solid rock underlying soils and regolith of varying depths.

Bedding (land): Ploughing or otherwise raising the surface of a field into a series of parallel beds separated by dead furrows or shallow drains. It is useful in improving field drainage. Beds and drains are parallel to the prevailing land slope; it is suitable for lands having < 1.5% slope and slowly permeable soils where tile drainage is not economical.

Belt of soil water: The part of the zone of aeration which consists of soil and other materials that lies near enough to the surface to discharge water into the atmosphere in perceptible quantities by the transpiration of plants or by evaporation from the soil.

Bench terrace: A bench terrace is shelf like embankment of earth with a level or nearly level top and a step or vertical downhill face constructed along the contour of sloping land.

Bench: Elevated portion of flat land; a topographic terrace.

Benchmark data: Data for a specific period used for comparative purposes.

Benchmark survey: A systematic study aimed at collecting baseline data, *e.g.* of existing crops, varieties, yields, socio-economic constraints, before a project begins. It represents the existing picture of the survey areas with regard to selected parameters and can be used to evaluate the results of the project.

Benchmarking: The process of identifying best practices indicating superior performance. Benchmarks are adopted as targets for optimal organizational performance, and may include standards or environmental management processes.

Benefit: cost ratio: The present value of benefits divided by the present value of costs. It is used to determine the profitability of a system.

Bentonite: Highly plastic clay consisting of the minerals montmorillonite and beidellite that swells when wet and is often used as a lining material to seal landfills and lagoons.

Berm: It is a shoulder or strip 6-10 ft. (2-3 m) wide made across the slope on downstream face of an earthen dam to control erosion.

Best management practice (BMP): Structural or managerial technique recognized as the most effective and practical means of controlling pollution for an agricultural, urban, forested, or mining area.

B-horizon: Soil horizon generally beneath A horizon, in which clay, iron or aluminium with accessory organic matter have accumulated and blocky or prismatic structure has developed. In distinct soil profiles, it is roughly equivalent to sub-soil.

Bhs horizon: A subsoil horizon notation whereby the 'B' refers to the B Horizon and the 'hs' to the humosesquic horizon. Iron and organic compounds (often referred to as 'coffee rock') are prominent within the horizon and the organic compounds are distributed as streaks, patches or lumps.

Binomial distribution: Also referred to Bernoulli distribution. It is a discrete probability distribution expressing the probability of one set of dichotomous alternatives that is success or failure.

Bioaccumulation: Referred to a condition when plants or animals collect contaminants in their tissues over time; when low amounts of contaminants are continually absorbed, they build up and can cause illness.

Biochemical oxygen demand (BOD): A laboratory test to measure the amount of oxygen consumed by microorganisms as they decompose organic matter. It indicates the amount of organic material in a water sample.

Biodegradable: Material that will decompose under natural, biological conditions and processes.

Biodiversity: Biodiversity is the variability among living organisms. It includes diversity within and among species and diversity within and among ecosystems (Millennium Assessment Framework). When linked to ecosystem function there are two key components of biodiversity; functional diversity (the diversity of functions and species that sustains a specific function) and response diversity (the diversity of ways in which organisms within an ecosystem function responds to change and disturbance).

Biodynamic agriculture: A view of agriculture based on a holistic and spiritual understanding of nature and humans' role in it, which considers a farm as a self-contained evolving organism.

Bioindicators: Organisms that are used to detect changes in environmental pollutant levels, such organisms are usually sensitive to changes in their surroundings.

Biological determinants of cropping systems: The biological factors such as crop species, varieties, weeds, insect pests, and diseases, which determine the crop configuration and performance of a cropping pattern at a given site.

Biological oxygen demand: The amount of oxygen used in the biochemical oxidation of organic matter; an indication of compost maturity and a tool for studying the composting process. A measure of the amount of pollution in water, shown by the amount of oxygen needed to oxidise the polluting substances.

Biological resources: A biological resource includes genetic resources, organisms or parts thereof, populations, or any other biotic component of ecosystems with actual or potential use or value for humanity.

Biological yield: Refers to total dry matter produced by a plant or a crop in a unit land area.

Biomagnification: An increase in concentration of a substance at each progressive link in the food chain (for example: berries, birds, foxes, bear; the concentration of a contaminant such as lead would be highest in a large meat-eater).

Biomass: The total mass of living organisms in a given volume or mass of soil. Any organic matter which is available on a renewable basis, including agricultural crops and agricultural wastes and residues, wood and wood wastes and residues, animal wastes, mineral wastes and aquatic plants, usually expressed as dry weight per unit area.

Biome: A major biotic unit of plant and animal communities with similarity in form and environmental conditions.

Bioremediation: A process to reduce contaminant levels in soil or water by using microorganisms or vegetation.

Biosphere: Zone incorporating all forms of life on earth. The biosphere extends from deep in sediment below the ocean to several thousand meters elevation in high mountains.

Biota: Refers to flora and fauna of an area.

Biotic factors: Factors resulting from the presence of plants and animals (including man), such as grazing of animals, tree cutting by man, soil bacteria and insects.

Biotic/abiotic stresses: Limitations imposed on development which occurs because of biological (biotic) or physical (abiotic) factors.

Black cotton soil: Refers to black colour soil having low organic matter and a high clay content, exhibiting a strong phenomenon of swelling and shrinkage; during dry periods develop deep cracks of several cm width and more than 50 cm deep.

Black water: Liquid and solid human body waste and the carriage water generated by toilet use.

Blind inlet: Inlet to a drain in which water enters by percolation.

Blocky like: These are cubes like 3 dimensions of about same size. When the edges or size are sharp, called as Angular blocky and when rounded, called as Sub-angular blocky. These usually found in the sub-soil horizon.

Blown out land: A miscellaneous type of land from which soil or soil material has been removed by wind erosion leaving shallow depressions in the underlying more resistant layer.

Blowout: Shallow, saucer-shaped hollow made by wind erosion on an aeolian deposit.

Bluff: A cliff with almost perpendicular front usually bordering a river. Bluffs are formed in valley sides by the cutting or scouring action of the river.

Bog soil: Great soil group in hydromorphic sub-order ofintrazon. Order, such as peat and muck. (1949 soil classification system).

Bog: Wetland that has no significant inflows or outflows, supports acidophilic mosses, particularly Sphagnum and in which peat is accumulating. A wetland characterized by peat deposits, acidic water, and extensive surface mats of sphagnum moss. Bogs receive their water from precipitation rather than from runoff, groundwater, or streams.

Boiling point: The temperature at which the vapor pressure of a liquid is equal to the applied pressure.

Border dikes: Earthen ridges to hold irrigation water within a field.

Border effect: In experiments, the difference in performance of plants planted at the edges of a plot and of those planted at the centre of the plot.

Border irrigation (border-strip irrigation): It is an efficient method of irrigating close growing crops and consists essentially of dividing the field by low flat levels into series of strips, each of which is flooded separately. These strips are made level transversely but follow a gentle down field slope longitudinally.

Border rows: A row of plants around test plots which protect test entries from a border row effect. These are outer few crop rows that are used to isolate the main plot. In case of seed plots these are the rows of male sterile parents but in case of commercial crops the same seed material is used for raising the border rows.

Bottom contraction: Vertical distance from weir crests to bottom of weir pond.

Bottom up approach: A management approach that emphasizes local decision making, participation at all level and grassroots mobilization. It is a consultative leadership style that promotes participation of lower level (hierarchy) in decision making and problem solving. Present guideline of participatory watershed management is mainly based on this approach in which beneficiaries participation in planning and decision making are ensured.

Boulder: Rock or mineral fragments, largest unit in sedimentary rocks, bigger than 10 cm.

Bound water: Form of water that is adsorbed strongly by colloids. This water is retained against forces of evaporation of over 1,000 atmosphere.

Box drains: Instead of pipes, underground drains may be made in V shaped cut or trench, sides of which are reverted with soil, restoring the surface of the field. Depth may be 90 cm below ground.

Brackish: Slightly saline or of salty nature.

Brake horse power: It is actual horse power required to be supplied by the engine or electric motor for driving the pump.

Broad base terrace: A broad base terrace has a ridge 25 to 50 cm high and 5 - 10 m wide with gently slopping sides and a dish stopped channel along the upper side constructed to control erosion by diverting runoff at non-erosive velocity. It is divided or classified as; Graded Terrace and Level Terrace.

Broad bed and furrow (B.B.F.) system: A land management system for successful crop production in vertisols (heavy black soil) by providing better drainage through raised broad beds (about 90-100 cm wide) and furrow (25-30 cm wide).

Broadcast sprigging: Vegetative turf establishment by broadcasting and covering of stolons, rhizomes, or tillers with soil.

Broadcast treatment: An application over an entire area of field.

Broadcast: To apply seeds or granules by hand or machine over a surface area. It involves scattering of agricultural inputs, such as seed, fertilizer and manure, on the surface of the soil by hand or by implements to provide uniform distribution of material over the entire field.

Broadcaster: A machine for sowing seeds by broadcast

Broad-spectrum herbicide: An herbicide effective against a wide range of weeds.

Brown earths: Soils having a mull horizon but no horizon with accumulation of clay or sesquioxides.

Brown forest soils: A great soil group of the intrazonal order and calcimorphic suborder, formed on calcium-rich parent materials under deciduous forest, and possessing a high base status but lacking a pronounced illuvial horizon.

Brown podzolic soils: Acid, predominantly brownish to yellowish soils, lacking or with a weak A_2 horizon and generally have weakly to moderately differentiated profiles with merging horizons.

Brown soils: A group of soils formed in semi-arid climate having a brown surface soil and zone of carbonate accumulation at a depth usually of 25 to 50 cm.

Browse line: Line on woody plants indicating height up to which browse has been removed by animals.

Browse: Twigs with or without leaves of shrubs, trees or woody vines etc. available for browsing animals.

Brush matting: Matting of brushes placed on badly eroded land to check erosion when trees etc. are being established: Also a matting of mesh wire and brush used for controlling stream bank erosion.

Brush: Growth of shrubs and small trees.

Buffer solution: Solution that resists change in pH; contains either a weak acid and a soluble ionic salt of the acid or a weak base and a soluble ionic salt of the base.

Buffer strip: Strip of grass or other erosion-resisting vegetation laid between or below strips of cultivated crop. Grass strip is usually of uneven width and serves as the correction strip to make crop strips even. It is more or less permanent. Buffer strip may also be placed on critical slope areas of the field.

Buffer zone: Neutral area which acts as a protective barrier separating two conflicting forces. An area which acts to minimize the impact of pollutants on the environment or public welfare. For example, a buffer zone is established between a compositing facility and neighboring residents to minimize odor problems.

Buffering capacity: The soils ability to resist change in pH. Soils with a high clay and organic matter content have a higher buffering capacity and can tolerate the addition of acidifying fertilisers over an extended period, or at a higher rate of addition without becoming too acid. But once it is acid, the soil will require a large amount of lime or dolomite to reverse the effect. The amount of lime or dolomite required varies from soil to soil depending on the pH

Bulk blending: Mixing dry, individually granulated materials to form a mixed fertilizer.

Bulk density, soil: Mass of oven dry soil (105°C) per unit bulk volume. It varies from 1.3 to 1.7 g/cc in sandy soils and 1.1 to 1.4 g/cc in clay soils.

Bulk fertiliser: Commercial fertilizer delivered to the buyer either in the solid or in the liquid form, in a non-packed form.

Bulk specific gravity: The ratio of the bulk density of a soil to the mass of unit volume of water.

Bulk volume: The volume, including the solids and the pores, of an arbitrary soil mass. The bulk volume is determined before drying to constant weight at 105°C.

Bulky organic manures: These are bulky in nature and supply plant nutrients in small quantities and organic matter in large quantities when applied to soil.

Bulky waste: Large items of refuse including, but not limited to, appliances, furniture, large auto parts, non-hazardous construction and demolition material, trees, branches and stumps which cannot be handled by normal solid waste processing, collection and disposal methods.

Bund cross section: It is the average of top & bottom width of bund multiplied by height of the bund.

Bund former: An implement used for making bunds or ridges by collecting the soil for trapezoidal shape.

Bund: An artificial earthen embankment made across sloping agricultural land to cut short lengthy soil slopes thereby and reducing run-off and soil erosion.

Buoyancy: The upward force excreted on the volume of fluid by virtue of the density difference between the volume of fluid and that of surrounding fluid.

Buried soil: Soil-covered by alluvial, loessal or other deposit to a depth more than solum thickness.

Buy-back center: facility where individuals bring recyclables in exchange for payment.

C

C horizon: Unconsolidated mineral horizon, beneath the solum excluding bed rock, relatively little affected by pedogenic processes and lacking properties diagnostic of 'A' or 'B' horizon.

C_3 plant: A group of plant in which the first product of CO_2 fixation is a 3-carbon compound; phosphoglyceric acid. They are comparatively less photo synthetically efficient, than C_4 plants, *e.g.* wheat, rice, barley etc.

C_4 plant: A group of plant in which the first product of CO_2 fixation is a 4-carbon compound, CO_2 oxaloacetic acid and is more photo synthetically efficient than C_3 plants. *e.g.* maize, sorghum, sugarcane etc.

Cadastral map: Large scale revenue map showing individual survey numbers and reference land marks like road, railway line, cart track, temple, cremation ground, tree grove etc. Map scale is 8"=1 mile (1: 7920) or 16"=1 mile (1: 3960). The map is useful for detailed land use planning.

Cadastral survey: To determine boundaries of field, estate and registration of landownership on maps.

Calcareous rock: Sedimentary rock having appreciable quantities of calcium carbonate such as limestone, chalk and tufa.

Calcareous soil: Soil that contains more than 5% free calcium carbonate. Soil containing sufficient calcium carbonate (often with magnesium carbonate) to effervescence visibly when treated with cold 0.1 N hydrochloric acid.

Canal: Artificial watercourse used for irrigation or inland navigation.

Canopy, crop: Portion of crop consisting of shoots and leaf foliage etc., as viewed from above the cover, which serves to intercept falling raindrops thereby protecting the soil against erosion.

Canvas dam: A device used for controlling flow of water in channels consists of triangular piece of canvas cloth fitted with a bamboo stick on one side.

Canyon: A narrow, deep valley with steep sides; gorge. It is formed by a river cutting through soft rocks in arid regions. Walls of a large canyon, however, are rarely vertical, irregularity of slope being due to inequalities in the hardness of the rock. (Grand Canyon of Colorado river).

Capillarity: The process by which moisture moves in any direction through the fine pore spaces and as films around particles.

Capillary action: The movement of a liquid upwards inside a narrow tube or upwards through the porous spaces in a solid, such as soil, plant roots, due to the forces of adhesion, cohesion, and surface tension.

Capillary conductivity: It is the movement of soil moisture under unsaturated conditions in a unit time and unit potential gradient.

Capillary fringe: It is the vertical distance above a water table in which moisture content varies from saturation to field capacity.

Capillary moisture: The amount of water that is capable of movement after the soil has drained. It is held by adhesion and surface tension as films around particles and in the finer pore spaces.

Capillary porosity: The volume of micro pores which holds water against the force of gravity, out of total porosity of the soil.

Capillary potential: The potential with which water is held by soil. Complex expressed in terms of work that must be done to move water against the capillary forces of the soil.

Capillary rise: The movement of water above the hydrostatic surface under the influence of capillarity.

Carbon cycle: The sequence of transformation where carbon dioxide is converted to organic forms by photosynthesis or chemosynthesis. The carbon utilized by an organism, later liberated upon the death and decomposition of the organism, and returned to its original state to be reused by another organism.

Carbon nitrogen ratio (C: N ratio): The ratio of the weight of organic carbon (C) to the weight of total nitrogen (N) in a soil or any organic material. It determines the composting potential of a material and serves to indicate product quality.

Cardinal points: Four main directions of the compass; north, south, east and west.

Cardinal temperatures: The maximum, minimum & optimum temperatures for plant growth. Between these limits of optimum temperature, growth proceeds at maximum rate. These three points are known as cardinal temperatures.

Carriage: It is a provision of adding carrying cost of material in preparing estimate of engineering measures, if construction site is located in remote.

Carry over soil moisture: The amount of moisture stored in root zone between two cropping seasons or before the crop is planted. This moisture influences to the water needs of succeeding crops.

Carrying capacity (grazing): Maximum number of animals that can be supported on an area in a given period of the year.

Cartography: Drawing of maps and charts.

Cascade: Small waterfall or a series of such falls resembling steps.

Cash crops: Crops produced by the farmer for sale and not for consumption such as sugarcane, tobacco, cotton, plantation crops, etc.

Castings, earthworm: Soil and plant remains excreted and deposited by earthworms in or on the turf surface or in their burrows. Castings form relatively stable soil granules that can, on closely mowed turf, produce an uneven surface. *Synonym:* earthworm casts.

Cataract: A big waterfall or series of falls.

Catch crop: A crop raised incidental to the main crop, occupying the area for a small period. A crop grown as a substitute of the main crop which has failed.

Catchment: An independent unit of land contributing runoff water to a common outlet.

Catena: A sequence of soils of about the same age, formed from identical parent material under similar climatic conditions, but exhibiting different characteristics due to variation in relief and drainage.

Cation exchange capacity: Total exchangeable cations that a soil can absorb on the surface. It is expressed in milli-equivalents per 100 gm of soil or clay.

Causeway: Raised road across a stream or river or wet place.

Cavern: Synonymous with cave, though sometimes it implies a cave of large dimensions.

Cementation: Process of binding soil particles by cementing materials like calcium carbonate, iron oxide, polysaccharides, organic acids etc.

Cemented layer: Indurated, having hard, brittle consistency as the soil particles are held together by cementing substances as oxides of silicon, iron and aluminium or calcium carbonate or humus. Hardness and brittleness persist even on wetting.

Chain survey: Chain survey is the simplest method of surveying. In this survey only measurements are taken in the field, and the rest work, such as plotting calculation etc. are done in the office. This is most suitable adapted to small plane areas with very few details. If carefully done, it gives quite accurate results. The necessary requirements for field work are chain, tape, ranging rod, arrows and some time cross staff.

Chain: Mountain system consisting of more or less parallel ranges. Term is loosely applied to other features occurring in a line such as chain of islands.

Chaining: Measuring distance with chain or rope is the most accurate and common method, called as chaining. For work of ordinary precision a chain is used. Where great accuracy is required, a steel tape is used.

Chalk: Soft white or greyish limestone, sometimes consisting of calcareous remains of small marine organisms and shell fragments; may contain up to 99% calcium carbonate.

Change point (C.P.): It is a point denoting the shifting of the level (instrument). It is a point on which is the fore and back sights are taken. It is also called a turning point (T.P.).

Channel stabilization: Prevention of erosion and stabilization of velocity distribution in a channel by using vegetation, jetting, revetments etc.

Check basin: In this method water is applied rapidly to fairly leveled plots surrounded by dykes. It is well known method generally used for heavy soils with low infiltration rate or high permeable soil like deep sand. Used for orchards grain & folder production.

Check dam: A small dam constructed in a gully or water course to decrease the velocity of stream flow, for minimizing channel scour and promoting the deposition of eroded material and to divert water from a channel.

Check leveling: It is the operation of running levels for the purpose of checking the series of levels, which have been previously fixed. At the end of each day's work, a line of level is run, returning to the starting point of that day with a view to check the work done on that day.

Check line: A check line also termed as a proof line is a line joining the apex of a triangle to some fixed points on any two sides of a triangle. A check line is measured to check the accuracy of the framework. The length of a check line, as measured on the ground should agree with its length on the plan.

Check row marker: A manually operated (usually pulled) light tool used to mark the soft rice field surface in perpendicular directions to form a grid; used as guide for transplanting of rice seedlings.

Check row planting: A planting pattern where each hill is aligned in rows and columns and if the row and column are equidistant, each hill has also diagonal alignments.

Chemical oxygen demand (COD): A measure of the oxygen equivalent of that portion of organic matter in a sample that is susceptible to oxidation by a strong chemical. A major objective of conventional wastewater treatment is to reduce the chemical and biochemical oxygen demand.

Chisel, sub-soil: A tiliage implement with one or more tyne(s) having knife like attachments used to shatter or loosen compacts soil layers below the plough layer.

Chlorination: Refers to the process of purifying/disinfecting water by adding chlorine.

Chronosequence: A sequence of soils differing in certain characteristics as a result of time as soil forming factor.

Chute: Sloping channel for conveying water over slope. The channel may be of masonry (masonry chute) or may be stabilized with grasses (sod chute) to prevent erosion.

Cipolette weir: It is contracted trapezoidal weir in which each side of notch has a slope of 1 horizontal to 4 vertical. It is named after its inventor "Cesare Cipolletti" an Italian engineer. It is used to measure medium discharges.

City survey: To locate premises, streets, water supply and drainage systems.

Class' A' pan (USWB evaporimeter): A standard evaporimeter measuring 120.7 cm in diameter and 25 cm deep maintained in agro meteorological observatories. It is helpful in generating data on evapo-transpiration, which in turn, can be used for scheduling of irrigation.

Class, soil: A group of soils defined by acidity, degree of slope, texture, structure, land-use capability, degree of erosion, or drainage.

Classes of structure: Aggregates/peds classified on the basis of their sizes as: Very fine, Fine, Medium, Coarse (or thick) and Very coarse (or very thick).

Classification, land capability: An interpretative classification of land based on land features, soil characteristics and environmental factors; helps in using the land according to its capacity and treating it as per its need for sustained production.

Classification of crops: It is the categorization of different crops as per requirement such as: botanical, use, agronomical or economic; erosion; growth period etc. For erosion the crops are classified as erosion permitting (such as cotton, potato, tobacco, maize etc. which are wide spaced, clean tilled and having inadequate canopy) and erosion resisting (such as grasses, close growing leguminous crops *e.g.* cowpea. green gram, velvet bean, kudzu etc.).

Classification soil: Systematic arrangement of soils into categories or divisions based on general characteristics and into subdivisions on the basis of detailed differences in specific properties.

Clay minerals: Clay-sized hydrous aluminium silicates having a large interlayer space that can hold significant amounts of water and other substances; they have large surface area allowing swelling and shrinking; examples are montmorillonite or smectite and kaolinite. Small mineral soil particles less than 0.002 mm in diameter.

Clay pan: A dense, compact, well defined, relatively impervious layer in the subsoil with much higher clay content than present in the overlying soil, formed by in-situ clay synthesis during soil formation or by downward movement of clay. It is hard when dry and plastic or stiff when wet. Its presence interferes with water movement and root growth.

Clay: A mineral soil separate having particles < 0.002 mm in equivalent diameter. It is ultra microscopic size having large surface area (10 to 1000^2 cm/g). The clay particles are smooth and in a colloidal state. Clay particles absorb and retain water, swell on wetting and shrink on drying, exhibit properties like flocculation (grouping/clustering), deflocculating, plasticity and stickiness. Soils with high clay are poorly drained, require very heavy draft for cultivation, can be worked in narrow range of moisture regime.

Clean cultivation: Periodic removal of all vegetation other than the crop being grown in the field by soil tillage operation.

Clean tillage: Cultivation of agricultural fields such that growth of all vegetation excepting the required crop is prevented.

Cleavage: Splitting of a rock into thin sheets or slabs, when submitted to great pressure. Direction of cleavage is usually inclined or at right angles to stratification of the rock and some-times parallel to it. Slate is an example of a rock having well developed cleavage.

Cliff: High, steep rock face (nearly vertical), occurring inland or along a coast.

Climate: The average weather for a particular region over a long time period.

Climatic analysis: Analysis of data over an extended period of time, including precipitation, maximum and minimum temperature, relative humidity, wind, and radiation.

Climatic index: A simple, single numerical value that expresses climatic relationships; for example, the numerical value obtained in Transeau's precipitation/evaporation ratio.

Climatology: The scientific study of weather patterns over time and space. It includes the integration of day-to-day weather over a period of time.

Climax community: The stable state of a species or community which is in complete equilibrium with the physical and biotic environment of habitat and is self-perpetuating.

Climax vegetation: A fully developed plant community that is in equilibrium with its environment. The most fully developed natural vegetation the climate can sustain.

Climax: A most advanced plant species (community) capable of development under, and in dynamic equilibrium with, the prevailing environmental conditions.

Climograph: A graph showing the differentiation between various types of climate.

Climosequence: A sequence of related soils that differ from one another in some characteristics primarily due to difference in climate as soil forming factor.

Clod: A compact, coherent soil mass varying in size from 5-10 mm to 200-250 mm produced mainly as a result of cultivation operations when the soil is too wet or too dry for tillage operations.

Closed drain: Sub-surface drain, tile or perforated pipe, which receives surface water through surface inlets.

Cloud burst: Abnormally heavy downpour usually associated with thunderstorm. It is frequent in mountains where upward movement of heated air may be suddenly stopped on crossing a mountain range. Rain drops and hailstones supported by the air fall down in a very small time. It can cause considerable erosion and damage to habitation.

Cloud: A mass of small water drops or ice crystals formed in the atmosphere due to condensation of water vapour at great height above the land.

Coarse fragments: Rock or mineral particles greater than 21 cm in diameter.

Coarse rejects: Waste rock that is produced early in a mine's processing stage; the rock is not further crushed or concentrated because it contains little or nothing of economic value.

Coarse textured: A broad textural grouping that refers to soils or materials dominated by sand, loamy sand, and sandy loam textural classes.

Coast: Land which borders a sea or any other large expanse of water, like lake, which is exposed to wave action and erosion.

Cobblestone: Rounded and partially rounded rock or mineral fragments having diameter 7.5-25.0 cm.

Co-compositing: Simultaneous composting of two or more diverse waste streams.

Coefficient of correlation: The ratio of the covariance of two variables to the product of the standard errors of two variables; the square root of the coefficient of determination. This value indicates how one variable is related to another.

Coefficient of variation (CV): A relative measure of variation estimated as the ratio of the standard deviation to the sample mean.

Cohesion: The tendency of a substance to cling together. The force of attraction that binds the molecules of the same kind.

Collapsibility, soil: A state of under consolidation related to the apparent cohesive strength of perennially unsaturated soils. When the soils become wetted, they slump. Clay soils have less tendency to collapse.

Colloid fraction: Organic and inorganic matter with very small particle size and a correspondingly large surface area per unit of mass.

Colloid: A particle, which may be a molecular aggregate, with a diameter of 0.1 to 0.001 μm (10^{-6} – 10^{-4} mm) which carries an electric charge. Soil clays and soil organic matter are often called soil colloids.

Colloidal clay: The smallest particle in a clay fraction; less than 1 micron (0.001mm) in diameter, which determines the physical and chemical properties of the soil.

Colloidal suspension: Suspension in water of particles so finely divided that they will not settle under the action of gravity but will diffuse, even in quiet water, under the random impulses of Brownian motion.

Colluvium: Deposit of broken rock and soil material accumulated on lower slopes and at the bottom of the hill due to gravitational force, and to some extent by soil creep, frost action or local wash.

Colorimeter: An instrument for chemical analysis of liquids by comparison of the color of the given liquid with its standard colors.

Command area: The total irrigable land area capacity of the canal dam or an irrigation project.

Committed water: Water reserved for use by the environment, downstream countries, or other downstream uses that have a right to the water.

Commodity-oriented research: Research focused on a given agricultural product.

Common land: Land belonging to village panchayat (council) and used for cattle grazing or any other community purpose.

Community forestry: A forest of the community by the community and for the community. It is exclusively managed for the interest of local community or a village and is run by them.

Compactor: A power-driven device used to compress materials to smaller volume.

Companion crop: One crop sown with another, used particularly of the small grains with which forage crops are sown. *Synonym* nurse crop.

Complementary enterprises: The enterprises in a production system which do not compete for resources among themselves viz land, labour, capital and management but mutually contribute to the production of each other.

Complementary intensive cropping: The cultivation of morphologically and physiologically different crops in an agricultural year under the sequential intercropping systems, so as to produce complementary effects upon each other and on succeeding associations.

Complete fertilizer: A product containing all three major plant nutrients (N, P, K) obtained by mixing different fertilizer materials.

Completely randomized design (CRD): An experimental design in which no blocking technique is employed and treatments could be randomly assigned to any experimental plot.

Complex fertilizers: A commercial fertilizer containing at least two or more of the major plant nutrients, obtained by a chemical reaction between the primary raw materials.

Component crops: The crops making up a cropping system are called component crops.

Component soil: The collection of polypedons or parts of polypedons within a map unit that are members of the taxon (or a kind of miscellaneous unit) for which the map unit is named.

Composite landscape: Landscape having topographic features developed as a result of more than one cycle of erosion.

Composition (volume) of soil: It is the relative percentage of three types of materials-solid, liquid and gas-constituting the soil. A silt loam soil has 50 per cent solids, 30 per cent liquid (water) and 20 per cent gas (air) by volume.

Compost: Organic residues or a mixture of organic residues and soil that have been piled, moistened, and allowed to undergo biological decomposition. A product obtained by the controlled decomposition of organic wastes, finally used as organic matter.

Composting: A biological process resulting in decomposition of the organic matter and lower the carbon: nitrogen ratio of the material. The result of composting is well-rotted manure known as compost.

Concentrate: A product containing a valuable mineral or metal and from which most of the waste material has been removed.

Concentrated flow: Flow of a large body of water over a relatively narrow course. It causes severe erosion and gullying.

Concretion: Crystallized calcium carbonate or iron oxide in the soil as a grain or nodule of varying colour, size, shape and hardness or other material cemented by calcium carbonate or iron oxide.

Conductivity: A measure of the ability of a liquid to transmit electrical current or heat.

Cone penetrometer: An instrument in the form of a cylindrical rod with a cone-shaped tip designed for penetrating soil and for measuring the end-bearing component of penetration/penetration resistance.

Configuration: Form of land surface with respect to horizontal outline and elevation.

Confined aquifer: An aquifer which is bounded above and below by formations of impermeable or relatively impermeable material. Water is confined aquifer is at pressure higher than atmospheric pressure. A water-bearing formation whose upper boundary is a layer which does not transmit water readily.

Conglomerate: Rock consisting of round water-borne pebbles cemented in a matrix of fine material, calcium carbonate, silica, iron oxide etc.; consolidated gravel or shingle.

Coniferous forest: A forest of ever green cone bearing trees yielding soft wood timber.

Conjunctive use: The use of more than one water source, systematically, to reduce overall environmental impacts. For example, someone might use groundwater instead of surface water during a drought period, and then return to using surface water when runoff became abundant again

Conservation cropping system: Growing crops in combination with minimum needed cultural and management practices. In a good conservation cropping system, the soil-improving crops and practices offset the effects of the soil-depleting crops and practices. Use of rotations that contain grasses and legumes and the return of crop residue to the soil, use of green manure crops of grasses and legumes, proper tillage, adequate fertilization, and weed and pest control are soil improving practices in conservation system.

Conservation tillage: A tillage system that does not invert the soil and that leaves a protective amount of crop residue on the surface throughout the year.

Conservation: The planning, management, and implementation of an activity with the objective of protecting the essential physical, chemical, biological characteristics of the environment and natural resources against degradation. Like soil, water, plants, animals etc. A balance between economic growth and environmental and natural resource protection.

Consistency (soil): The degree of cohesion and adhesion of soil material and its resistance to rupture and to penetration; plasticity, toughness, and stickiness of puddled soil material; and the manner in which the soil material behaves when subject to compression.

Consistency: Resistance of a material to rupture or deformation.

Consumptive use: The quantity of water used in plant growth by the combined processes of evaporation, transpiration, and retention in the plant expressed in units of volume per unit area.

Contaminant: Any foreign material physical, chemical, biological, or radiological substance lending impurity to a primary material; physical contaminants of compost include glass and plastic, chemical contaminants include heavy metals and toxic organic compounds.

Contiguous drought: Drought resulting from irregular precipitation patterns which cause a moisture deficit during the rainy season.

Contingency cropping: Cultivation of crops under abnormal situations like drought and floods as a mitigation strategy by producing some food, feed and fodder to encounter emergency conditions.

Continuous cropping: Cultivation of crop one after the other without seasonal fallowing. If not properly fertilized, leads to fertility degradation.

Contour border irrigation: An irrigation system practiced along the contour border.

Contour bunding: It consists of building earthen embankments across the slope of the land, following the contour as closely as possible. A series of such bunds divide the area into strips and act as barriers to the flow of water, thus reducing the amount and velocity of the runoff.

Contour cropping: Sowing of crop in rows or strips along contour.

Contour cultivation: It refers to all the tillage practices, mechanical treatments like planting, tillage and interculture performed nearly along the contour of the area (across the land slope).

Contour ditch: Irrigation ditch made on approximate contour.

Contour farming: Carrying out agricultural operations like ploughing, sowing/planting, intercultivation along the contour. It helps conserve soil moisture and reduce water erosion.

Contour flooding: Irrigation from contour ditches.

Contour furrow: A furrow ploughed on the contour on pasture or rangeland to prevent soil loss and so as to allow water to penetrate the soil; sometimes used in planting trees and shrubs on the contour.

Contour interval: The difference in elevation between adjacement contours on a map.

Contour irrigation: A system of irrigation where water is applied to a field along the contours.

Contour map: An elevation map in which lines connect points of equal elevation.

Contour or contour lines: "A contour is an imaginary line of constant elevation on the surface of the ground". Contours are represented on the map by contour lines. The contour and contour lines are often used interchangeably.

Contour planting: Planting sowing of row crops along the contours in a hilly terrain.

Contour ploughing: Ploughing along the contours.

Contour strip cropping: It is the cultivation of wide row agricultural crops (maize, cotton etc.) and close growing crops (green gram, black gram, cowpea, groundnut etc.) in narrow alternate strips on the contour on slopy lands to reduce soil erosion. On lands which are slightly or moderately wet, the strips are graded (grade < 1 %) (graded strip cropping). This helps in proper drainage as well as reduction of erosion.

Contour terrace: A terrace formed along the contours on steep mountain slopes with inadequate natural cover to prevent erosion until natural cover is established.

Control structure: A regulating structure to maintain water at a specified elevation, generally installed in gravity flow systems.

Convectional rainfall: Refers to the rainfall caused by vertical ascent of air due to excessive heating of the earth's surface.

Conventional planting: Planting that takes place days to months after a fallow period; usually involves primary and numerous secondary tillage operations. *Synonym:* delayed planting.

Conventional tillage: The combined primary and secondary tillage operations normally performed in preparing a seedbed for a given crop grown in a given geographical area.

Conveyance efficiency (Ec): The ratio between water received at the inlet of a field and that released out. Expressed in percentage.

Conveyance loss: Water that is lost in transit from a pipe, canal, or ditch by leakage or evaporation.

Coppice farming: Coppice farming is a practice of utilizing land capability by regular harvesting of such trees which produce numerous shoots from the stump after cutting. Coppice sprouts usually grow vigorously because they are served by roots big enough to feed the former tree.

Coppice mound (microrelief): Small mound of stabilized soil material around desert shrubs formed as a result of deposition of wind borne material.

Coppice: A plantation of trees which are periodically cut to provide fuel, poles etc. Shoots (coppice) grow from the cut stump.

Core trench: Excavation for core wall of an earthen embankment.

Core wall: A wall of masonry, sheet piling or compacted soil inside an earthen embankment to reduce seepage from a water reservoir.

Corrasion: Mechanical erosion of bed and banks of a river due to loose solid material (pebbles and sand etc.) being transported by water. Bed erosion is vertical corrasion and bank erosion is lateral corrasion.

Correction strip: Irregular area of land lying between consecutive contour strips.

Correlation coefficient (r): A measure of the degree of association between two variables and is computed as the ratio of the covariance of the two variables to the product of their standard errors. The degree of correlation ranges from +1 to -1. A correlation coefficient of 0 means that the two variables are not linearly interrelated. An 'r' value of +1 or -1 indicates complete association. A positive (plus) correlation means that high values of one variable are linearly associated with high values of the other. A negative (minus) correlation means that as one variable increases the other tends to decrease.

Corrosion: Wearing away of rocks by chemical action such as solution in carbon dioxide containing water.

Corrugation irrigation: Application of irrigation water in graded furrows or channels so spaced as to ensure adequate lateral water spread by the time required amount of water has entered the soil.

Cove: A small creek, inlet or steep sided recess in the side of a mountain.

Cover (ground): Vegetative growth producing a protective mat on the ground for reduction of soil erosion. Low growing shrubs and herbs constitute ground cover in forest areas.

Cover crops: Refers to the close growing crops which are grown primarily to cover the soil and reduce the loss of moisture due to leaching and erosion by wind and water. They also often reduce the weed growth. Effectiveness of the cover crop depends on close spacing and development of good canopy for interception of raindrops so as to expose minimum soil surface for erosion.

Cradle knoll: (micro relief): Small knoll formed by earth which is raised and left by an uprooted tree.

Crater: Funnel shaped hollow on the top of the cone of a volcano. Bottom of the funnel is the opening or vent through which lava finds its way to the surface.

Creek: Small stream or tributary of a river; narrow coastal inlet.

Creep: Slow mass movement of soil and soil material along relatively steep slopes primarily under gravity, facilitated by saturation with water and alternate freezing and thawing.

Crevasse: Wide crack in embankment of a river or canal; deep vertical crack in a glacier due to increase in bed slope, turning or different velocities in the middle and sides.

Crib dam: A barrier of timber forming bays or cells that are filled with heavy material like stone.

Critical area: A severely eroded and sediment producing area requiring special management for vegetation establishment and stabilization.

Critical difference: It is the difference above or equal to which all differences between variable are considered significant. The standard error of difference when multiplied further by 2 and t-value (at required level of significance) at the error degrees of freedom is critical difference.

Critical length: An approach for fixing the spacing of bunds by determining the critical length of land between adjacent bunds. Increase in drainage area increases both velocity and amount of runoff gathering in narrow channel. But the critical length approach, the attempt is to space bunds in such a way that the velocity remains within non-erosive limit.

Critical level: The level of a factor which is just limiting to plant performance; sometimes specifically defined as 95% of the performance when the factor is non limiting. Widely used in plant and soil analysis for evidence of nutrient deficiency or toxicity. In case of leaf-area index, the term used as the index sufficient for near-maximum light interception or growth rate.

Critical period (water): It is the period during which a crop is most sensitive to moisture stress and the loss can not be compensated by adequate moisture supply at a later stage.

Critical temperature: The temperature above which a gas cannot be liquefied; the temperature above which a substance cannot exhibit distinct gas and liquid phases.

Crop coefficient: Crop coefficient is the ratio between evapotranspiration of crop and potential evapotranspiration.

Crop residue management: Use or management of crop residue left after harvest for protection or improvement of the soil.

Crop residue: Portion of a plant left in the field after harvest. It can be used to serve as vegetative mulch to reduce erosion and induce conservation of moisture.

Crop rotation (sequential cropping): The planned cultivation of different crops on a piece of land in succession. System of cultivation where crops such as cereals & legumes that need different nutrients or management are grown one after the other. Principles of good land and crop management, *i.e.* utilization of moisture and nutrients from different soil depths are observed. Conservation of soil with good crop canopy during periods of high rainfall, inclusion of leguminous crops amongst cereal and cash crops, control of insect pests, weeds and crop diseases etc.

Crop season: The most favourable weather condition for the growth & yield of a crop.

Crop water depletion: The amount of water depleted for the process of crop production by transpiration (T), evaporation from soils (E) and field ponds and canals. Originating from rainfall (green water), irrigation (blue water) or a combination of both, it is a consumptive use defined as the water is no longer available for other use because it has evaporated, transpired, or incorporated into crops.

Crop water requirements (ETcrop): The depth of water needed to meet the evapotranspiration requirements of a disease-free crop, growing in large fields under non restricting soil conditions and achieving full production potential under the given growing environment.

Crop water use efficiency: The ratio of crop yield to the amount of water used by the crop plants to meet evapo-transpiration requirement.

Cropping intensity: It is the ratio between total cropped area and actual net cultivated area expressed in percentage. For individual plot, cropping intensity is number of crops taken in sequence in a crop year expressed as per cent. One crop, two crops and three crops indicate 100 per cent, 200 per cent and 300 per cent cropping intensity respectively.

Cropping pattern design: The crop pattern for year-round land utilization at a given area considering available physical, biological, and socio-economic factors. The spatial and temporal combination of crops on a plot and the management used to produce them.

Cropping pattern: Arrangement or method of raising crops in an area, *e.g.* mono, double, multiple, relay, mix cropping etc. Crop rotation also constitutes a cropping pattern.

Cropping scheme: The plan of raising different crops on individual plots of a farm with an object of getting the maximum returns without impairing soil fertility.

Cropping season: The period during the year when the environment is favourable for the growth of agricultural crops. In regions that have bimodal rainfall, there will be two such seasons.

Cropping sequence: The time course of events among crop components utilizing the same unit of land. Cropping sequence can be coincident, concomitant, interpolated or overlapping.

Cropping system (farming): The pattern of crops taken up for a given piece of land, or order in which the crops are cultivated on piece of land over a fixed period and their interaction with farm resources and other farm enterprises and available technology which determine their make up.

Cropping systems research: The research activities, that focuses on the evaluation of farmers existing cropping systems; design, testing, and development of new improved cropping pattern and component technologies for selected environments to efficiently utilize available farm resources.

Cropping, double: Practice of raising two consecutive crops in a crop year on the same piece of land.

Cropping, mix: Practice of sowing two or more crops simultaneously on the same piece of land. Admixed seed may be broadcast or seed of different crops may be sown in different lines. Examples-maize+black gram; sorghum + red gram; cotton+groundnut: wheat+gram.

Cropping, mono: Practice of raising the same crop year after year on a piece of land.

Cropping, multiple: Practice of raising more than two crops (generally three), one after the other, in a crop year on the same piece of land. It may be done under irrigation.

Cropping, relay: Practice of a rising three to four crops in a crop year in a sequence such that the next crop is sown in the standing earlier crop to save time and ensure optimum growth for each crop. It is a practice for irrigated areas. Example maize-potato-wheat-green gram.

Crop-residue management: Use of the non-commercials portion of the plant or crop for protection or improvement of the soil.

Cross sectioning: It is the operation of levelling to determine the surface undulation or outline of the ground transverse to the given line and on either side of it.

Crown: Foliage portion of the tree consisting of branches, leaves, flowers and fruit.

Crumb structure: Soil structure in which most of the peds are crumbs.

Crumb: Soft, porous and more or less rounded ped with 1-5 mm diameter. The aggregates are small and are weakly held together and are like crumbs of breads, found in pasture soils or grassy lands.

Crust: Surface layer on soils having thickness from a few milli-metres to 2.5 cm which is much more compact, hard and brittle when dry, than the lower material.

Crystalline rock: Rock made up of minerals which have crystallized in place from magma.

Cubic foot: A volume equal to that of a cube 1 foot in length, 1 foot in breadth and 1 foot in thickness. One cubic foot of water = 28.37 liters or 6.23 gallons or 0.0283 cubic meters.

Cubic meters: A volume equal to that of a cube one meter in length, one meter in breadth and one meter in thickness. One cubic meter of water = one kilo liters or 1000 liters or 220 gallons or 35.3 cubic feet.

Cultivation: Normally shallow tillage operations to improve, drainage, water conservation, aeration, or to control weeds. It includes any labour and care taken in the raising of plants, such as stirring soil, fertilizing etc.

Cultivator: An instrument or small machine for cultivating small areas of land.

Culturable command area: The area which can be irrigated from a scheme or facilities created and is fit for cultivation.

Culvert: Channel or conduit conveying water across and under a road.

Cumec: A unit of flow or discharge equivalent to cubic metre per second.

Cumulative effects: the combined environmental impacts that accumulate over time and space as a result of a series of similar or related individual actions, contaminants, or projects.

Cumulative infiltration: Total volume of water infiltrated per unit area of soil surface during a specified time period.

Cumulative run-off: The total volume of ron-off over a specified period of time.

Cup anemometer: A device used for measuring the wind speed from the speed of rotation of wind mill (set of cup rotating around vertical axis).

Curbside collection: A system where recyclable materials are collected at the curb, often from special containers, to be taken to various processing facilities.

Current: Movement of water in a channel or river; vertical movement of an air-mass.

Cusec: A unit of water flow or discharge of cubic foot per sec.

Cut and fill: Process of excavating part of an area and using the excavated material to fill adjacentareas in order to attain relatively levelled surface.

Cut off time (irrigation): The time at which the supply of water is cut off at the top end, leaving the water already supplied to flow down the slope in case of surface irrigation.

Cut off: The digital number in the histogram of a digital image which is set to zero during contrast stretching. Usually this is a value below which atmospheric scattering makes a major contribution.

Cut-off drain: Surface drain, sub-surface drain or a combination of both, constructed to intercept flowing water. Same as interceptor drain.

Cut-off: It is a natural or artificial channel which serves to shorten a meandering stream. It shortens the stream length. Increases velocity of water and decreases the length of any levees required.

Cutthroat flume: It is just like a Parshall flume without throat section. The flumes has flat bottom, vertical walls and a zero length throat section. Mmost advantage of this flume is economy. It can operate either as a free or submerged flow structure.

Cycle of erosion: Course of development in evolution of landscape: comprising of stages youth, maturity and old age. During youthful stage the valley formation is under vigorous development, rivers flowing rapidly and having irregular beds, rapid waterfalls and lakes. During maturity, the landscape relief attains maximum amplitude. Lakes, rapids and waterfalls have vanished and the river beds, gorges have widend into- V-shaped valleys. In old age, the width of the valley floor is several times the meander-belt and there are widespread low lands with relatively faint relief (peneplane). If these lands are uplifted, youthful activity is re-established and the cycle would repeat.

D

Dam: A man made structure across a river or stream to control its flow for a number of useful purposes like flood control, irrigation, production of hydro-electricity etc.

Darcy's law: Law describing the rate of flow of water through saturated porous media. A volume of water passing through a unit area per unit time is proportional to the cross sectional area and to the difference in hydraulic head and inversely proportional to the thickness of the medium. In this law, hydraulic conductivity (K) is taken as proportionality constant.

Data acquisition system: The system used to measure and record the data.

Data: The collection of facts of experiments, instruments, and surveys that are calculated statistically to give measured statistical results.

Database: Relational data structure used to store, query, and retrieve information.

Datum line: Zero or based level with reference to which altitudes of land surfaces and sea depths are described.

Datum surface or line: It is any arbitrarily assumed level surface or line from which vertical distances are measured. In India the datum adopted for G.T.S. bench marks is the mean sea level at Mumbai.

Dead furrow: It is an open trench left in between adjacent strip of land after completion of ploughing.

Dead storage: The maximum capacity of a reservoir below the outlet level. Dead storage are not useful as it cannot be drain out.

Debris dam: A barrier constructed across a stream or channel for stopping transport of debris along the bed.

Debris guard: Screen at the entrance of a channel for stopping debris. Also trash rack.

Debris: Material formed by disintegration of rocks and vegetative material; transportable by streams, ice. gravity etc.

Decalcification: Removal of calcium carbonate or calcium ions from the soil by leaching.

Deciduous forest: Forest having trees which shed leaves in hot season (monsoon forests) to reduce moisture loss by transpiration and in autumn (cool temperate forests) to protect themselves against cold and frost. Examples is teak (monsoon forest) and oak (temperate forests).

Decomposition gases: Gases produced in the breakdown of garbage or other material. Some, such as methane, are flammable.

Decomposition: Breaking down into component, parts or basic elements.

Deep percolation: Water which percolates below root zone of plants and hence is not available for their growth.

Deep placement: Refers to the application of fertilizer or nutrients below the soil surface or furrow at a depth of 20 cm or more before planting of crop.

Deep ploughing: Ploughing very deep into the soil, used when reclaiming previously virgin land for agricultural purposes.

Deep seepage: The part of collected run-off which escapes from a reservoir through the underlying earth or rock strata below any possible intercepting cut out constructed at the dam.

Deep soil: A soil having a profile solum depth of more than 1 meter.

Deep tillage or subsoiling: Tillage operation that loosens the soil up to a depth of 40 cm or more for the purpose of conserving moisture in the monsoon season or for breaking hard pans.

Deferred grazing: Discontinuation of grazing on an area for specified time period during growing season in order to encourage plant reproduction etc.

Deflation: Removal and transport of fine soil particles by wind erosion.

Deforestation: Large scale clearance of forests.

Degradable: capable of being chemically reduced or broken down.

Degradation: Wearing down or deepening of a valley by scouring action of the flowing water (river, stream etc.). It also refers to reduction in functionality of a resource due to over exploitation.

Delineation of watershed: Watershed delineation is to describe or sketching out the area bounded by ridge line, contributing runoff at common point and dividing or separating it from the adjoining area.

Delineation: An individual polygon shown by a closed boundary on a map that defines the area, shape, and location of a map unit within a landscape.

Delivery ratio, sediment: Ratio of sediment yield (tonnes/unit area year) to gross erosion (tonnes/unit area/year). It is less than 1.

Delta (water): Refers to the total depth of water required by a crop from sowing to maturity.

Delta: A body of alluvium deposited at or near the mouth of a river or stream where it enters a body of relatively quiet water, generally a sea or lake.

DEM : Digital Elevation Model. A GIS raster layer representing elevation.

Demonstration plot: A plot planted specifically as a demonstration at a research station.

Demonstration trial: Refers to a non-replicated trial conducted for the purpose to demonstrate some established technology or principle.

Demonstration: Refers to the practical explanation or showing of a potential technology to the user by displaying working of a particular practice or technology, developed and established on a research farm.

Dendritic drainage pattern: Tree branches like pattern of tributaries of a stream.

Denitrification: Biochemical or chemical reduction of nitrite or nitrate into gaseous nitrogen as molecular nitrogen or an oxide of nitrogen.

Denudation: Combined process of weathering, erosion and transport of the weathered surface material, resulting in sculpturing of land surface and degradation of hills to base level.

Depletion: Refers to continued withdrawal of water from body of water stream, reservoir. Also used for nutrient in soil.

Deposit: Material left at a new place by natural transport agencies such as water, wind, ice, gravity or by human activity.

Depth of cut: Refers to the maximum depth of the penetration with reference to the initial soil surface.

Depth of irrigation: Refers to the quantity of water in terms of depth (cm) required to bring soil water content of root zone to field capacity.

Depth, effective soil: Depth of soil up to which plant roots penetrate to draw water and plant nutrients; depth to a layer which retards root growth.

Desert climate: Type of climate characterised by aridity or lack of regular precipitation. It is unproductive and unable to support settled, independent communities.

Desert crust: A hard surface soil layer containing calcium carbonate, gypsum or any other binding material exposed in desert areas.

Desert pavement: Layer of gravel or stones left on the surface in desert areas due to removal of fine material by wind erosion.

Desert soil: A zonal great soil group characterised by a thin, light coloured surface horizon (may be vesicular) underlain usually by calcareous material formed under sparse shrub growth in arid climate. Soils are rich in soluble salts. Low in N and organic matter has a high pH.

Desert varnish: Glossy sheen on stones and gravel in arid regions due to abrasion by wind borne soil particle.

Desert: Almost barren land having arid hot or cool climate, resulting in sparse vegetation. A desert may have a poor grassland or scrub. In rock desert, the rocks are exposed due to wind erosion, in stony desert, rocks are broken into fragments due to diurnal temperature changes, in sandy desert, sand dunes are present. Area where lack of vegetation is due to high altitude and low temperatures is called cold desert (Ladakh in Jammu & Kashmir, India).

Design of experiment: The complete sequence of steps taken ahead of time to ensure that the appropriate data will be obtained, which will permit an objective analysis and will lead to valid inferences regarding the stated problem.

Design: Refers to the method of arranging sample or experimental plots to minimize the effects of uncontrolled variations in fertility and other natural factors and to make possible estimate of such effects in relations to those due to variations in treatment & draw conclusions.

Desilting area: An area with growing grass, shrubs or other vegetation for depositon of silt and other debris from run-off going into a pond or area needing protection from sedimentation.

Detachment: Removal of fragments of soil material from soil mass by agencies of erosion like water, wind, ice directly or borne particles.

Detention dam: A structure constructed for temporary storage of stream flow or run-off for subsequent controlled release.

Determinants of cropping pattern: It includes all the factors (biotic and abiotic) that influence the performance of cropping pattern and are not readily modifiable by changes in cultural techniques of crop production.

Determinate growth: Type of growth characterized by the cessation of growth of plants after initiation of flowering in plant species uniformly within certain time limits. The plant first completes its vegetative phase and then enters into reproductive phase, thereby making a clear-cut distinction between these two growth phases, *e.g.* cereals and grasses.

Deterministic model: A non-stochastic model in which no random variables are recognized. Exact relationships are postulated, and the output is predicted by the input with complete certainty.

Detritus: Fragmentary material such as sand and mud formed by disintegration of pre-existing rocks.

Dew point: Temperature at which the atmosphere becomes saturated with water vapour which at lower temperature condenses to form drops of dew on soil surface or vegetation near the surface.

Diagnostic horizons: Combination of soil horizons with typical characteristics indicative of classes of soils. Those occurring at the surface are called epipedons and those occurring below the surface are called subsoil diagnostic horizons or endopedon.

Diamond drill: A piece of equipment used to drill through hard rock, the drill has a diamond on the drill bit and can cut through hard rock better than a metal drill bit.

Diaphragm type embankment: In this type of embankment pervious material occupy bulk but a diaphragm of impermeable material like plastic, butyl, puddle clay steel wood etc is provided. Diaphragm cutoff extends from above waterline to down impervious foundation

Difference in elevation (H): It is the vertical distance between two different points.

Differential leveling: It is the operation of leveling to determine the elevations of points some distance apart or to establish bench marks.

Digital data: Can possess only discrete values. In the usual binary scheme these values are high/low, on/off or 1/0.

Digital display: A form of data display in which values are shown as arrays of numbers.

Digital image processing: Computer manipulation of the digital-number values of an image in order to get meaningful information.

Digital image: An image where continuous range of analogue values of the object or property are converted to a range expressed by a finite number of integers, usually recorded as binary codes from 0 to 255, or as one byte.

Digital number (DN): Value assigned to a pixel in a digital image, according to the variation in property observed by sensonr.

Digitization: Process of converting an analog display into a digital display.

Digitizer: Device for scanning an image and converting it into numerical format.

Digitizing: Process and operations for encoding graphic data into some numeric system (*e.g.*, X, Y - coordinates) and storing it on a computer.

Dike (levee): An embankment to confine or control water to prevent overflow in lowlands.

Dilution: to decrease the concentration of a substance by mixing it with another or by adding water

Dip: Angle which a stratum, vein, dyke or sill makes with the horizontal.

Direct runoff: The part of runoff which enters the stream quickly after the rainfall or snow melting.

Disc harrow: A type of harrow, with two or more sets of saucer-shaped discs

Disc plough: A type of plough with large rotating discs in place of the mould board.

Discharge: The volume of water that passes a given location in unit. Usually expressed in cubic feet per second (cusec) or cubic meter per second (cumsec)

Disinfection: to destroy or prevent the growth of micro organisms. To remove/control infection.

Disintegration: Reduction of rocks into smaller pieces predominantly by mechanical means.

Disperse: To break compound particles of soil (aggregates) into individual primary particles. To distribute or suspend fine particles, such as clay, in a dispersion medium like water.

Dispersion medium: Portion of colloidal system in which disperse phase is distributed.

Dispersion ratio: The ratio of silt plus clay in soil suspension after limited shaking and settling, to actual silt plus clay determined by mechanical analysis. Greater this ratio, more easily the soil is dispersed and eroded.

Disposal: The relocation and/or containment of unwanted materials. Putting away unusable substance.

Dissolution: The process of dissolving a solid in a liquid

Dissolved oxygen (DO): The oxygen dissolved in water and readily available to fish and other aquatic organisms.

Dissolved solids: Total quantity of dissolved material organic as well as inorganic, contained in water.

Distributary: A channel leaving a river and not rejoining it, carrying water to a lake or sea. Such channels are formed in delta areas or on alluvial fans. Terms also use for small channel receiving water from a canal for delivery to farmers' fields.

Ditch: A water channel dug to assist drainage or the mark a boundary.

Diversified cropping: A cropping system including cultivation of two or more crops where no single crop contributes 50% or more towards the total crop production or monetary income annually.

Diversified farm: A farm in which diversified farming system is practiced and no single product or source of income equals as much as 50% of the total receipt.

Diversion (or diversion terrace): A ridge of earth, generally a terrace, built to protect down slope areas by diverting runoff from its natural course.

Diversion boxes: A water control device used for diverting irrigation water in different directions available in 2-way, 3-way or 4-way diversion structure.

Diversion canal: A canal that diverts water from one point to another from the point of diversion at the main canal to the beginning of the distribution system.

Diversion dam: A barrier or structure built for diverting all or part of water in a stream into a different course.

Diversion rate: A measure of the amount of waste material being diverted for recycling compared with the total amount previously thrown away.

Diversion: It is a channel constructed for diverting run-off from above a gully head and causing it to flow in a controlled manner to a protected outlet. Process of diverting run-off from a hill side away from habitation and agricultural lands.

Diversity index: The measurement of multiplicity of farm products. Computing as reciprocal of sum of squares of the share of gross revenue received from each individual farm enterprise in a single year.

Dominant (ecology): Species having considerable influence upon the conditions of existence of associated species due to number or behaviour.

Double cropping: A type of multi-cropping. Cultivation of two crops a year in sequence from the same piece of land.

Draft: The effort required to pull an implement through the soil. Also the control on a modern tractor which keeps this load constant by raising or lowering the implement.

Drag: Force retarding the velocity of water or wind over the ground surface. Forced applied on particle or surface due to horizontal component of force of flowing fluid.

Drain tile: Concrete, ceramic, PVC or clay pipe laid underground for drainage of excess water from an area.

Drain: A structure constructed remove excess water from the land through open ditches or sub-surface tile drains. To lose water from the soil by percolation.

Drainage channel: A small ditch made to remove water from the soil surface.

Drainage class (natural): Frequency and duration of saturation or partial saturation during soil formation, as opposed to altered drainage, which is commonly the result of artificial drainage or irrigation but may be caused by the sudden deepening of channels or the blocking of drainage outlets. Seven classes of natural soil drainage are recognized:

Drainage coefficient: The rate of water drained off from a given area in 24 hrs is known as drainage coefficient expressed as depth, in cm.

Drainage density: It is defined as the ratio of the total channel length [L] in the watershed to total watershed area [A]. Greater drainage density gives more runoff. Drainage density = L/A.

Drainage of surface water: Diversion or removal of excess water from the surface of the land by means of improved natural or constructed channels, supplemented when necessary by the shaping and grading of land surfaces to such channels.

Drainage requirement: The amount of water that a drain must remove in a given time from a field for satisfactory crop growth.

Drainage water: Refers to the water that soil is unable to hold against the force of gravity also called gravitational water, free water, and excess water.

Drainage way: A general term for a course or channel along which water moves in draining an area. A term restricted to relatively small, linear depressions that, at some time, move concentrated water and either lack a defined channel or have a small, defined channel.

Drainage: Removal of excess gravitational water from the soil by artificial means to enhance crop production. Surface drainage and Sub surface drainage or underground drainage are two types.

Drawdown: Phenomena of lowering of the ground-water surface in a channel or water table as a result of pumping or withdrawal of water.

Drip irrigation: Method of irrigation in which the required quantity of water is applied by means of mains, sub mains, manifolds & plastic laterals, with equally spaced emitters usually laid on the ground surface pressure and at low discharge to the root zone of the crop.

Drizzle: Rainfall in which water drops are very small *i.e.* 0.2 to 0.5 mm diameter.

Drop inlet spillway: Overfall structure, where water drops through a vertical riser into a discharge conduit.

Drop spillway: Overfall structure where water drops over a vertical wall into an apron.

Drop structure: A device made up of wood, iron or cement concrete installed wherever there is drop in the field channels for controlling safe and non-erosive flow of water downstreams.

Drosometer: A instrument used for measuring dew.

Drought avoidance: The capacity of a plant/species to grow for a longer time in a given moisture-stress conditions. The process is performed by special adaptations such as deep root system, less canopy area etc.

Drought escape: The process which enables the plant to complete its life cycle before serious moisture stress can cause damage to crop growth and yield.

Drought recovery: The ability of plant to resume normal growth upon alleviation of drought.

Drought resistance: The capacity of a plant to maintain growth and yield under moisture-stress conditions.

Drought stress: Effect on growth/yield of a plant due to water limitation.

Drought tolerance: Ability of plants to grow and produce grain, with part of its life cycle under water stress.

Drought year: Refer to a year in which rainfall of particular place is deficit by more than twice the standard deviation of long range normals.

Dry aggregate: Compound or secondary soil particle which is not destroyed by dry sieving.

Dry farming or dry land farming: A method of farming in arid and semi-arid areas without using irrigation, the land being treated so as to conserve moisture. The practice of crop production entirely with rain water received during the crop season or on conserved soil moisture in low rainfall (<800 mm) areas of arid and semi-arid climate and the crops may face mild to very severe moisture stress during their life-cycle.

Dry-bulb thermometer: Thermometer kept in Stevenson's screen used to determine current air temperature. This measurement and the reading from a wet-bulb thermometer are used for the determination of relative humidity or dew point from a psychrometric table.

Duff: More or less firm organic matter layer over mineral soil, consisting of vegetative matter in different stages of decomposition.

Dug out pond: A pond formed by excavation rather than by constructing a dam.

Dumpy Level: The dumpy level is simple, compact and most commonly used instrument for measuring elevations of points relative to a bench mark level. It is cheaper, and easier to maintain in adjustment. It measures horizotal bearing not vertical.

Dune: It is a mound or ridge of sand in desert areas or along the sea-coast formed by deposition of wind borne material. Initially the sand particles may have accumulated against an obstacle and the heaped material grew with more deposition. Dune may be crescent shaped or a narrow ridge extending parallel to the prevailing wind direction. In areas of variable winds, dunes have no particular shape. Smaller dunes usually move, but the bigger dunes may get fixed up due to rain water (as and when rainfall occurs) percolating to the lower sand layers. The sea-coast dunes usually resemble desert dunes in profile.

Duration curve: Graphical representation of number of times certain flows are equalled or exceeded in a period of record.

Duripan: A subsurface diagnostic horizon cemented by silica.

Dust devil: A local dust whirl of few metres in diameter, in which particles are swept around the centre and lifted to great heights (600-900 metres) above the earth's surface.

Dust mulch: Shallow layer of loose granular or powdery soil created in agricultural fields by shallow cultivation in order-to reduce moisture loss from soil surface by breaking capillaries continuity from deeper layer.

Dust storm: Refers to a storm caused by turbulent wind producing a thick mass of dust reducing visibility (even up to zero) in arid dusty areas. The storm is preceded by a wall of dust sometimes over 3 km high. The air is dry and any rain in the initial stages may evaporate before reaching the ground. Later, the rain may shorten the duration of the dust storm by washing down the dust.

Duty of water: The area covered by one cusec of water flowing continuously throughout the growing season of a crop. It is therefore varies with kind of crop, season, nature of soil, method of irrigation and method of cultivation.

Dyke: Embankment of soil or stones raised along the banks of a river to prevent overflow of low lands.

E

Earth pillars: Conical pillars of soil capped by relatively flat stones left on the ground due to erosion of the surrounding area under high rainfall. Flat stones protect these pillars from the beating action of raindrops.

Earthworm: An invertebrate animal with a long thin body divided into many segments, living in large numbers in the soil. They are essential to the health of the soil, they draw organic matter down, bring subsoil up and their burrows assist drainage and aeration.

Ecoclimate: The climate observed under crop canopy.

Ecofarming: Farming land by using practices that maintain biological diversity and conserve the soil resource base. It aims at the maintenance of soil chemically, biologically and physically the way nature would do it left alone. Soil would then take proper care of plants growing on it.

Ecological amplitudes: The range of environmental factors (tolerance limits) within which an organism or a physiological process can function.

Ecological crop geography: The study of broad spatial distribution of crop plants and the rationale of such distributions in terms of physical and socio- economic environment influencing the production of crops.

Ecology: Science which deals with interrelations of organisms and their environment.

Economic efficiency: It is the allocation of resources in the economy that yields an overall net gain to society as measured through valuation in terms of the benefits of each use minus its costs.

Economic viability: Economic viability of a watershed can be determined by a budget analysis. The analysis includes cost of labour, works and purchased inputs for all operations specified as well as benefits obtained. It includes the environmental and social benefits deriving from the watershed, and is a pre-requisite for wider adoption of sustainable watershed management practices

Economic yield: It is the economically useful part or consumable part of total dry matter produced by a plant or crop.

Ecosystem approach: An approach based on the application of appropriate scientific methodologies focused on levels of biological organization, which encompass the essential structure, processes, functions and interactions among organisms and their environment. It refers to a strategy for the integrated management of land, water, and living resources that promotes conservation and sustainable use in an equitable way.

Ecosystem assessment: A social process through which the findings of science concerning the causes of ecosystem change, their consequences for human well-being, and management and policy options are brought to bear on the needs of decision-makers.

Ecosystem services: Refers to the benefits people obtain from ecosystems. These include provisioning services such as food and timber; regulating services such as flood and disease control, and ground water recharge; cultural services such as spiritual, recreational, and cultural benefits; and supporting services, such as nutrient cycling, that maintain the conditions for life on Earth.

Ecosystem stability: A description of the dynamic properties of an ecosystem. An ecosystem is considered stable if it returns to its original state shortly after a perturbation (resilience), exhibits low temporal variability (constancy), or does not change dramatically in the face of a perturbation (resistance).

Ecosystem: An ecological entity consisting of the biological community and the non-living environment functioning together in an interacting system. It is a dynamic complex of plant, animal, and microorganism communities and the nonliving environment, interacting as a functional unit. Humans are an integral part of ecosystems. A well-defined ecosystem has strong interactions among its components and weak interactions across its boundaries.

Ecotone: A transitional vegetation strip between two communities, having characteristics of the neighbouring two types of vegetation and its own characteristics.

Ecotype: Population of a locally adapted species having distinctive limit of tolerance to environmental factors of a particular locality.

Edaphic factors: Edaphic factors are those related to the soil. It includes chemical and physical nature of the soil, the availability of air and water in it, its temperature, alkalinity and acidity etc. which affect plant growth through effect on nutrients, water supply and anchorage.

Edaphic: Pertaining to soil. A term that describes the influence of soil on plant growth and development.

Edaphology: The science that deals with the influence of soils on living things; particularly plants, including humankind's use of land for plant growth.

Effective irrigation: Refers to an artificial, controlled and uniform application of water to a crop in required amount at required time, to produce optimum yields without waste of water and adverse effect on soil at lowest cost.

Effective precipitation: Part of the total precipitation which becomes available for plant growth.

Effective rainfall: Effective rainfall is a part of rainfall available for the consumptive use of the crop.

Efficiency: It is the ratio of power output to power input.

Efficient cropping zone: A cropping zone characterized by relative yield index of 200% and relative spread indices varying from 90 to 200%.

Effluent: Treated or untreated liquid gas waste material that is discharged into the environment from a structure such as a settling pond or treatment plant.

Elevation: It is vertical distance of a point above or below the datum (mean sea level). It is also known as the reduced level (R.L.)

Eluvial horizon: Horizon which has lost material from the soil by solution or suspension within the soil profile.

Eluviation: Refers to the process of removal of soil material in suspension or solution, from a layer or layers of soil.

Emergency spillway: A spillway constructed for discharging runoff in excess of the given design flood. It protects the embankment from overtopping action by passing the water in excess of temporary storage capacity of reservoir due to unexpected runoff event.

Emission spectrum: A spectrum of electromagnetic radiation containing narrow spectral lines from an element.

Emission: A substance discharged into the air, especially by an internal combustion engine.

Emulsifier: A surface active substance which promotes the suspension of one liquid to another.

Emulsifying agent: Refers to a substance that coats the particles of the dispersed phase and prevents coagulation of colloidal particles.

Enclosure: An area which is fenced to confine animals.

End contraction: Horizontal distance from end of weir crests to side of weir pond.

End products of weathering: Refers to chemically stable materials produced as a resultants of rock decomposition. They may be quartz, clay (silicates of alumina derived from felspars), calcium carbonate (from lime felspars) and salts in solution.

Energy cropping plantation: The cultivation or plantation of crops and trees in the field for energy purpose *e.g. Leucanea, Casuarina, Eucalyptus,* etc.

Energy farming: Cultivation of crops that will provide fuel, or energy products for example, close-planted, fast-growing tree species such as poplar, leucaena, eucalyptus etc.

Energy productivity ratio: It is the ratio that expresses food yield per unit of energy input and is most often used in evaluating the energetic of agricultural systems.

Energy recovery: The conversion of waste energy, generally through the combustion of processed or raw refuse (incineration), to produce steam.

Energy: The ability of a system to do work. It exists in many different inter-convertible forms such as heat, light, motion and electricity.

Energy-efficiency index: The index that estimates the rate at which the use of energy inputs generates energy outputs.

Engineering survey: To collect detailed data for the design for of projects involving roads, railways, etc.

Enriched compost: Compost fortified with nutrients through addition of fertilizers during its production to improve nutrient content and narrow down the C: N ratio.

Enrichment ratio of a soil constituent: Ratio of concentration in soil material in run-off to concentration in soil from which, run-off originated.

Entisols: An order of soil classification including those soils which have no diagnostic pedogenic horizons. They may be found under any climate on recent geomorphic surfaces or recent alluvium. Those soils that have natal, if any, profile development are known as entisols. Soils in desert belong to this classification. The productivity of these soils varies with their location and properties. With controlled water supply and proper fertilization, these soils have good productivity and good for vegetables, groundnut, citrus, wheat, paddy, etc.

Environment: Sum total of all external conditions (biotic and abiotic) influencing the existence or development of an organism or a community.

Environmental impact statement (EIS): A report submitted by an organization to describe the possible positive or negative impacts of its actions on the environment, and its plans to reduce, mitigate or avoid these impacts.

Ephemeral stream: A stream which flows only in response to precipitation and receives no water from springs or snow. Its channel is always above the water table.

Epipedon: A diagnostic horizon occurring at the soil surface.

Equalizer: A barrier constructed at regular interval in continuous contour trenches for the purpose to avoid breaching due to excessive accumulation of runoff. Equalizers of 20-30 cm width are placed at regular interval in CCTs.

Equivalence factor (intercropping): The equivalence factor is the number of plants of component 'a' which is equally competitive to one plant of component 'b'. A equivalence factor of less than one, indicates that component 'a' is more competitive then 'b'.

Erode: To wear away or remove the land surface by water, wind, ice, gravity etc.

Erodibility: The lack of resistance or susceptibility of soil to erosion.

Erodible: Susceptible to erosion by water, wind, ice, gravity etc.

Erosion (accelerated): Erosion much more rapid than geologic erosion, mainly as a result of human or animal activities or of a catastrophe in nature, for example, fire, that exposes the surface.

Erosion (geologic): Erosion caused by geologic processes acting over long geologic periods and resulting in the wearing away of mountains and the building up of such landscape features as flood plains and coastal plains.

Erosion class: Grouping of erosion conditions in accelerated erosion based on degree of erosion or on characteristic patterns.

Erosion index: The product of kinetic energy and maximum 30 minute rainfall intensity of a rain storm. It reflects the combined potential of raindrop impact and run-off turbulence to erode soil particles.

Erosion pavement: A layer of coarse fragments, such as sand or gravel, remaining on the surface of the ground after the removal of fine particles by erosion.

Erosion potential: A numerical value expressing the inherent erodibility of a soil or maximum potential erosion. In the Universal Soil Loss Equation (under clean tillage, up and down slope) EP= *RKLS*

Erosion resistant crop: A crop that provides effective protection against soil loss by erosion because of its dense foliage & soil binding ambition of that root system etc.

Erosion rill: Refers to a type of erosion due to water by producing very small number of channels that can be obliterated by tillage operations.

Erosion sheet: Removal of a fairly uniform layer of soil from earth surface, often scarcely perceptible especially when caused by wind.

Erosion splash: A type of soil erosion under the influence of falling rain drops resulting from soil splash.

Erosion surface: A land surface shaped by the action of erosion, especially by running water.

Erosion: Detachment and movement of soil or rock by running water, wind, ice, gravity etc.

Erosive velocity: Velocity of the erosive agent necessary to cause erosion.

Erosive: Tending to cause erosion. Water or wind having sufficient velocity to cause erosion.

Erosivity: The measured or predicted ability of water, wind, gravity, or any other erosion agent to cause erosion.

Error variance: A measure of experimental error.

Error, experimental: The deviation of a randomly occurring observation from its true or expected value.

Escrapment: A steep face of high land; the escarpment of a hill or- mountain is generally on side nearest the sea.

Esker: A narrow ridge of sandy or gravelly drip deposited due to the combined action of a stream and glacier ice.

Estuary: Mouth of a river where tidal activity is evident and fresh water and sea water mix. Estuary is developed mainly in areas recently submerged by the sea. It acts as breeding ground and habitat of large number of species and display great biodiversity.

Eutrophication: Refers to the degradation of water quality due to enrichment by nutrients, primarily nitrogen (N) and phosphorus (P), which results in excessive plant (principally algae) growth and decay. Low dissolved oxygen (DO) in the water is a common consequence.

Evaporation (E): The process of the change in the state of a liquid or solid to a gas or vapour.

Evaporation losses: Refers to the loss of water in the form of water vapour from land and water bodies. The process of evaporation of water in nature is one of the fundamental components of the hydrological cycle by which water is converted from liquid state to vapour through absorption of heat energy. This is the only form of moisture transfer from land and oceans into the atmosphere.

Evaporation pan: Evaporimeter composed of a fairly deep tank or pan with a rather large surface in which lowering of the water level caused by evaporation can be measured.

Evaporation rate: The rate at which a particular substance will vapourize (evaporate) when compared to the rate of a known substance such as ethyl ether. This term is especially useful for health and fire-hazard considerations.

Evaporative cooling: Temperature drop caused by evaporation of water from a moist surface.

Evaporimeter: Device used for measuring the quantity of water evaporated into the atmosphere during a given time interval.

Evaporization: Vaporization of a liquid below its boiling point.

Evapotranspiration: Combined loss of moisture from soil by evaporation and from vegetation by transpiration from a given area in a specified time period.

Evapotranspirometer : An instrument used for measuring evapotranspiration, consisting of a soil tank in which vegetation (a crop) is planted; the tank is designed so that all the water added to it and all the water left after evapotranspiration can be measured.

Evergreen: Perennial plants which are never entirely without green leaves.

Ex situ: Away from the natural or original position/place.

Excessively drained: A soil that loses water very rapidly because of rapid percolation.

Exclosure: An area which is fenced to exclude animals.

Exfiltration: Process of water exiting the soil surface.

Exfoliation: A weathering process consisting of peeling off of thin layers of rock due to alternate expansion and contraction during day and night. Rock corners get rounded-off. The process is accelerated by chemical weathering of the outer- layers and by expansion of frozen water in the rock fissures.

Exothermic: Refers to a processes that release heat energy.

Exothermicity: The release of heat by a system as a process occurs.

Experiment: A planned investigation to obtain new facts or to confirm or refine the results of previous work. Such an investigation will aid in decision making, recommending of new processes, procedures, plant varieties, and so on. This type of research sets the circumstances and is controlled by the researcher.

Experimental design: The plan of conducting an experiment. It involves the assignment of treatments to the experimental units that will help in obtaining results with some precision.

Experimental error: The difference in results between experimental plots treated alike; uncontrollable random error.

Experimental farms: Government or institute-controlled farms where experiments are conducted.

Experimental plot: The smallest area unit in field studies that receives an experimental treatment.

Experimental site: A specific location where field experiments are conducted.

Experimental station: A place with land and buildings where various facilities and trained staff are available for scientific experiments.

Experimental units: A unit to which one treatment is assigned or applied.

Experimental yield: The yield level of crop & variety obtained at experimental stations where yield maximization is the major objective using all possible sophisticated technology.

Ex-situ conservation: *Ex-situ* conservation means the conservation of components of biological diversity outside their natural habitats.

Extension forestry (India): It includes mixed forestry on wastelands and community lands, raising of shelterbelts in dry and arid regions, and raising of plantations of quick growing species on lands along the roads, canal banks and railway lines.

F

F layer: Layer of partially decomposed litter on forest floor below the L layer in forest soils. A layer of partially decomposed litter with portions of plant structures still recognizable (hemic material).

F test: A test of statistical significance consisting of the ratio of two independent variances of normally distributed variables.

Factorial design: An experimental design in which two or more treatments are being tested and are combined in every possible combination.

Factorial experiment: An experiment where treatments are combinations of two or more factors. The treatments can be either complete factorial combinations or incomplete factorial combinations.

Factors of soil formation: Refers to various agents responsible for soil formation such as climate, parent material, organisms, relief and weather, which influences the physical and chemical properties of soil.

Fahrenheit (°F): A temperature scale in which the freezing point of water is taken as 32° and the boiling point of water as 212° under standard atmospheric pressure.

Fallow land: A land left unfarmed for one or more growing seasons to kill weeds, make the soil richer.

Fallow systems: It is the sequence of crop years with fallow years. Extensive fallow systems are shifting cultivation systems Intensive fallow systems are bush fallow and grass fallow systems.

Fallow: It is the practice of allowing crop land to lie idle during a growing season to build up the soil moisture and fertility contents, so that a better crop can be produced the following year. It is usually worked periodically to control weeds and improve moisture infiltration.

Family Farm: The 'traditional' idea of farming where a relatively small farm is owned and managed over several generations by one family. Normally two or more generations are working simultaneously. Most are very efficient and environmentally benign.

Fan: Accumulation of debris brought down by a stream on a steep gradient and deposited on a gently sloping plane in the shape of a fan.

Farm budgeting: A process of estimating costs, returns and net profit on a farm.

Farm enterprise: An individual crop or animal production function within a farming system which is the smallest unit for which resource use and cost return analysis is normally carried out. *e.g.* Dairying, poultry, Honey bee keeping, sericulture, Laculture, Piggery, Sheep & Goat raising, Fishery.

Farm forestry: A farm management system in which trees are grown specifically for fuel, food and for a variety of other resources on a farm. It is a three dimensional farming which provides an alternative to monoculture grain farming. The three dimensions are defined as the trees themselves, the harvest from the trees which is used to feed livestock's and the animals and their products.

Farm irrigation efficiency: It is the ratio expressed in percentage of irrigation water available for crop production of source to that delivered at the farm head gate.

Farm management: A branch of agricultural economics which deals with the business principles and practices of farming with the objective of obtaining the maximum possible return from the farm as a unit under a sound farming programme.

Farm planning: A complex process involving multiple decisions to be consideration in respect of the kinds of crops to grow, rotations, mixtures, soil and water conservation practices to be followed and building, bullocks, machinery purchase etc.

Farm pond: A small body of water constructed for retaining rain water in a pit dug in the ground by water-harvesting techniques.

Farm receipts: The total revenue received from the sale of farm products, the increase in inventories of livestock, feed suppliers and receipt from outside labour, rent of building etc. in a given time.

Farm resources: Land, labour, water, capital & infrastructure that one used for production purpose.

Farm system: Each individual farm has its own specific characteristics arising from variations in resource endowments and family circumstances. The household, its resources, and the resource flows and interactions at this individual farm level are together referred to as a farm system. The biophysical, socio-economic and human elements of a farm are interdependent, and thus farms can be analysed as systems from various points of views.

Farm: A piece of land used for agriculture either to raise a crop or pasturage or maintain livestock.

Farming system research: A location-specific research which is multi- and interdisciplinary in nature and uses whole farm approach and used improved technologies to enhance and stabilize agricultural production. The research strategy includes base data analysis, on-centre research and on-farm research.

Farming systems: It represent an appropriate combination of farm enterprises *viz.* cropping system, live stock, poultry, fisheries, forestry, bee keeping, sericulture and the means available to the farmer to raise them for increasing profitability.

Fault plane: Surface along which a fault has occurred.

Fault: It is a fracture or fracture zone in earth's crust, rocks on one side having been displaced relatively to those on the other side. Therefore the rock strata on the two sides do not match. The displacement is usually vertical but may be in any direction, including horizontal.

Fencing: A device that demarcates the boundary of the individual farm and helps to prevent the encroachment of the land and provides protection from wild animals and cattle.

Fertility (soil): The inherent capacity of soil to supply nutrients in balanced and proportionate amount in a form readily available to plants.

Fertility capability classification: a classification based on quantitative topsoil and subsoil parameters directly relevant to plant growth; various soil condition 'modifiers' define specific types of soil adversity or complexes of edaphic problems.

Fertility gradient: Refers to the variation in natural fertility in any direction across an area of land.

Fertility index: Refers to the relative sufficiency expressed as a percentage of the amount of nutrient adequate for optimum yields. It is related with soil test values and crop response with a fertility index of 0-10, 10-25, 25-50, 50-100 and 100+ for soil test rating of very low, low, medium, high and very high.

Fertilization (foliar): Foliar application of a dilute solution of liquid (usually nitrogen and micronutrients).

Fertilization (soil): Making soil fertile with the application of fertilizer that aid in the nutrition of plants.

Fertilizer grade: An expression showing minimum guarantee of available plant nutrients contained in a fertilizer expressed as percentage of plant nutrients; *e.g.* a 20-10-5 grade of fertilizer indicates 20% nitrogen, 10% phosphoric acid (P_2O_5) and 5% potash (K_2O).

Fertilizer mixture: Refers to a product obtained by physically mixing different fertilizers and essentially contain more than one of the three major nutrients, *viz.* nitrogen, phosphorus and potassium.

Fertilizer ratio: Refers to the relative proportion of three major plant nutrients in a fertilizer material, keeping the percentage of nitrogen as one in the ratio. Thus, a 10-5-5 fertilizer mixture which contains 10% nitrogen, 5% P_2O_5 and 5% K_2O, has a nutrient ratio 2 : 1 : 1.

Fertilizer requirement: The quantity of plant nutrient/ elements required to be appied in addition to the amount of nutrients supplied by the soil, to increase plant growth or crop yield to a desired level.

Fertilizer, complete: A term to denote fertilizer containing appreciable quantities of N, P, and K; it now includes secondary and micronutrients essential to plant growth.

Fertilizer: Natural or synthesised organic or inorganic material added to the soil to supply certain elements essential for plant growth.

Fibrous root system: A plant root system constituted by small, finely divided, widely spreading roots. There is no individual large root.

Field border plantings: Vegetation established on border of fields in order to conserve soil and provide cover and food for birds etc.

Field capacity (F.C.): Field capacity is the moisture content in percentage of a soil on oven dry basis, when it has been completely saturated and downward movement of water has practically ceased.

Field moisture deficiency: Refers to the quantity of water which would be required to bring the soil- moisture content to field capacity.

Field sampling: A field is divided into particular proportions and a grid is used for even sampling of different sections of the field.

Field screening: Evaluating varieties for resistance in the field in contrast to greenhouse and screen house evaluations.

Field strip cropping: A system of cropping for soi land water conservation in which crops are grown in parallel strips across the general slope of the land rather than on the contour. Strips of close growing crops (erosion resisting) are alternated with those of wide spaced cultivated crops (erosion permitting).

Field water balance: An expression of all gains and losses of water over a given period of time expressed in terms of mm/period.

Field water capacity: The maximum amount of capillary water that a particular soil is able to hold.

Field-channel efficiency: Ratio between water received from channel at the field inlet to that at the inlet of a block of fields; fraction.

Field-irrigation efficiency: The ratio of irrigation water available for use of crops to that delivered to a field expressed in the percentage.

Film, water: A layer of water around soil particles, having thickness equal to 1-2 to 100 or more molecular layers. It is the water left in the soil after drainage has practically ceased.

Filter strip: A strip of permanent dense vegetation of sufficient width and vegetation density above farm ponds, diversion terraces and other structures to retard the flow of runoff water, causing it to deposit soil, thereby preventing silting of water bodies.

Filtration: The process of separating liquids from solids by passing the liquids through a porous barrier (filter)

Fine texture (soil): Soil consisting of large quantities of fine fractions of the soil (silt and clay). It includes all clay loams and clays, such as sandy clay loam, silty clay loam, clay loam, sandy clay, silty clay and clay.

Fine textured group: A broad textural grouping that refers to soils or materials dominated by clay, sandy clay, silty clay, and heavy clay textural classes.

Fire break (forestry): A fire barrier made in a forest, by removing inflammable materials, in order to stop creeping or running fires. It also serves as a line from which to work with men and equipment for control of forest fires.

Fire, ground: A fire that burns all organic materials of the forest floor and also burns into soil itself- such as peat fire. It is different from surface fire wherein flames are visible and burning is accelerated by wind. In ground fire wind is normally not a serious factor.

Firm: It is a consistency of moist soil, which has noticeable resistance to crushing but could be crushed with moderate pressure between the thumb and forefinger.

First bottom: Normal flood plane of a river or stream.

First flushing device: It is an essential part of roof top harvesting system. It is a valve that ensures flushing off the runoff from early rains and donot allow entry in storage facility as early rain and runoff contain large quaintly of pollutants

Fish pond management: It is the practice of creating a pond environment suitable for fish production and manipulating fish population or mixtures to increase production. The practice: includes fertilization and control of undesirable pond weeds.

Flag stone: Relatively thin fragment 15-38 cm long, of sand stone, limestone, slate, shale or (rarely) of schist.

Flocculent: A chemical when added to water attaches to small particles and helps them sink; the material that settles on the bottom can be removed to improve the clarity of the water

Flood control: Facilities or methods to reduce floods.

Flood irrigation: Application of irrigation water by covering the entire surface of the soil by a sheet of water, the flow being directed by border dikes etc.

Flood peak: The highest stage or discharge attained by a flood.

Flood plain: Land bordering a stream, made up of sediments from overflow of the stream and subject to inundation at the flood stage of the stream. It is generally highest near the stream, and insensibly slopes away from the banks. During its formation the flood plain is characterised by marshes and meandering streams. In case the drainage gets diverted, the flood plain is left as smooth, fertile lands.

Flood routing: It is the process of determining stage height, storage volume and outflow rate from detention and storage reservoirs or streams for a particular hydrograph. Factors considered in flood routing are (*i*) inflow hydrograph (*ii*) outflow (*iii*) available storage and (*iv*) outflow hydrograph.

Flood stage: The stage at which overflow of stream banks begins to cause damage in the reach where elevation is measured

Flood tide: Advancing or rising tide.

Flood water retarding structure: A structure meant for temporary storage of flood water and subsequent controlled release.

Flood way: A channel, natural or excavated with or without dykes or levees, utilized for carrying excessive flood flows thereby reducing flooding.

Flood: Temporary inundation of lands that are used or usable by mankind and usually not covered by water. Inundation is by overflow from a river, stream, lake, or ocean, causing or threatening to cause damage.

Flooding: It consist of opening a water channel in a plot or field so that water can flow freely in all directions and cover the surface of the land in a continuous sheet. It is the most inefficient method of irrigation.

Flora: Plant life of a region or geological period.

Flume: An open conduit made of wood, stone, concrete or metal on a prepared grade, trestle of bridge for the purpose or carrying water across creeks, gullies, ravines or other obstructions. Also used in reference to calibrated devices meant for measuring water flow in open conduits.

Fluvial or Fluviatile: Refers to rivers, streams etc.

Fluvioglacial: Pertaining to streams coming from glaciers or to deposits made by these streams.

Fold: It is a bend in rock strata on account of movement in earth's crust. The bends take the shape of arches (anticline) and troughs (syncline). Denudation by water which occurs simultaneously with folding wears away the anticlines of the fold more rapidly than the synclines. The Himalayas, the Pyrenes, different Alpine chains are folded mountains.

Forage: Refers to herbaceous food used for grazing or harvested for feeding animals.

Forb: A herbaceous plant, that is not a sedge, grass or rush.

Force of adhesion: It is the attraction of solid surface of water molecules (It is the attraction of unlike materials to each other). Due to the force of adhesion, the water molecules are attached to the surface of soil particles and thus a thin film of water is tightly held around the soil particles. Finer the soil particles, greater the surface area and consequently, the water film is held or retained more tightly.

Force of cohesion: It is attraction between similar molecules of like characteristics. Cohesion is attraction of water molecules for each other. When more water is added to the moist soil, the cohesive force comes into action and the freshly added molecules get attracted towards already existing water molecules. This results in thickening of water film around the soil particles.

Ford: Shallow portion of a water body which can be crossed by wading.

Foresight: It is a staff reading on a point whose elevation is to be determined or on a change point. It is also termed as minus sight. It is the last staff reading denoting the shifting of the instrument. Also called a foresight reading.

Forest floor: Dead organic matter, including litter and unincorporated humus, lying over the mineral soil surface under forest vegetation.

Forest influence: The influence of forests on soil, water supply, climate, environment etc.

Forest soils: Soils developed under forest vegetation.

Forest: Trees and associated woody vegetation covering a large area of land usually with closed canopy.

Forestry: The art of growing and cultivating forest trees and their systematic utilization, reproduction and improvement of the productive capacity in masses, including the planting and culture of new forests.

Formulation: the combination of active and inactive (inert) ingredients which make up a pesticide.

Fragipan: Natural subsurface horizon with high bulk density relative to the solum above, appearing to be cemented when dry, but showing moderate to weak brittleness when moist. The layer is low in organic matter, mottled, slowly or very slowly permeable to water, and usually shows occasional or frequent bleached cracks forming polygons. Fragipan may be found in profiles of either cultivated or virgin soils but not in celcareous material.

Free board-(Hydraulics): Vertical distance between the maximum design elevation of water surface and top of retaining banks or structures. It is provided to prevent overtopping of structures due to wave action or any unforseen circumstances.

Free flow: A condition where in the rate of discharge is solely dependent on the length of crest and depth of water in the converging section of the parshall flume. In case of weirs the criterion is the depth of water at 4H (crest height) distance away from the weirs. There is no back pressure of water in a free-flow condition.

Free ground water: Refers to the ground water in the interconnected interstices in the zone of saturation, it extends down to the impervious barrier, and moves freely under the influence of gravity in the direction of the slope of the water-table.

Freely drained: A soil that allows water to percolate freely.

Frequency of irrigation: The interval that can be safely allowed between two successive irrigations is known as frequency of irrigation. It depends on consumptive use rate of a crop and on the amount of available moisture in the crop root zone. It is function of crop, soil and climate. Irrigation interval = Allowable soil moisture depletion/Daily water use.

Fresh mulch: Primary layer of largely undecayed herbage residuum on the soil surface.

Friable: Consistency (moist soil) pertaining to ease of crumbling of soils.

Friction head: It is the equivalent head expressed in meters of water required to overcome the friction caused by flow through the pipe and pipe fittings.

Fumigant: Refers to gaseous materials that kills insects, pathogens, or other pests in soil or grain bins by producing fumes

Fungicide: Chemicals used for control of fungal diseases.

Furrow crown: The peak of the turned furrow slice.

Furrow face: The vertical side of the furrow made in the soil which ploughing, away from which the turned soil is thrown.

Furrow method: Water is allowed to flow in furrow opened in crop rows. It is suitable for sloppy lands where the furrows are made along contours. The length of furrow is determined mostly by soil permeability. It varies from 3 to 6 meters. Row crops such as potatoes, cotton, sugarcane, vegetable etc. can be irrigated by furrow method.

Furrow planting: Plating of seeds or seedlings in the bottom of furrows.

Furrow slice: The ribbon of soil cut, lifted, pulverized, thrown, or turned to one side by the plow bottom.

Furrow sole: The bottom of the furrow on which the plough bottom slides.

Furrow wall: The undisturbed soil surface left by the side of a furrow.

Furrow: A trench or long narrow cut in the soil after a plow passes through it, a trench or ditch dug by hand.

G

G horizon: Layer of intense reduction having ferrous iron and grey to brown mottlings.

Gabion: A cylindrical or rectangular wire mesh cage filled with rock and used as apron, revetment etc. to check erosion.

Gallon: A gallon is 0.1602 cubic foot. One gallon of water weighs about 10 lb

Garbage: Refers to all waste materials that is thrown away, generally defined as wet food waste. The term is also used to describe all products discarded, regardless of their reusability or recyclability.

Gauge height: Level of water surface above a datum such as channel bottom.

Gauge: Device for registering precipitation, water level, discharge, velocity etc.

Gauging station: Selected section of a stream channel provided with a gauge, stage level recorder, silt sampler etc. for monitoring discharge, soil loss etc.

Geib divisor: Similar to multi slot divisor used for sediment sampling.

Genesis soil structure: The causes and method of formation of the structural units or aggregates of soil.

Genesis, soil: The mode of origin of the soil. Refers especially to the processes or soil-forming factors responsible for the formation of the solum, or true soil, from the unconsolidated parent material.

Genetic: Resulting from or produced by soil forming processes. genetic profile, genetic horizon.

Geodetic surveying: In geodetic surveying the curvature of the earth is taken into consideration. It is extended over a large area greater than 250 km^2. The line joining any two points considered as a curved line. Very refined methods and instruments are used in this type of surveying. In this method very high precision or accuracy is required.

Geographic range: Geographic limits of the ecologic range; geographic extent of actual occurrences of a species.

Geography: The subject dealing with earth's surface like physical features, soils, 'vegetation, climates, products, people etc. It has a number of sub-divisions such as mathematical geography, physical geography, human geography, political geography, economic/ commercial geography and historical geography.

Geological erosion: Natural erosion due to geological processes occurring over geologic periods resulting in wearing away of mountains and building of floodplain and coastal planes.

Geometric correction: Image-processing procedure that corrects spatial distortions in an image.

Geometric mean: A type of mean indicating the central tendency in a set of data or number. It is the nth root of the product of n items or values.

Geometrical isomers: Compounds with different arrangements of groups on either side of a bond with restricted rotation, such as a double bond or a single bond in a ring; for example: isomers of certain alkenes. Stereoisomers that are not mirror images of each other; also known as position isomers.

Geomorphic surface: A mappable area of the earth's surface that has a common history; the area is of similar age and is formed by a set of processes during an episode of landscape.

Geomorphology: The study of the characteristics and configurations and evolution of rocks and land forms.

Georeferencing: Assigning map coordinates to an image. Usually involves resampling of pixels to extrapolate the values for the new pixels.

Geostationary: Refers to satellites travelling at the angular velocity at which the earth rotates; as a result, they remain above the same point on earth at all times.

Geyser: A spring consisting of a jet of hot water and steam thrown into the air at regular or irregular intervals. Geysers indicate waning phase of volcanic activity.

Gilgai: Micro relief consisting of a succession of micro basins and micro knolls in nearly level areas, formed due to expansion and contraction of clay soils with changes in soil moisture. Micro relief in sloppy areas consists of micro valleys and micro- ridges parallel to slope. Gilgai micro relief has been observed in black clay soils having predominantly montmorillonitic clay.

GIS: A geographic information system (GIS), also known as geospatial information system, is any system for capturing, storing, analyzing, managing and presenting data and associated attributes which are spatially referenced to Earth. In certain countries such as Canada, GIS is well known as Geomatics. The other definition is, GIS is a system or tool or computer based methodology to collect, store, manipulate, retrieve and analyse spatially (georeferenced) data.

Glacial drift: Rock debris transported by glaciers and deposited directly from ice or melt water. Debris may or may not be heterogeneous.

Glacial soil: Soil derived from glacial drift.

Glacial till: Unstratified drift deposited by ice consisting of intermingled boulders, gravel, sand and clay.

Glacier table: A block of rock perched on a pedestal of ice on the surface of a glacier, the rock protects the ice below from melting as quickly as the surrounding ice.

Glacier: Refers to huge mass of ice, formed on land by the compaction and re-crystallization of snow, that moves very slowly down slope or outward due to its own weight.

Gley soil: Soil developed under conditions of poor drainage leading to reduction of iron and other elements and presence or grey colours and mottles.

Gleyzation: Soil forming process leading to the formation of gley soils.

Global climate change: Refers to the gradual warming of the earth caused by the greenhouse effect. As a result of man-made emissions of greenhouse gases such as carbon dioxide, chlorofluorocarbons (CFC) and methane, although there is no agreement among the scientific community on this controversial issue.

Global radiation: The sum total of direct solar radiation and diffused radiation received per unit of horizontal surface.

Global warming: The overall increase of atmospheric temperature due to a build up of greenhouse gases and reduction in ozone layer.

Global water cycle: The global water cycle involves major transports that link the Earth's atmosphere, land mass and oceans. The water cycle can be divided into two parts a portion that is accessible to humans and that which is not.

Gorge: A deep, narrow valley with steep walls. It is not very different from a canyon, though the latter is much bigger in size. Sides of a small gorge are approximately vertical.

GPS: Global Positioning System. A receiver that calculates its absolute geographic position by determining its relative position to a set of at least three satellites.

Grab sample: A single water or wastewater sample taken at a single point in time and location

Grade (fertilizer): It is the minimum guaranteed content of plant nutrients in a fertilizer material, content expressed as whole numbers in terms of total nitrogen (N), available phosphoric acid (P_2O_5) and water-soluble potash, (K_2O).

Grade profile: The longitudinal profile of a river course in which the sediment, velocity and volume of water are in equilibrium and no down-cutting or scour occurs. Such a river is at grade and the profile conforms to a smooth logarithmic curve. The graded profile is a slope of transportation.

Grade stabilization structure: A structure made for stabilizing the bed slope of a gully or stream, in order to check further head; cutting or bed lowering.

Grade: Slope of a channel, natural ground or road.

Graded bunding: Graded bunds are the bunds or terraces laid along a pre-determined longitudinal grade very near the contour but not exactly along contour. They are used for the safe, disposal of excess runoff in high rainfall areas and regions where the [Clay] soil is relatively impervious. Farming operations are not done on bunds or bund channels.

Graded strip-cropping: Growing crops in strips that grade toward a protected waterway.

Graded terrace: A terrace having a constant or variable grade (slope) along its length. It is suitable for high rainfall area or fine textured soils.

Grades of structure: Depending upon the stability, distinctness, durability, the aggregates are classified onto the four grades as: Structure less, Weak, Moderate and Strong.

Gradient: Change in elevation, velocity, pressure etc. per unit length; slope.

Granular fertilizer: A fertilizer material measuring about one-tenth of an inch in diameter and composed of particles of roughly the same composition. This kind of fertilizer is superior in efficiency compared to the fine or powdery fertilizer, due to ease in handling and less fixation in soil.

Granular structure: A soil in which the individual grains are grouped into spherical aggregates with indistinct sides. Highly porous granules are commonly called crumbs. A well- granulated loamy soil has the best structure for most crop plants.

Granular: Similar to crumb except that the aggregates are harder, less porous and the individual soil particles are more strongly held together than in the crumb structure. Commonly found in cultivated fields.

Granule: Natural granular soil aggregate or ped that is relatively non-porous.

Grassed water way: A natural or constructed water way usually broad and shallow covered with erosion-resistant grasses used for safe disposal of surface water from crop land.

Grassland farming: A farming system that involves cultivation of grasses and legumes in livestock and land management in which the legumes are the keystones and grasses form the backbone of the grassland farming.

Grassland: Land on which the vegetation is dominated by grasses. or any plant community in which grasses and/or legumes make up the dominant vegetation. Grassland is intermediate in status between forest or woodland on one hand and the desert on the other.

Gravel envelope: Selected gravel aggregate placed around a subsurface drain to facilitate entry of water into the drain. It is also put around well casing to facilitate water entry.

Gravel filter: Graded sand and gravel aggregate placed around sub-surface drain or well screen to prevent entry of fine materials from the aquifer into drain or well.

Gravel: A deposit of rounded stones or pebbles.

Gravelly soil: Soil containing 15-90 percent pebbles by volume.

Gravimetric water content: Ratio of the mass of water in a soil to the mass of oven dry (105°C) soil.

Gravitational head of water (z): It is the elevation of the point with respect to an arbitrary datum or reference point in the soil.

Gravitational water: The water that flows freely through soils in response to gravity. It is the excess water above field capacity in a soil moving down under the influence of gravity.

Gravity dam: Dam that resists over turning due to its weight.

Gravity irrigation: Irrigation in which water flows and is distributed by gravity.

Grazing capacity: The highest stocking rate possible without damage to vegetation and related resources.

Grazing system: Manipulation of grazing animals to allow adequate growth of vegetation for use by the animals. Rotational grazing; deferred rotational grazing etc.

Great soil group: One of the higher categories in soil classification.

Green belt: Strip of land kept in natural or relatively undeveloped state around a habitation, to break up the monotony of urban development. It may be put to agricultural use also.

Green manure: Plant material incorporated into the soil while still green (generally before flowering), in order to ameliorate the soil *e.g. sesbenia, glyricedia* etc. It improves the physical condition of the soil or for adding nitrogen and increases organic carbon in the soil.

Green water resource: The soil moisture generated from infiltrated rainfall that is available for root water uptake by plants, and which constitutes the main water resource in rainfed agriculture.

Grey water: Wastewater from clothes washing machines, showers, bathtubs, hand washing, lavatories and sinks.

Grid format : The result of interpolation from values of a variable measured at irregularly distributed points, or along survey lines, to values referring to square cells in a rectangular array. It forms a step in the process of contouring data, but can also be used as the basis for a raster format to be displayed and analyzed digitally after the values have been rescaled to the 0-255 range.

Grit: Coarse grained sandstone or sandstone made up of angular grains.

Gross irrigation requirement: The total amount of water applied through irrigation including losses during conveyance, distribution and application of water in the fields etc.

Gross primary productivity (GPP): Total carbon assimilation by plants. GPP = NPP + respiration losses.

Ground cover: Vegetation like grasses or other plants grown to save soil from water or wind erosion.

Ground data: Supporting data collected on the ground, and information derived there from, as an aid to the interpretation of remotely recorded surveys, such as airborne imagery,

Ground moraine: Rock fragments which drop to the bottom of the glacier through crevasses and are dragged with other fragments plucked from the valley floor beneath the ice.

Ground swath: Width of the strip of terrain that is imaged by a scanner system.

Ground truth: A term used for data, information, and observations obtained on the surface or subsurface about features or classes, used to aid in interpretation of remotely sensed data.

Ground water run-off: Part of ground water which discharges into a stream as spring or seepage water.

Ground water: Portion of the total precipitation either passing through or standing in the soil and the underlying strata, free to move under the influence of gravity. Most of the ground water exists within a few hundred feet of the earth's surface.

Ground-control point: A geographic feature of known location that is recognizable on images and can be used to determine geometric corrections.

Ground-Truthing: Acquiring data about features of interest in remote sensing by collecting ground-truth data in the field, inspecting aerial photography, additional maps, other ancillary data.

Ground-water recharge: Inflow of water to a ground-water reservoir from the surface. Infiltration of precipitation and its movement to the water table is one form of natural recharge. Also, the volume of water added by this process.

Grove: A natural or planted small group of trees, usually without, under storey.

Gully control plantings: Sowing of seed, planting rhizomes, cuttings, transplants or seedlings in gullies in order to establish, vegetative cover for control of run-off and erosion. Vegetation established may provide useful products like fuel, forage and industrial wood like bamboo.

Gully erosion: Process of erosion by which running water accumulates in narrow channels which go on deepening and widening as the process continues.

Gully: A channel or miniature valley formed as a result of erosion and caused by concentrated but intermittent flow of water usually during or immediately after heavy rains. The channel' is deep enough to interfere with tillage operations. It cannot be obliterated by tillage (unlike rill). Gully may be dendritic or branching or linear (long, narrow and of uniform width). Gully may be U, V or W shaped (cross-section).

Gullying: Removal of soil by running water, with formation of channels that cannot be smoothed out (and often cannot be crossed) during normal tilling by wheeled vehicles.

Gypsum block: An instrument for *in situ* moisture measurement. Made up from plaster of paris with the help of two electrodes parallel to each other in a medium of gypsum. The resistance reading is about 400-600 ohms at field capacity and 50,000-75,000 at wilting point.

Gypsum requirement: The quantity of gypsum or its equivalent required to reduce the exchangeable sodium fraction of a given amount of soil to an acceptable level where dispersion of soil colloids does not take place.

Gypsum: A hydrated calcium sulphate ($CaSO_4 . 2H_2O$). It is used as a soil amendment.

H

H layer: A layer of well decomposed organic matter of unidentifiable origin in mor humus. The 02 horizon.

Habitat: A specific area in which a particular type of plant/animal lives of found.

Hail: Refers to a solid precipitation in the form of ice pellets from cumulo-nimbus clouds due to severe updraughts ranges from 5-50 mm in diameter and has onion-like cross section.

Hailstorm: Refers to a storm, consisting largely of hails or frozen raindrops ranging in diameter from 5 to 10 mm or more, the ice particles are precipitated either separately or as aggregates of irregular size and shape.

Hair hygrometer: Equipment used for measurement of humidity of the air in which the sensing element is a strand of hair, the change of its length is a function of humidity of the air.

Half-life: Time required for one-half of a specified radioactive substance to decompose.

Halomorphic soil: A suborder of the intrazonal order consisting of saline and alkali soils developed under inadequate drainage in arid areas. Great soil groups Solonchak or saline soils. Solonetz soils and Soloth soils are examples.

Halophytic vegetation: Salinity loving or tolerant vegetation, generally having fleshy leaves or thorns like desert vegetation.

Hammermill: Crusher or shredder used to break up waste materials into smaller pieces.

Hanging valley: A tributary valley which does not slope into the main valley on account of over-deepening of the latter. Water from the hanging valley enters the main valley by waterfalls or rapids. Hanging valleys are particularly common in glaciated regions.

Hard pan: A hardened soil layer in lower A or B horizon, caused by cementation of soil particles by organic matter, silica, sesquioxides or calcium carbonate. Hardness of the layer does not change appreciably with variation in moisture content and its pieces do not slake in water. The hard pan may have any texture. (duripan, caliche).

Hard woods: A botanical group of trees having broad leaves, in contrast to conifers.

Hardness: A characteristic of water which describes the presence of dissolved minerals. Carbonate hardness is caused by calcium and magnesium bicarbonate;

noncarbonate hardness is caused by calcium sulphate, calcium chloride, magnesium sulphate, and magnesium chloride.

Harrow A shallow working tillage implement used to break down clods for smoothening and pulverizing the soil as well as to cut the weeds and to mix materials with the soil. Disc harrows may be used for primary cultivation whereas tined harrows are used pre or post sowing.

Harrowing: A secondary tillage operation, which pulverises, smoothens and packs the soil for seedbed preparation and helps in control of weeds.

Harvest index (H.I.): The ratio of grain weight to total aboveground plant dry weight. Yield of the plant parts of economic interest (economic yield) as percentage of total biological yield in terms of dry matter.

Harvesting: The process of gathering in a crop; in the case of rice, the gathering in of mature rice panicles from the field. Includes the operation of cutting, picking, plucking or digging, or combination of these for removing the useful part or economic part from the plants.

Hay: Stems and leaf parts of plants cut and dried such as alfa-alfa, clovers, and other forage legumes and thin stemmed leafy grasses for animal feed.

Hazardous waste: A waste containing any substance (solid, liquid, or gaseous) that is harmful or potentially harmful to life or the environment; this type of waste includes toxic, flammable, corrosive and oxidizing substances and is subject to special handling, shipping, storage, and disposal requirements.

Haze: Fine dust or liquid particles dispersed in the atmosphere, rendering it opalescent.

Head land: An uncultivated strip left at the end of crop rows or along a fence. Also a steep crag or cliff jutting out into the sea.

Head: Depth of water flowing over the weir crest measured at some point in weir pond or the height of a column of water above a standard datum such as mean sea level.

Headwaters: The source and upper tributaries of a stream or river.

Heavy soils: Clayey soils are called as heavy soils as they are difficult or heavy for cultivation.

Hectare centimetres: Volume of water necessary to cover an area of one hectare (10,000 sq. meters) to a depth of one centimetre (1hectare centimetre = 100 cubic meters = 100,000 litres)

Hectare metre water: Water column having vertical depth of one meter stored over an area of one hectare, assuming subject to no leaching, percolation, seepage or evaporation of water. It is equivalent to 10,000 m^3 water.

Hectare: A measurement of land area in the metric system equivalent to 10,000 m^2. Equal to roughly 2.47 acres of land.

Hedge, hedgerow: A barrier of bushes, shrubs or small trees planted close together in a line.

Height of instrument (H. I): It is the elevation (or the R.L.) of the plane of collimation (or plane of sight) when the instrument is correctly levelled. It is also called the height of plane of the collimation.

Herb: Plant having no persistent parts above the ground, unlike a, shrub or tree.

Herbage: Sum total of all herbaceous plants growing at a site.

Herbicide: A chemical used to destroy or inhibit undesirable plant growth.

Herd: Group of cattle collectively as a unit for grazing.

High analysis fertilizer: A fertilizer material containing 25% or more of the major plant nutrients, namely nitrogen, phosphorus (as P_2O_5) and potassium (as K_2O).

High inputs: Crop production involving advanced technology, high capital resources; fertilizers for maximum economic return; chemical weed and pest control at advanced technical levels; modern method of mechanization are employed to maximize yields or economic return.

High-input farming: Intensive agriculture which uses fertilizers, pesticides and modern machinery to guarantee a large crop output.

Highway erosion control: Prevention and control of erosion along the highways by mechanical and vegetative soil conservation practices.

High-yielding varieties (HYVs): Varieties developed through a breeding program that possess desirable agronomic characteristics, resistance to insects and diseases, and tolerance for environmental stresses like soil problems, temperature, and drought; nearly all HYVs are short-statured or semi-dwarf.

Hill type Bench Terraces: It is used for hilly areas with a reverse grade towards the hill.

Hill: A small portion of the earth's surface raised above its surroundings.

Hillock: A mound or a small hill.

Histic epipedon: Thin organic soil horizon saturated with water at some period of the year, unless artificially drained, occurring at or near the surface of mineral soil.

Histogram: A bar diagram representing a frequency distribution.

Histosols: These are organic soils (pleats and mucks) consisting of variable depths of accumulated plant remains in bogs, marshes and swamps that have developed under water saturated environment. Highly rich in organic matter *i.e.* organic corbon ranges from 12 to 18% in soils with low to more than 50% clay content.

Holding pond: Earthen pond built for storing polluted run-off.

Horizon, soil: A layer of soil or soil material approximately parallel to the land surface and different from adjacent layers in physical, chemical and biological characteristics such as texture, colour, pH, consistence, structure, microbial population etc. Very few soils have all the horizons.

Horizonation: It is the process of differentiation of soil in different horizons along the depth of the soil body. The differentiation is due to the fundamental processes.

Horizontal line: It is any line lying in the horizontal plane. It is a straight line tangential to a level line.

Horizontal plane: It is a plane tangential to the level surface at that point. It is perpendicular to direction of gravity (plumb line).

Household hazardous waste: discarded or unused portions of home cleaning products, workshop and outdoor chemicals, automotive fluids, and personal care products that contain toxic chemicals.

Humic acid: A mixture of dark coloured organic substances of variable or indefinite composition precipitated on acidification of a dilute alkali extract of the soil.

Humid: Region or climate in which moisture when distributed normally throughout the year is not a limiting factor for the production of most crops.

Humidity index: Refers to surplus as a percentage of annual potential evapo-transpiration in dry climates.

Humidity: Dampness, the amount of water or water vapour in the air.

Humification: Processes whereby the carbon of organic residues is transformed and converted to humic substances through biochemical and chemical processes.

Humus form: A group of soil horizons located at or near the surface of a pedon, which have formed from organic residues, either separate from or intermixed with, mineral material.

Humus: It is the fraction of organic matter which is left after most of the plant or animal residues have decomposed. It is 'characterized by dark colour, high cation exchange capacity, carbon nitrogen ratio approximately ten, high water adsorption and swelling etc. Humus includes F and H layers in undisturbed forest soils.

Hurricane: A wind blowing with a mean velocity of more than 75 miles (120 km) per hour.

Hydraulic conductivity: The proportionality factor in Darcy's law in relation to viscous flow of water in the soil. It is the flux of water per unit gradient of hydraulic potential (see Darcy's law).

Hydraulic equilibrium: Hydraulic equilibrium is the condition for zero flow rate of water film in soil.

Hydraulic fill dam: Dam built from earth material pumped into place with water, the fines being washed towards the centre for ensuring more imperviousness.

Hydraulic gradient: Slope of free surface of flowing water in an open channel.

Hydraulic gradient: The decrease in hydraulic head per unit distance in the soil in the direction of the greatest rate of decrease of hydraulic head.

Hydraulic head: It is the vertical elevation with respect to a standard datum at which water stands in a riser or a manometer connected to a point in question in the soil.

Hydraulic jump: Sudden turbulent rise of water level from a flow stage below critical depth to a stage above critical depth. The velocity reduces from critical to sub-critical during this rise in water level.

Hydraulic non equilibrium: Condition in which movement of water occurs between flow regions, *e.g.*, macropore to micropore, as a result of gradient in hydrualic potential in the soil.

Hydraulic radius: The area of cross-section of a stream divided by its wetted perimeter.

Hydrocarbons: Refers to substance containing carbon and hydrogen in various combinations (*e.g.* gasoline and oil).

Hydrogeology: The study of groundwater, with particular emphasis on the chemistry and movement of water.

Hydrograph: A graph showing variation in stage (depth) or discharge of water in a stream over a time duration.

Hydrography: The study of water on earth's surface, particularly with reference to its physical features, position, volume etc. and the precipitation charts of seas, lakes, rivers, contours of the sea bed, shallows, deep currents etc.

Hydrologic equation: It is the water inventory equation (inflow = outflow + storage) that expresses the basic principle that during a given time interval the total inflow to an area must equal the total outflow plus the net change in storage.

Hydrological cycle: Continuous circulation of water between hydrosphere, atmosphere and lithosphere is known as hydrological cycle. This has neither a beginning nor an end.

Hydrological soil groups: Categorization of soils into four groups depending on run-off potential. Deep sands (low run. off) (final infiltration rate 8 to 12 mm/hour) are included in group A and clay soils (final infiltration rate less than 10 mm/hour) are included in group D, other groups band C having values 4-8 and 1-4 mm/hour respectively.

Hydrology: The science dealing with the properties, distribution, and flow of water in relation to its occurrance in wells, lakes, streams etc.

Hydrolysis constant: An equilibrium constant for a hydrolysis reaction.

Hydrolysis: The reaction of a water molecule with another larger molecule, resulting in the splitting of the larger molecule. For ex. $CH_3COONa + H_2O = CH_3COOH + NaOH$.

Hydromorphic soils: A sub-order of intrazonal soils, which includes great soil groups formed under poor drainage conditions in marshes, swamps, seepage areas and flats.

Hydrophyte: A plant which requires lot of moisture for its growth and, therefore, lives in water or in a very humid region. The roots are generally shallow, the stem is long and fragile having little woody fibre and the leaves are thin and wide. Banana, lotus, water hyacinth are examples. Syn. hygrophyte.

Hydrosphere: Oceans, lakes, rivers and other water bodies of the Earth are called Hydrosphere, most of the earth's total water is contained in oceans (96%), small portion (2%) as snow and ice and rest (2%) in the water bodies of the continents.

Hygrometer: Instrument for measuring the relative amount of moisture in the atmosphere and for determining the dewpoint.

Hygroscopic coefficient: The quantity of moisture contained in dry soil when it is equilibriated with some standard relative humidity near a saturated atmosphere (about 98 %) expressed in terms of percentage on oven dry weight basis.

Hygroscopic fertilizer: Fertilizer which absorb water from air and become moist and sticky for example urea, CAN etc.

Hygroscopic water: Water adsorbed by a dry soil from the atmosphere of high relative humidity.

Hygroscopic: A term used to designate materials that absorb moisture from the air, *e.g.* urea.

Hygroscopicity: The ability of a dry materal to readily take up and retain moisture.

Hygrothermograph: An equipment that automatically records both temperature and relative humidity on a single chart continuously.

Hypothesis: An assumption, supposition, or postulate drawn before all the facts have been discovered or investigated and adopted for the time being as a guide for further investigation. Something not yet proven or assumed to be true for the sake of testing its soundness or in order to bring out new evidence.

Hypoxic: Insufficient availability of oxygen in an environment to support aerobic respiration.

Hypsometry: A measurement of the elevation of land above sea level.

Hysteresis: The relation between energy status and moisture content can be obtained in two ways, (i) in desorption by taking an initially saturated soil sample and applying increasing suction to dry the soil gradually and (ii) in absorption by gradually wetting an initially dry soil. The measurement of energy status and moisture content during this process are taken and plotted on graph. The curves obtained through desorption and sorption is different for the same soil sample. The moisture content at a given suction is greater in desorption than in absorption and this phenomenon is known as hysteresis.

I

Igneous rock: Rock formed as a result of cooling and solidification of magma, and that has not appreciably changed since its formation, such as granite and basalt etc.

Ignitable: A material capable of burning or causing a fire.

Illite: A hydrous aluminium silicate clay mineral having 2 : 1 lattice structure and containing considerable amount of potassium.

Illuvial horizon: Horizon in a soil profile in which soil material carried from an upper horizon has been deposited as a result of precipitation from solution or separation from suspension.

Illuviation: The process of deposition of soil materials (removed from the eluvial horizon) in the lower layer (or horizon of gains having the property of stabilizing translocated clay materials) is termed as Illuviation. The horizons formed by this process are termed as illuvial horizons (B-horizons, especially *Bt*) The process leads to textural contrast between E and Bt horizons, and higher fine: total clay ratio in the Bt horizon.

Image dissection: The breaking down of a continuous scene into discrete spatial elements, either by the receptors on the retina, or in the process of capturing the image artificially.

Image enhancement: Any of a group of operations (*e.g.*, contrast stretch, spatial filtering) that improve the delectability and presentation of targets or categories in an image.

Image processing: Manipulation of an image to improve or change some quality of the image.

Image: Pictorial representation of a scene recorded by a remote sensing system.

Imagery: General term for base map or reference map materials.

Impedance: The total opposition of a material (*e.g.*, soil, copper wire) to items (*e.g.*, roots, coleoptiles, water, electrons) moving through it.

Impeded drainage: A condition that hinders the movement of water through soils under the influence of gravity.

Impermeable layer: A layer of solid material, such as rock or clay, which does not allow water to pass through.

Impervious soil: Soil through which water, air or roots cannot penetrate. No soil is ever completely impervious.

Impervious surfaces: Land where water cannot infiltrate back into the ground such as roofs, driveways, streets, and parking lots. Total imperviousness means the actual amount of land surface taken up with impervious surfaces, often stated as a percentage. Interestingly, a site with a total imperviousness of 60% can act like a site with only 10% imperviousness if strategies such as channeling roof runoff into a garden and using swales to capture rainwater are used.

Impoundment: a structure or location used for confined storage, such as a pond, lake or reservoir

Improvement cutting: Cutting of undesirable species, unsatisfactory growth or plants having insect infestation or disease for the purpose of improving the quality and vigour of other trees in an immature stand.

Impurity: Refers to presence of any unwanted material or chemical substance that is present within another substance or mixture

In situ: When applied to tree plantations, refers to seed planted in the same area as it was collected. In the natural or original position or location.

Inceptisols: Soils that are generally moist, having pedogenic honzons of alteration of parent material but not of illuviation. The profile development has just started and better developed than entices.

Incinerator: A facility in which the combustion of solid waste takes place.

Income equivalent ratio (lER): The ratio of area required under sole cropping to produce the same gross income as one hectare of intercropping at the same management level. It is the conversion of LER into economic terms.

Incomplete fertilizer: A classification of fertilizers that contains only 1 or 2 of the major fertilizer elements out of N, P, and K.

Incomplete tillage: The result of omitting one or more of the elements of a complete tillage system.

Increment: Increase in diameter, height, volume etc. of a tree or stand during a specified period.

Indicator plant: It is the plant, which reflects specific growing condition by its presence or character of growth.

Indigenous vegetation: Vegetation native to an area; not introduced from outside.

Indore process: Anaerobic composting method of Indian origin in which alternate layers of organic wastes and human or animal excreta are placed in a pit or pile, pile being turned twice in six months. Compost is maintained moist by allowing: necessary drainage.

Indurate soil: Cemented soil mass that does not soften on wetting.

Industrial waste: materials discarded from industrial operations or derived from manufacturing processes.

Infiltrability: The flux (or rate) of water infiltration into soil when water at atmospheric pressure is maintained on the atmosphere–soil boundary, with the flow direction being one-dimensionally downward.

Infiltration capacity: The maximum rate at which water can infiltrate into a soil under a given set of conditions.

Infiltration flux (or rate): The volume of water entering a specified cross-sectional area of soil per unit time.

Infiltration velocity: It is the actual rate at which water is entering the soil at a given time. It may be less than the infiltration rate when the supply of water is limited. (rainfall or irrigation). It has the same units as infiltration rate.

Infiltration: The entry of water through the soil surface into the soil profile.

Infiltrometer: Apparatus used for measuring the rate of entry of a fluid into a porous body such as water into the soil. It generally consists of single or double rings with variable or constant water head, embedded into the soil.

Inflorescence: Arrangement of a plant's flowers on the stem. *e.g.* umbel, receme, spike, panicle etc.

Informal survey: Field study in which interviews with farmers, direct observations and existing information are used to develop an understanding of the farming system's constraints and potential.

Inner capillary water: It is that part of capillary water, which is nearest to the hygroscopic water and is in the form of a thinner film, held more tightly and moves rather very slowly than outer capillary water.

Inorganic chemicals: natural or synthetic chemicals that contain no carbon.

Insecticide: Chemical substance that kills insects.

***In-situ* conservation:** In-situ conservation means the conservation of ecosystems and natural habitats and the maintenance and recovery of viable populations of species in their natural habitats.

***In-situ* surface water treatment:** The in-situ application of a substance other than a pesticide to surface water, except in a dugout, for restoration, enhancement or other purposes.

Institutional waste: Refers to material originating in schools, hospitals, prisons, research institutions, and other public buildings.

Intake rate: Rate of entry of water into the soil.

Integrated natural resources management: It is a conscious process of incorporating multiple aspects of natural resource use into a system of sustainable management to meet explicit production goals of farmers as well as goals of the wider community.

Integrated solid waste management: practice of using several alternative waste management techniques to manage and dispose of specific components of the municipal waste stream. Waste management alternatives include source reduction, recycling, composting, energy recovery, and land filling.

Integrated water resource management (IWRM): Refers to a process which promotes the co-ordinated development and management of water, land and related resources, in order to maximize the resultant economic and social welfare in an equitable manner without compromising the sustainability of vital ecosystems.

Intensive agriculture: A method of farming in which as much use is made of the land as possible by growing crops close together, growing several crops in a year or using large amounts of fertiliser.

Intensive cropping: Maximum use of the land by multiple cropping in the same price of land.

Inter cultivation: The tillage operation done in the field after sowing or planting and prior to the harvesting of crop plants known as inter cultivation.

Inter tillage: The tillage operations that are carried out in the standing crop are called inter tillage operations.

Inter-basin transfer: A transfer or diversion of water (either groundwater or surface water) from one basin to another. This may also be referred to as water export/import. Constructing facilities to transport water from the basin it naturally occurs into another river basin.

Interception channel: Channel dug at the top of an earthen cut or at the foot of a slope or at other critical site for interception of run-off; catch drain; interception ditch.

Interception, precipitation: Stopping, interrupting and temporary' holding of precipitation by vegetative canopy or vegetation" residue.

Interceptor drain: Surface or sub-surface drain or of both for intercepting flowing water.

Intercropping, interplanting: Sowing or planting of an auxiliary crop between lines of the main crop so as to reduce weed growth and improve utilization of land for higher total production *e.g.* Pulse crops-black gram or green gram sown between maize or cotton lines.

Interculture: It includes gap filling, thinning, weeding, mulching, top dressing of fertilizers, hoeing, earthling up etc. unless these are carried out at right time, with suitable implements mainly hoes & hand tools the crop will not attain a vigorous growth.

Interdisciplinary research: Research that integrates two or more scientific disciplines with the goal of advancing the understanding of complex cognitive and practical problems.

Inter-flow: Fraction of rainfall that infiltrates into the soil and moves laterally through upper soil horizons until intercepted by a stream or it appears on the surface at a lower point down slope.

Intermediate sight (I.S.): It is any other staff reading taken on a point of unknown elevation from the same set up of the level. All sights taken between the back sight and the foresight are intermediate sights.

Intermittent grazing: Alternate grazing and resting of a pasture etc. for variable time periods.

Intermittent stream: A watercourse that does not flow continuously, or flows during spring and summer only.

Internal soil drainage: Downward movement of water through the soil. Rate of movement depends on soil texture, structure, underlying layers and height of perched or permanent water table etc.

Internode: The space in plant stem between two successive nodes. Internode decreases with proximity to terminal node.

Intersection: In this method the point is fixed on plane by the intersection of the rays drawn from the two instrument stations. The line joining at these stations is called the base line.

Intra-basin transfer The diversion of water within a drainage basin. Constructing facilities to transport water between sub-basins within a major basin. This water would have ended up in the same downstream place under natural conditions.

Intrazonal soil: Soil having characteristics which reflect the dominating influence of a local factor like relief, parent material or age over the normal effect of climate and vegetation.

Intrinsic permeability: The property of a porous material that expresses the ease with which gases or liquids flow through it. Often symbolized by $k = Kn/pg$, where K is the Darcy hydraulic conductivity, n is the fluid viscosity, p is the fluid density, and g is the acceleration of gravity. Dimensionally, k is an area $[L^2]$.

Invader plant species: Plant species that are absent in undisturbed parts of the plant community but will invade the plant community under continuous overuse or disturbance.

Inverse nitrogen yield concept: According to Wilcox, the yield of the crop is inversely proportional to its nitrogen content, *e.g.* $Y=K^{-n}$ where Y = yield; n = N (%) in crop; and K= constant (318Ib/acre).

Inversion: Refers to the condition in which there is abrupt rise instead of fall in temperature with height is called inversion.

Inverted siphon: Pipeline with ends higher than the middle portion laid under a road etc. for conveyance of water across the road. No syphon action is involved, but the configuration of the pipe resembles a syphon in inverted position.

Iron pan: A hardened or indurated soil horizon in which the main cementing agent is iron oxide.

Irrigable area: The proportion of the arable area of an irrigation project which is subject to irrigated farm use. It excludes lands required for non-productive uses.

Irrigable land: A land under existing or potential irrigation development which by reason of topography, quality of land and other characteristics is physically suitable for sustained irrigation and for which an adequate and suitable water supply can be provided at reasonable cost.

Irrigated bench terraces: Level benches are adopted under irrigated conditions. The level table top terraces are referred to as irrigated bench Terries.

Irrigated dryland: Dryland having well-drained soils where water does not accumulate and irrigation is used mainly for dry land crops such as wheat, maize, potato, and other cash crops. Dry- land rice may also be grown with intermittent type irrigation.

Irrigated rice: Rice which is supplementary or fully supported with water supplied by artificial means.

Irrigated wetland: Areas subjected to pounding during rainy season where invariably a rice crop is grown with irrigation. Availability of irrigation water may be year- round or seasonal. Other non-rice crops, particularly high-value crops, may be grown with irrigation in rice-based patterns.

Irrigation application efficiency: It is the percentage of irrigation water applied to an area which is stored in the soil for use by the crop.

Irrigation district: An organization that owns and manages a water delivery system for irrigating a given region.

Irrigation efficiency: Irrigation efficiency is the ratio usually expressed as percent of the volume of irrigation water transpired by plants, plus that evaporate from the soil, plus that necessary to regulate the salt concentration in the soil solution and that used by plants in building plant tissue to total volume of water diverted, stored or pumped for irrigation.

Irrigation frequency: Time interval between successive irrigations.

Irrigation interval: Refers to time in days between the start of successive field irrigation application on the same field.

Irrigation period: Number of hours or days required to apply one irrigation to a given design area during the peak consumption use period of a crop to be irrigated.

Irrigation requirement: It is the total quantity of water applied to the land surface in supplement to the water supplied through rainfall and soil profile to meet the water needs of crops for optimum growth. IR = WR – (ER + S)

Irrigation response: The rate of increase in crop yield per unit of increase in water applied.

Irrigation structure: It is the structure or device necessary for the proper conveyance, control, measurement or application of irrigation water.

Irrigation water requirement: The net irrigation water requirement of across divided by the irrigation efficiency of a system.

Irrigation water: Refers to the artificial application of water by the process of irrigation.

Irrigation, automatic: Hydraulic-electric control of irrigation in response to a transducer that senses plant needs. The term is commonly used more loosely to refer to hydraulic or electrically actuated valves manually present on a time-based controller.

Irrigation, semiautomatic: An irrigation system in which valves respond directly to a manually operated remote-control switch.

Irrigation: The artificial application of water to soil to fulfill the water needs of growing crops by gravity or pumped systems in areas where natural precipitation is insufficient to assist in the production of crops, especially during stress periods.

Isobars: Lines of equal pressure.

Isobath (water-table): A line on a map or ground connecting pcints of same height or elevation of water-table.

Isocline: A line or curve connecting the least cost combinations of inputs for all output levels is known as isocline.

Isogenic: Differing in genotype by only one or a very few genes.

Isohyte: A line on a map joining places having equal rainfall in a certain period.

Iso-quants: All the possible combinations of two- inputs, physically capable of producing the same amount of output.

Isotach: A line representing equal wind speed.

Isotherm: Line connecting points of equal temperature. Isotherm maps are used to portray surface-temperature patterns of water bodies.

Isotone: Nuclides having the same number of neutrons in the nucleus but differing in the number of protons. Usually it cannot any one such nuclides.

Isotope: Different form of the same element containing the same number of protons and electrons, but differing in the number of neutrons.

IW: CPE ratio: In climatological approach, scheduling of irrigation water is done and the depth of irrigation water is fixed for different crops on the basis of this ratio.

J

Jetty: A structure made up of piles, rocks etc. extending into a stream or sea in order to induce scouring or bank building or for protection.

Jhum cultivation: Refers to the slash-and-burn type of shifting cultivation in the hill tracts of North –Eastern states in India and in parts of Bangladesh. Specific type of mixed cropping involving 3-15 crops are grown simultaneously in the same field. A complex diversified form of agriculture aimed at minimizing risk but have accelerating effect on soil erosion and environmental degradation.

Joint: A fracture or parting which interrupts the continuity of a rock.

Judging distance: This is very rough method of determining distance. It is used reconnaissance survey may differ from person to person depending on skill and experience.

Jungle: A term of Indian origin for wild, uncultivated land having thick under-growth. Sometimes applied to monsoon forests.

Juvenile A phase in the sexual cycle of a plant characterized by differences in appearance from the adult and by inability to respond to flower-inducing stimuli.

Juvenile phase: The phase of vegetative growth of a plant before which it cannot be induced to produce flowers. This period may vary from plant to plant, *e.g.* rice plants have a juvenile phase of one month.

Juvenile water: Water that has come to earth's surface from great depths for the first time (through a hot spring etc.).

K

K: Soil erodibility factor in Universal Soil Loss Equation.

Kame: A mound of sand or gravel deposited by a stream as it flowed from beneath a glacier and generally found on the outwash plane of a glacier.

Kankar: Concretionary masses of calcium carbonate commonly found in alluvial soil.

Kaolinite: A hydrous aluminosilicate whitish clay mineral of 1 : 1 crystal lattice consisting of one silicon tetrahedral layer and one aluminium oxide-hydroxide octahedral layer.

Kelvin scale: Scale for expressing temperature. In this scale, absolute zero is 0° Kelvins; water boils at 373.15° Kelvins and freezes at -273.15° Kelvins. (0° centigrade = 273.15°k)

Key grazing area: A sample of a pasture that represent the grazing use of the entire area.

Key terrace: The staked terrace line that serves as a reference for laying out other terraces.

Key utilization species: A forage species whose use indicates the extent or degree of use of key grazing areas.

Kilocalorie (Kcal): Unit of energy equal to 1,000 calories.

Kilopascal (kPa): A unit for quantifying pressure (force per unit area). Used to measure atmospheric pressure.

Kilowatt: It is a unit of power equal to 1,000 watts and it equals to energy consumption at the rate of 1,000 joule/sec. It is usually used for electrical power.

Kinetic energy: Energy by virtue of motion of a body and is proportional to the square of velocity.

Kinetic temperature: Internal temperature of an object determined by random molecular motion. Kinetic temperature is measured with a contact thermometer.

Knoll: A small, rounded mound or hill.

Koppen's classification (climate): A classification system that relates climate with vegetation to provide an objective numerical basis for defining climate types in terms of climatic elements.

Kurtosis: Deviation of a symmetrical frequency distribution from the normal by excess (platy kurtosis) or deficiency (lepto kurtosis) in its shoulders as opposed to tail and centre.

L

L layer: It is the O_1 horizon in soil profile that comprise of surface layer of forest floor includes freshly dropped leaves, needles, twigs, stems, bark and fraits etc. During growing season, this horizon may be very thin or absent.

Lacustrine deposit: The sedimentary material deposited from lake water. The deposit is shingly on the margin and has clay and limestone in deep water. Presence of fresh water snails and algae is an indication of lacustrine origin. The deposit may be subsequently exposed due to lowering in water level or elevation of land.

Lag phase: First stage of the sigmoidal growth curve where growth declines within a brief span of time.

Lagoon: A shallow pond or lake, a small artificial body of water usually composed of several compartments. Sometimes used to treat wastewater to a secondary level of treatment.

Lake: An extensive body of water, bounded by land on the earth's surface. In case quantity of water entering a lake exceeds the evaporation loss excess water flow out through an outlet channel. No outlet may be seen in areas of low rainfall and high evaporation.

Laminar flow: When water movement can be expressed in planes parallel and sliding over one another without mixing. Different imaginary planes have different flow velocity.

Lamination: Stratification in thin layers (fraction of an inch thick). It is exhibited by fine grained sandstone and shales.

Land (sub marginal): Refers to a land that does not give enough return to meet cost of operation for a specific use.

Land (super marginal): Refers to a land that shows profit after meeting all expenses on its use.

Land (wild): Refers to uncultivated land which may or may not be maintained by owner for productive vegetative purposes.

Land capability class: One of the eight classes of land in the land capability classification distinguished according to the capability of land to be used and limitations/risk associated.

Land capability classification: It is the interpretative grouping of land based on inherent soil characteristics, associated land features and environment (climate) into classes, sub-classes and units for optimum sustained production, without damage to the land or soil. Eight classes have been identified by Soil

Conservation Service of United States of America. Other countries have varied the number of classes to suit local conditions.

Land capability map: A map showing land capability units, subclasses and classes. Different land classes are shown in different colours such as light green, yellow, red and blue for lands suitable for agriculture as well as other less intensive use and dark green, orange, brown and purple for less intensive use (grassland, forest, wild life). The mapping unit coloured light green denotes land with little or no hazard of erosion and is suitable for most intensive use (intensive agriculture) while the Mapping unit coloured purple has the maximum hazard and limitation for use and may be allowed to establish ecological equilibrium with: the environment (climate and indigenous vegetation) without biotic interference.

Land capability subclass: Groups of capability units within classes of the land capability classification that have the same kinds of dominant limitations for agricultural use. The domination erosion (e), wetness, overflow, drainage (w) root zone problem (s) and climatic limitation (c) Expressed as subscript of land capability classes of III_s, VI_e etc.

Land capability unit: A group of soils with almost similar suitability for plant growth limitation and response to soil management. Capability unit provides more detailed information for management of specific fields, than the sub-class.

Land capability: Refers to the suitability of land for use without damage. It is an expression of the effect of physical land conditions on the total suitability of land for different uses without damage. For example intensive crop cultivation for grazing, for woodland for wildlife and other recreations. Capability of land is determined considering (a) risks or hazards of land damage due to erosion or other factors and (b) difficulties or limitations for different types of land use due to land characteristics and climate.

Land characteristic: Refers to any attribute of land that can be measured or estimated and that can be employed as a means of describing land qualities or distinguishing between land units of differing suitabilities for use.

Land classification: Systematic grouping of land on the basis of its physical characteristics (including vegetation) without explicit assessment of suitability for kinds of land use. Categorization of land units based on properties of the land or its suitability for some specific purpose.

Land cover map: Map of ground features that can be differentiated on a scene (*e.g.*, urban areas, bare land, pasture, etc.).

Land disturbing activity: Any activity that results in change in water or wind erosion and movement of sediment.

Land drain: A drain for removing water from land.

Land drainage: The removal of free water from the land surface as well as root zone of the soil.

Land form: A recognizable natural landscape such as plateau, stream terrace, flood plain, valley etc.

Land grading: Reshaping of the field surface to a desired elevation and slope to control the flow of water, to check soil erosion and to provide surface drainage.

Land levelling (irrigation): Reshaping of land surface for a more uniform spread of irrigation water. This would increase water-use efficiency.

Land preparation: The process of preparing the soil for planting, to provide a favourable soil environment for seed germination and plant growth.

Land reclamation: The process of changing general character of land like drainage of wet land, leaching of saline land, irrigation of semi-arid or arid land, recovery of submerged land from sea, lake or river. In order to improve land suitability for intensive use.

Land resource area: An area of land with similar potential on problems in soil and water conservation in relation to agriculture and are target area for specific treatment.

Land resource region: A generalized grouping of land resource areas having regional relationships to agriculture with emphasis on problems in soil and water conservation.

Land resource unit: It is a sub-division of land resource area with emphasis on specialized agriculture and soil and water conservation problems.

Land resting: Temporary discontinuation of cultivation for a specified period on a piece of land for specific purposes such as restoring fertility, weed removal, erosion control etc.

Land side: Cultivation part of plough that slide along the face of the furrow wall. It helps to slice on the ground and in stabilizing the plough while it is in operation. Land side is fastened to the frog, with the help of bolts.

Land slide: Rapid movement of a soil mass along with rock or debris from upper part of the slope to a downstream. Slipping of mass of material downhill under the influence of gravity. Sloping topography, water seeking material existence of slip surface are assisting factor.

Land suitability rating: Scaling suitability of a land for a land-utilization type, based on a set of land qualities. Land-suitability ratings are combined to give a land-suitability class.

Land use patterns: Different methods to utilize available land resources over the time for agricultural production.

Land use plan: Plan showing location with recommended land use and intensity of development of a piece of land for habitation, recreation, agriculture, plantation etc.

Land use planning: Refers to the development of plans for the uses of land over long periods, together with the formulation of ways and means for achieving such uses.

Land utilization index: The index expressing temporal utilization of land. It is analogous to land occupied by crop and expressed as the number of days during which the crops occupy the land during a year divided by 365 and can be expressed as a fraction or as a percentage.

Landsat: A series of unmanned earth-orbiting NASA satellites that acquire multispectral images in various visible and IR bands.

Landscape: Natural land features such as hills, forests, fields, water etc. which distinguish one part of the earth's surface from another. The landscape is usually confined to an area which can be comprehended by the eye in a single view.

Large watersheds: Large watersheds are those in which peak flows are greatly influenced by channel characteristics and basin storage.

Laser levelling: Land levelling technique wherein the levelling device, normally tractor-drawn, is controlled by a laser beam set at a certain bench mark or level in order to achieve higher accuracy.

Lateral moraine: Fragments of rock, broken off by frost etc. fallen down from the valley sides on to the glacier ice.

Lateral: Refers to secondary or side channel in drip irrigation or canal irrigation system.

Laterite: A reddish rock material, formed by weathering illuviation & eluviation in humid tropical regions. It consists mainly of hydrated oxides of iron and aluminium.

Lateritic soil: A suborder of zonal soils developed in warm, temperate and tropical regions under conditions of high rainfall with alternate wet and dry periods. Soils are rich in iron and aluminium hydroxide low in N, P, K, lime and magnesia. It includes the great groups, yellow podzolic, red podzolic, yellowish brown lateritic and lateritic.

Latosol: A great soil group of zonal soils including those formed under forested, tropical and humid conditions. They have low silica sesquioxide ratio of clay fraction, low base exchange capacity, low clay activity and a high degree of aggregate stability. The colour is usually red.

Lava: Refers to the eruption of molten rock or magma from a volcanic vent or a fissure and solidified on the surface of the land. Lava may vary in chemical composition and may be acidic, intermediate or basic depending upon the parent material.

Law of diminishing returns: When other factors in production do not change, each successive increase in the input of one factor results reduced increase in output. In operates after a certain point known as point of inflection in production curve.

Law of minimum: When a character such as yield is controlled by number of separate factors, the rate of growth process is limited by the most limiting factor. (Present in relative minimum)

Leachate: Water or other liquid that has percolated through the soil or washed (leached) from a solid material, such as a layer of soil or waste, having dissolved or suspended substances.

Leaching efficiency: It is the ratio of average salt concentration in drainage water to an average salt concentration in the soil water of the root zone at near field capacity.

Leaching requirement: The quanlity of water applied to the soil that must pass through the root zone so as to maintain soil salinity to a specified value.

Leaching: It is removal of dissolved or suspended substances or soluble material by the passage of water through the soil. This takes place when a liquid (*e.g.* water) passes through a substance, picking up some of the material and carrying it to other places.

Leaf area index: It is the ratio between surface area of leaves of vegetation and the corresponding land area covered by the leaves. LAI = Leaf area/Ground ore.

Leeward side: Sheltered/protected side of mountain barrier.

Legend: A list indicating explanation or identifying symbols used in a map, usually given in the margin of the map.

Legume inoculation: Inoculating legume seed or soil on which legume is to be grown with proper strain of nitrogen fixing bacteria. Bacteria can be added from pure culture or through the soil of a field where the legume crop has already been grown.

Legume: A member of the pulse family-leguminosae. The fruit (pod) opens along two sutures when ripe. Leaves are alternate, have stipules and are generally compound whereas the flowers are butterfly like (papilionaceous). Includes important food and forage crops such as beans, pea, groundnut, alfalfa, kudzu. Almost all legumes fix atmospheric nitrogen and the herbaceous species are used as cover and green manure crops and also for soil building.

Length of run: Distance that water has to traverse in furrows or between the borders over the surface of a field between two head ditches or between a head ditch and end of the field.

Lentic: Pertaining to standing water bodies like swamps, ponds, lakes etc.

Lethal Dose (LD): Minimum amount of a substance required to cause death in a targeted organism.

Levee: Natural bank of a river formed by deposition of sediment during flooding. As the flood subsides, the levee forms the highest portion of the flood-plain along the river course. It is a earthen embankment used to hold irrigation water within certain limits so that uniform irrigation of the entire field is obtained. The term also used for an earthen dam placed at varying distances from the bank of a river to serve as barrier to adjacent low lying land during floods.

Level line: In surveying (levelling) the line lying in a level surface. It is normal to the plumb line at all points.

Level surface: Any surface parallel to the mean spheroidal surface of the earth *e.g.* surface of a still lake. A level surface may be regarded as a curved surface, every point on which is equidistant from the center of the earth. It is normal to the plumb line at all points.

Level terrace: A terrace that strictly follows the absolute contour, without any grade, practiced on permeable soils where conservation of moisture for crop use is particular importance where it is impossible to provide outlet channels.

Leveling (soil): The operation in which the soil surface is worked to established a desired uniform slope.

Leveling (survey): Determining the relative vertical distance of different points on the surface of earth.

Measurements are taken only in the vertical plane by means of one of the several instruments like, IOP level, Dumpy level, thedolite, total station etc.

Leveling rod: Leveling rod is used with the level to obtain the vertical distance between the plane of sight and the surface or point on which the level rod is held.

Levellers: Equipment commonly used for the fine grading of small and medium-size fields. Two wheeled automatic leveller are in common use now

Ley farming: A system of farming in which arable crops requiring annual cultivation are sown in land fit for cultivation (arable land) in rotation on the field with two or more years of sown pasture.

Ley pasture: A temporary pasture grown as a specific phase in a defined crop rotation sequence.

Life saving irrigation: The irrigation given to a otherwise rainfed crop to save it from total failure due to long dry spells. The source of irrigation generally is harvested water. It is practiced in water scarce area.

Lime (agricultural): A soil amendment consisting mainly of calcium carbonate and containing quantities of magnesium carbonate and other materials (oxides, hydroxides etc.) Primarily added for neutralizing acid soils and satisfying the calcium and magnesium need of crops.

Lime concretion: An aggregate of precipitated calcium carbonate or of other soil material cemented by precipitated calcium carbonate.

Lime pan: A hardened layer due to cementation by calcium carbonate.

Lime requirement: The amount of agricultural limestone or the equivalent of any other liming material required to raise pH of the surface soil (6 inches or 2000,000 lbs in one acre) to a desirable value under field conditions. For maintaining a high degree of availability of most of the nutrient elements soil pH 6.5 is desirable.

Limestone: A sedimentary rock consisting essentially of calcium carbonate (at least 50 per cent). Different types of limestone are distinguished by name according to texture, mineral composition, origin, geological age etc. Most of them are partly or wholly of organic origin, and contain hard parts of many organisms like shells of molluscs and skeletons of corals.

Line of collimation: It is the line joining the intersection of cross hairs of the optical centre of the object glass to the object under right. It is also called the line of sight.

Lining: A process of covering over all or part of the bottom surface of a pond, reservoir etc. to reduce seepage and conserve water.

Liquid limit: Minimum percentage of water (by weight) at which a small sample of soil would barely flow under a standard treatment. Water content corresponding to an arbitrary limit between liquid and plastic consistency states of a soil expressed as mass by mass basis.

Lister: An equipment that yield double plough depositing soil in opposite directions making a series of alternate ridges and furrows in the field. The operation is helpful in conservation of moisture.

Lithosequence: A group of soils that differ, one from the other, in some characteristics resulted due to differences in the parent rock as a soil forming factor.

Lithosols: A great soil' group of a zonal soils characterized by incomplete solum or no clearly expressed soil morphology. They consist of freshly and imperfectly weathered rock or its fragments.

Lithosphere: The outer solid crust of earth enveloping the central core is called Lithosphere. It consists of the thin loose layer of soil and the mass of hard rock, several kilometres thick, on which the soil lies.

Litre: An unit of volume which is equivalent to 0.22 imperial gallons or 0.0353 cubic feet or 1/1000cubic meters or 1000 millilitre (ml).

Litter (forestry): A surface layer of loose organic debris that includes freshly fallen, or slightly decomposed leaves, twigs, fruits etc. in the, forest.

Littoral deposits: Deposits on the shore line between high and low tide levels. They consist of much sand and well-rounded pebbles due to strong current and wave action resulting in, intense marine abrasion. Littoral region of the ocean comprises shallow waters near the coast, and has the richest vegetation and supports abundant animal life.

Live storage: The water stored above the outlet in a reservoir.

Load discharge: Release of contaminants, usually expressed as kg/day, at levels or concentrations above the level that can be removed though application of best available technology economically achievable.

Loading (soil, water, air): amount of a substance entering the environment (soil, water, or air).

Loam: Soil material containing 10-25% clay, 10-25% silt and 50-75% sand as per textural classification by the International system for textural designations. The composition is 7-27% clay, 28-50% silt and 23-52% sand vide United States System for textural designations.

Loamy: Intermediate in texture and properties between fine and coarse textured soils. The term includes all textural classes having loam or loamy as part of their names such as clay loam, silty clay loam, sandy clay loam, sandy loam, loamy sand, silt loam, loam etc.

Loess: Soil material transported and deposited by wind. It is primarily of silt sized particles, and may contain some fine sand and clay. The deposited material is uniform and unstratified.

Loose rock dam: A dam made of loose rock without using mortar also called rubble dam. It is a perforated structure.

Loose: A consistency of dry or moist soil.

Lopping: Pruning or cutting away aerial parts of shurbs or trees. It is practiced to accelerate fresh growth of tree.

Lotic: Pertain to flowing water bodies like streams and rivers.

Lower plastic limit: The minimum moisture content (percent by weight) in a soil material at which it could be deformed without rupture.

Lysimeter: A device for measuring quantity or rate of water movement through a soil column, generally undisturbed, and collecting the percolate for analysis. It is used to estimate actual evapotranspiration through water balance method.

M

Macro scale (Meteorology): The long systems ranging from few hundreds to 10000 km in size and a lifetime is of few days to several weeks. It is divided into two scales, Synoptic scale and Planetary scale.

Macroclimate: The climate over a large area such as a region or country.

Macronutrient: Element required in large quantities (usually> 1 ppm) for plant growth. It is applied in the form of fertilizer or liming material. 'Macro' refers to quantity and not to essentiality of the element.

Macropore: Larger soil pores, generally having a minimum diameter between 30 and 100 micrometers (> 60 microns) from which water drains readily by gravity.

Made land: Land filled with earth or mixed earth and trash under the control of man. A miscellaneous land type.

Main stations (survey): Main stations are the end of the lines, which command the boundaries of the survey, and the lines joining the main stations are called the main survey line or the chain lines.

Major project (irrigation): A project which can irrigate more than 10,000 ha is called major irrigation project.

Management practice: Practical ways of using management decisions to organise the use of resources or materials.

Man-day of labour: The amount of work expected from a farm worker in a 8 hours operating at the average rate of performance using adequate equipment.

Mangum terrace: A type of broad-base terrace initially constructed and used in Franklin County, North Carolina, U.S.A. in 1885, named after inventor priestly magnum.

Manning's formula (hydraulics): It is a formula for predicting velocity of water in an open channel or pipeline is given by formula $V = \frac{R^{2/3} S^{1/2}}{n}$ Where, V is mean velocity of water flow (m per second); R is hydraulic radius (m of crossection/wetted perimeter); S is channel slope (m per m) and n is roughness coefficient or retardance factor of the channel lining.

Mantle rock or regolith: Layer of loose unconsolidated rock of varying thickness, which covers the earth's land area found beneath the soil and subjected to weathering.

Manual separation: Refers to the separation of recyclables or compositable materials from waste by hand sorting.

Manure: Excreta of animals, with or without an admixture of bedding or litter, fresh or at various stages of decomposition or composting. In some countries the term is broadly used to denote any fertilizer material. The decomposed manure is called farmyard manure or farm manure or barnyard manure. The average composition of well rotted farmyard manure is 0.5 % nitrogen, 0.3% P_2O_5 and 0.5% K_2O

Map scale: Relationship between a certain distance on the map and the corresponding distance on the ground. It is expressed as (i) two distances or (ii) arithmetic ratio or. Fraction known as representative fraction (*e.g.* 1:10,000, which means 1 cm on the map equals to 10,000 cm or 100 m on the ground).

Map units: Measurement units used to define quantities depicted on a map, such as offset distances, pattern and shade spacing, and text and symbol size.

Map, planimetric: A map showing the horizontal position of features of land with sufficient accuracy for measurement.

Map, topographic: A representation of the physical features of land on which terrain relief is shown by contour lines.

Marble: Lime stones which have completely crystallized (coarse grained) due to metamorphism, which may be polished for decorative purposes.

Marginal (bund): Earthen embankment made between the gullied area and the above lying non gullied land so as to facilitate different types of land use in both the areas and divert run-off water from the upper land into the gullied area at desired locations. This would reduce erosion.

Marginal benefit (cost ratio): An index of the economic advantage of a new pattern, used to evaluate a series of alternatives to the existing pattern. It is the ratio of benefit incurred on last unit of input to the cost of that input.

Marginal product (MP): It is the ratio of change in total output as related to the last unit of input addition..

Marking station: Surveyor fixes up the required no stations at places from where maximum possible stations are covered.

Marl: Soft, unconsolidated calcium carbonate usually mixed with clay or other impurities. Some of the marls are marine deposits while others are fresh water deposits.

Marsh, tidal: A low, flat area having interlacing channels and tidal sloughs, being periodically inundated by high tides. Vegetation is characterised by salt tolerant plants.

Marsh: Periodically wet or continually flooded areas with the surface not deeply submerged. Dampness is due to impermeable nature of the soil and poor drainage. Vegetation consists of hydrophytes like sedges (*Cirrus spp.*), cattails (*Typha spp.*), and rushes etc. Sub-classes are fresh water marsh and marine marsh. The term is often used synonymously with swamp.

Masonry dam: A dam built of bricks or rocks and mortar. It is a permanent type structure.

Mass burn: municipal waste combustion technology in which solid waste is burned in a controlled system without prior sorting or processing.

Mass diagram: Graph showing cumulative quantities such as an integral of a time-flow curve where every point is the sum of all preceding values. The diagram is useful in water-storage analysis. Infiltration characterization etc.

Matric potential: Portion of the total soil water potential due to the attractive forces between water and soil solids as represented through adsorption and capillarity. The amount of work that an unit quantity of water in an equilibrium soil water (or plant water) system is capable of doing when it moves to another equilibrium system identical in all respects except that there is no matrix present.

Mattress (engineering): A blanket of brush or other material interwoven or otherwise joined together and weighted with rock concrete etc. or otherwise held in place to cover an area exposed to scour.

Mature soil: A soil with well-developed, distinct horizons as a result of soil forming processes. It is in equilibrium with its present environment.

Maximum available water: The maximum quantity of water that can be held in the soil between field capacity and wilting coefficient expressed in weight/weight basis. This is the moisture that can be readily extracted by the plant and used for normal growth.

Maximum capillary capacity: The maximum moisture content in the soil beyond which any addition of water gets percolated down by the force of gravity. This is the point of maximum capillary capacity.

Maximum contaminant level (MCL): The MCL is the enforceable standard for greatest amount of a contaminant that can be present in drinking water without causing a risk to human health.

Maximum daily limit (MDL): The absolute maximum allowable load or concentration of a substance in a facility's effluent. This limit is based on water quality and technological limits.

Maximum residue limit (MRL): The maximum concentration of a residue legally permitted or recognized as acceptable in or on a food, agricultural commodity or animal feedstuff.

Maximum thermometer: A thermometer used for measuring the highest temperature attained during a day. It is usually a mercury glass thermometer with an index.

Maximum water holding capacity: Maximum amount of water can be held until all micro and macro pores are filled with water. This stage is called the maximum water holding capacity.

Meadow strip: A sloping field or strip of grassland, which in addition to yielding hay, also serves as a broad, shallow channel for run-off disposal. It is many times used as terrace outlet channel. Usually much larger than a grassed waterway.

Meadow: A field growing natural or planted vegetation (dominated by grasses) for hay making.

Mean depth (hydraulics): Cross-sectional area of a channel divided by surface or top width.

Mean deviation: Sum of the deviation of each score from the mean, without regard to sign divided by number of scores.

Mean sea level: The mean plane at which the tide oscillates the average height of the sea for all stages of the tide. At any particular place, it is derived by averaging the hourly tide heights over a 19 year period.

Mean square: It is the average of the squared deviations from the arithmetic mean of a series of values also called variance.

Mean velocity: Flow rate (discharge) divided by cross-sectional area of channel. The average velocity of flow expressed as discharge divided by area of cross section of channel.

Mean: The arithmetic average of a series of observations or measurements. The arithmetic average obtained when the sum of the values of individuals in the data is divided by the number of individuals in the data.

Meander belt: Belt of land along the valley floor which lies between outermost meanders of a stream.

Meander land: Unsurveyed land along a lake shore or stream border, which has developed by the receding of shoreline or stream since the last revenue or cadastral survey.

Meander: A curve in the course of a river as it continually swings from side to side in large loops in flat country. The concave bend is worn away by the current and the bank is often steep while the convex bend gradually gets deposition and the bank has a relatively gentle slope. The meander-belt is fifteen to eighteen times the river width. Meanders of a river move side to side and also downstream.

Measuring weir: Rectangular, triangular or trapezoidal notch through which water flow is measured.

Mechanical practices: Soil and water conservation practices that are based on mechanical structure, which primarily modify the land surface or store, convey, or dispose of run-off without causing excessive erosion.

Mechanical separation: sorting of waste into various components using mechanical means, such as cyclones, trommels, and screens.

Medial moraine: When two glaciers join, the two adjacent lateral moraines combine to form the medial moraine.

Median: The median is the middle of a series when the observations are arranged in order of magnitude and it divides the series into two equal halves, half the number of observations lying above it and half below. In case of even number of observation of middle two observations is called median.

Medium texture: Intermediate texture between coarse and fine texture (soils). It includes the textural classes-very fine sandy loam, loam, silt loam and silt.

Mellisols: Soils having thick surface horizon of dark colour, dominated by divalent cations associated with grasslands granular or crub structure, friable consistency and with moderate fertilization soil are productive.

Mellow soil: A very soft, very friable, porous soil having no tendency towards hardness or harshness.

Mesoclimate: The climate over a specific locality such as a hillside or valley, extending no more than a few kilometres in radius.

Mesophyte: A plant requiring average amount of moisture and hence growing in climates of moderate rainfall and temperature.

Mesoscale (Meteorology)**:** The systems are approximately 10 km in size and a lifetime is of few hours [up to 5 hrs] *e.g.* Thunder storm.

Metal: Refers to a group of elements possessing certain qualities including metallic luster, malleability, ductility, high specific gravity and good conductivity of heat and electricity; metals are mined from the Earth

Meteorology: The Science deals with the physics, chemistry and dynamics of atmosphere and also their direct and indirect effects upon the earth surface, oceans and thereby Life in general

Micro irrigation: Method of applying low volume of water at low pressure & high frequency usually at an interval of 1 to 4 days. The system has extensive network of pipes operated at low pressure. Emitters are provided at pre-determined spacing for emission of water.

Micro-pores: Soil pores size having diameter ranging from 3 to 30 microns (< 60μ) which plays an important role in water and nutrient retention with slow capillary flow.

Micro-scale (Meteorology)**:** A process operating within vegetation canopies near earth surface its size is in few cm and Life span is few seconds.

Micro-environment: The environment around surface of a living or non- living object.

Microclimate: The climatic condition of a small area on the ground or area around plants (up to 2 m height), resulting from the modifications of the general climatic conditions by local difference in relief exposure and cover etc.

Micrometer: One millionth of a meter, or 10^{-6} meter, the unit usually used for measuring microorganisms also called micron.

Micronutrient: Chemical element essential for growth but required in extremely small quantities, usually < 100 mg kg^{-1} in a plant. These elements consist of B, Cl, Cu, Fe, Mn, Mo, and Zn. 'Micro' refers to the quantity required and not to essentiality of the elements.

Micro-relief: Small-scale, local differences of topography including mounds, swales or pits a few feet in diameter and having up to 6 ft. elevation differences.

Mid-day depression or mid-day deficits: Phenomenon of severe water stress during periods of high radiation and low humidity even though plants growing in soils nearing field capacity known as mid day depression or water deficits.

Milling process: Refers to the process by which the valuable components of the ore are separated from waste material. Rice milling is done for separating grain from paddy.

Mine dumps: Areas covered with waste materials from quarries, ore mines, coal mines and smelters and usually having little or no vegetative cover as a result of the mining activity.

Mine wash: Water based deposition of sandy, silty or clay material recently eroded as a result of mining activity. It may clog streams or other channels and damage the land over which it gets deposited.

Mine water: The water that is pumped or flows out of any underground working or open pit

Mineral soil: A soil consisting predominantly of, and having its characteristics dependant mainly on mineral matter, and having less than 20 percent organic matter.

Mineral water: Water containing large amounts of dissolved minerals such as calcium, sodium, magnesium, and iron. Some tap waters contain as many or more minerals than some commercial mineral waters. There is no scientific evidence that either high or low mineral content water is beneficial to humans.

Mineral: A naturally occurring inorganic substance possessing definite physical and chemical properties and chemical composition.

Mineralization: The microbial conversion of a chemical element from an organic (containing carbon) to an inorganic (not containing carbon) state.

Minimum thermometer: Thermometer used for measuring the lowest temperature attained during a day. It is generally a alcohol or spirit in glass thermometer.

Minimum tillage: Crop production where soil cultivation is kept to the minimum necessary for crop establishment and growth. Weed control, where necessary, is done by using herbicides, by pulling or scraping, or by mulching.

Mining water use: Water use during quarrying rocks and extracting minerals from the land.

Minor project: An irrigation project with a capacity to irrigate less than 2,000 ha.

Miscellaneous land type: A mapping unit for areas of land that have little or no soil, that are too nearly inaccessible for orderly examination, and it is not feasible to classify their soil for any leason. Examples are bad land, made land, meander land, mine dumps, mine wash, river wash, rough broken land, rubble land, scoria land, slickens, stony land, swamp, tidal flats, urban land, volcanic ash and wasteland.

Misfit river: A river which appears to be too small in relation to the valley it has carved. The river has probably lost its headwaters by river capture.

Mitigation: Actions taken for the purpose of reducing the negative impacts on the environment of a particular land use or activity. Climate change mitigation through plantation of tree.

Mixed cropping: Growing of two or more crops simultaneously on the same piece of land, without any definite row arrangement. It is a risk averting practices in rainfed drought prone area.

Mixed farming: Mixed farming is a type of farming under which crop production is combined with livestock raising. The livestock enterprise is complementary to crop production programmes so as to provide a balanced and productive system of farming.

Mixed fertilizers: Fertilizers containing two or more of the major fertilizer elements. The percentages of these nutrients are expressed as fertilizer grade, like 10: 5: 5. (N.P.K)

Mixed forest: A forest having two or more tree species so that at least 20 percent trees belong to other than the dominant species.

Mixed intercropping: Growing two or more crops simultaneously with no distinct space allotted for one crop.

Mode: The most frequent values from observation or data. In a frequency table the modal class is the class which has the greatest frequency.

Model: A small imitation of the real thing; a system of postulates, data, and inferences presented as a mathematical description of an entity or state of affairs. Mathematical expression to use data to project result.

Moderately coarse texture: Predominantly of coarse particles includes all the sandy loams excepting the very -fine sandy loam.

Moderately fine texture: It consists predominantly of intermediate size (soil) particles or has relatively small amounts of fine or coarse particles. It includes clay loam, sandy clay loam.

Moist soil: Soil having moisture content greater than friable limit.

Moisture availability index: It is the ratio of assured rainfall (weekly or monthly) at 50% probability level to potential evapotranspiration of the corresponding period.

Moisture content: The amount of water present in the soil or plant expressed as the mass of water per unit dry mass of the material when dried at 103°C (217°F) for eight hours or more.

Moisture deficit index (MDI): The measure to estimate dryness of a region. and is expressed by the formula $MDI = \frac{P - PE}{PE} \times 100$, *where,* P = Precipitation and PE= Potential evapotranspiration

Moisture equilibrium: The condition reached by a sample seed when it no longer takes up moisture from, or gives up moisture to, the surrounding atmosphere. *Synonym:* hygroscopic equilibrium.

Moisture equivalent: The moisture retained in soil which has been wetted and centrifuged for 30 min. in a centrifugal field equal to 1,000 times gravity. Moisture equivalent is expressed as moisture percentage on a dry weight basis and approximates field capacity for many medium and fine textured soil.

Moisture percentage: The weight of water per 100 units of weight of dried material or on basis of depth as the equivalent depth of free water per 100 units of depth of soil. Numerically this value approximates the volume of water per 100 units of volume of soil.

Moisture regimes: The different levels of the available soil moisture (ASM as %), a testing factor or unit inputs used in conducting irrigation experiments, such as ASM at 100, 80 60, 40 % etc.

Moisture release curve or characteristic curve: It is the functional relationship between soil moisture tension and soil moisture content.

Moisture retentive soil: A soil that retains a high percentage of water. Clay soils are more moisture retentive than sandy soils.

Moisture stress: When the plant suffers from a lack of water to support good growth and development.

Moisture tension (or pressure): The equivalent negative pressure in the soil or the equivalent pressure required to be applied to soil water to bring it in equilibrium, through a porous permeable wall or membrane with a pool or water of the same composition.

Moisture volume percentage: Ratio of volume of water in a soil to total bulk volume of the soil expressed as percentage.

Moisture weight percentage: Moisture content of soil expressed as percentage of oven dry (105°C) weight of soil.

Mole drains: Cylindrical channels artificially formed in the sub soil using a mole plough without digging a trench from the surface. A mole drain should be at least 75 cm below the surface to prevent closing of the holes by compaction from farming operations.

Monoculture: Practice of raising the same crop repeatedly over a piece of land.

Monsoon: It is defined as reversal of wind direction a seasonal accompanied by changes in precipitation.

Montmorillonite: 2:1 type of alluminosilicate clay mineral having expanding crystal lattice structure, in which two silicon tetrahedral layers enclose an aluminium octahedral layer. Considerable expansion occurs along the C-axis by water moving between silica layers of contiguous units.

Mor: A type of forest humus characterized by an accumulation or organic matter on the soil surface in matted Oe(F) horizons, reflecting the dominant mycogenous decomposers. The boundary between the organic horizon and the underlying mineral soil is abrupt. Sometimes differentiated into the following groups: Hemimor, Humimor, Resimor, Lignomor, Hydromor, Fibrimor, and Mesimor.

Moraine: The rock material brought down by a glacier.

Mosaic: Assemblage of overlapping aerial photographs or satellite imageries having matched edges to give a continuous photographic representation of the area. Mosaicing is a practice of image interpretation.

Most probable number (MPN): A statistical expression for estimating the number of microorganisms in a culture or a volume of water.

Mottled (soil): Soil horizons having spots of colour. It may be due to impeded drainage, soil development from an unevenly weathered rock or weathering of different kinds of minerals.

Movable dam: A movable barrier which may be fully or partly opened to allow flow of water through or over the dam.

Muck soil: A soil containing 20-25 per cent organic matter.

Muck: Highly decomposed organic matter in which original plant parts are not distinguishable. It contains more mineral matter and is usually darker than peat.

Mulch farming: A system of farming in which organic residues or other materials are left on the surface (without mixing) to serve as mulch for the purpose of soil and moisture conservation and weed control.

Mulch tillage: Preparation of soil in such a way that plant residues or other mulching materials are specially left on or near the surface.

Mulch: A loose surface horizon consists of either inorganic or organic materials such as saw dust, straw, paddy husk, groundnut shell, crop residues, leaves, plastic film, paper, stones, loose soil etc. applied or induced to form for stabilizing the surface and improving soil microclimatic conditions. Mulch reduces erosion and water loss from the soil. It moderate soil temperature and can be used to control weeds.

Mulching: Application of a layer of compost or sawdust paddy husk or other material to the surface of the soil, creating an interface that accepts water readily but reduces evapotranspiration.

Mull: A type of forest humus in which F layer may or may not be present and in which there is no H layer. The A_1 horizon is constituted by an intimate mixture of organic matter and mineral soil and has a gradual transition to the horizon below. (May be differentiated into firm mull, sand mull, coarse mull, medium mull and fine mull).

Multicropping: The cultivation of more than one crop on the same piece of land in one year.

Multidisciplinary approach: An approach in which a number of disciplines are involved in a project or programme with common general objectives.

Multiple correlation coefficients (R): A estimate of influence of two or more variables (combindley) on dependent variable commonly used for evaluating regression model.

Multiple correlation: Linear relation of more than two variables. The collective association of several variables with one another usually linearly.

Multiple cropping index: It is the sum of area planted to different crops and harvested in single year divided by the total cultivated area times 100 expressed in percentage.

Multiple cropping: Growing two or more crops on the same field in the same year. It is the intensification of cropping in time and spacc dimensions with minimum deterioration of soil.

Multipurpose project: Project with more than one purpose for example an irrigation project to serve more than one objective such as flood control, irrigation, power generation, navigation etc.

Multislot divisor: A device used to divide the run-off into multi units (3, 5, 7, 9, 11, 13, 15 aliquots) depending on the number of slots in divisor. One aliquot is measured for volume of run-off and quantity of soil loss and multiplied suitably to get values per unit area.

Multispectral classification: Process of classification of satellite imageries based on their spectral characteristics in multiple band of electromagnetic wavelengths.

Systematic grouping of pixels based on spectral similarity.

Munsell colour system: System of designating/assigning colour to a soil specifying relative degrees of three simple variables of colour-hue, value and chroma. A colour (soil) of 10 YR 6/5 indicates hue 10 YR, value 6 and chroma 5. On the basis of these notations, different colour names are given.

N

Nappe: The sheet of water flowing over a weir. The term also applied in geology for a sheet like rock moved from its original position.

National Agricultural Innovation Project (NAIP): It is a project launched by the ICAR to facilitate accelerated and sustainable transformation of Indian agriculture in support of poverty alleviation and income generation by collaborative development and application of agricultural innovation by the public research organizations in partnership with the farmer's groups, the private sector, the civil society organizations and other stakeholders.

National Agricultural Research Project (NARP): It is a project launched by the ICAR to strengthen the regional research capabilities of the agricultural universities in India, with an objective of conducting need based, location-specific and production-oriented research in all the agro climatic zones identified in the area of its jurisdiction.

National Agricultural Technology Programme (NATP): It was an initiation of government of India with World Bank Assistance. It was launched in November, 1998. Its purpose was to make the extension serious, broad based, holistic beyond agriculture technology transfer besides to consolidate earlier weakness and gaps. The Research component of NATP is being implemented by the Indian Council of Agricultural Research (ICAR) and the Extension component by the Department of Agriculture and Co-operation.

National demonstrations: The national demonstration project was launched by the ICAR in 1965 as an instrument of transfer of technology. The main objectives are (i) demonstrating to the farmers the production potential of land by adopting high yielding varieties, multiple-cropping programmes and other scientific package of practices, (ii) providing research workers a first-hand information on problems faced by farmers and factors limiting crop yields.

Native pasture: A pasture covered with native plants or naturalized exotic plants.

Native species: A species in the original fauna or flora of an area.

Natural bridge: A bridge or arch of natural rock, which is sometimes formed when the tough, unjointed rocks of a valley spur are cut through by a stream. The phenomenon is more common in limestone.

Natural erosion: Refers to erosion (without the interference of man and undisturbed environmental condition under the cover of vegetation). When the land is in its perfect equalibrium also known as geological erosion.

Natural farming: The system of farming in which the plants are grown as natural entities without manipulation of soil, uses no machines, no prepared fertilizers and no chemical but yields normal harvests.

Natural vegetation: The vegetation of a region as it exists at present or which existed before any marked modification by man.

Naturalized flow (Re-constructed Flow): The flow that would have occurred in the absence of any man-made effects. For the purposes of water management, natural flow is a calculated value based on the recorded flows of contributing rivers.

Naturalized plant: A plant introduced into an area from outside, which has established and adapted itself in the area by long continued growth.

Naturally occurring wetland: An area where water has or does accumulate due to the lower elevations documented to have occurred under natural conditions.

NDC (National Data Centre): It is a section of National Remote Sensing Centre, Hyderabad, responsible for processing providing (selling) remote sensing data to Indian user. Even for procuring remote sensing data from foreign agency one has to go through National Data Centre of NRSC

Nephelometric turbidity unit (NTU): Unit of turbidity of water. Essentially, a measure of the cloudiness of water as measured by a nephelometer. Turbidity is based on the amount of light that is reflected off particles in the water.

Net area sown: Actual extent of land (revenue classification) sown to crops during a given year, when cropped more than once in any year, its area is added to the net area sown to arrive at the total area sown during the year.

Net duty of water: The amount of irrigation water delivered to the farm for raising a crop; measured at the point of delivery.

Net irrigation requirement: Amount of irrigation water just required to bring the soil moisture content in the root zone depth of the crops to field capacity. It is the difference between the field capacity and soil moisture content in the root zone before application of irrigation water.

Net positive suction Head [NPSH]: It is the total suction head minus the vapor pressure of water at the pumping temperature both expressed in meter.

Netting dam: A type of dam in which wire netting is used to from a small check dam usually constructed at the head of the gully. Bottom and side of net is fixed by means of burying and wooden post. Brush or straw is loosely piled toward upstream side of netting wall to form a porous barrier but slowdown flow velocity.

Neutral soil: A soil in which the surface layer, up to at least the normal plough depth, is neither acid nor alkaline in reaction. (pH 6.6-7.3).

Neutralization: Moderation of soil pH towards neutrality. It is done by raising the pH of an acidic material or lowering the pH of an alkaline material to a nearly neutral pH level (7)

Neutron moisture meter (depth probe): A radiation based soil moisture measuring device in which fast neutron released from source is thermalized primarily by H^+ from water and detected. Neutron source and detector compacted in a cylindrical container that is lowered down a tube in soil indicate moisture content.

Neutron scattering: A means for thermalization of last neutrons by multiple collisions with hydrogen atoms. The slow neutrons are caught by a detector and counted by a counting unit.

Nitrification: Refers to biochemical oxidation of ammonia (NH_3), ammonium (NH_4), or atmospheric nitrogen (N) to nitrate (NO_3) or nitrite (NO_2).

Nitrogen cycle: The sequence of biochemical changes undergone by nitrogen, when it is utilized by a living organism, liberated, upon its death and decomposition, and converted to its original state of oxidation.

Nitrogen fixation-(Soils): The conversion of atmospheric elemental nitrogen (N2), into organic compounds by organisms in the soil. These compounds are utilized by the plants.

Nitrogen fixing plant: Plants that can assimilate and fix free atmospheric nitrogen with of bacteria in root nodules. Legumes are important nitrogen fixing plants.

Nivation: Erosion due to the action of snow. Erosion of soils or rock beneath a snow patch and on its margin due to frost action, chemical weathering and solifluetation.

Non discharge systems: A wastewater disposal systems that do not discharge to surface waters, such as spray irrigation, land application, or conventional septic systems.

Non-consumptive Use: A use of water in which all of the water used is directly returned to the source from which it came. For example, water used in the production of hydroelectricity is a non-consumptive water use.

Non-graded sediment: Loose or cemented detrital sediments containing appreciable quantities of more than one grade.

Nonpoint source (NPS) contamination: Refers to water contamination derived from diffuse sources such as construction sites, agricultural fields, and urban runoff.

Non-renewable natural resource: A natural resource, which once used, cannot be replaced.

Normal erosion: Gradual erosion of land that does not greatly exceed natural erosion.

Normal water level: The level at which water is stored normally in farm pond or reservoir is called normal water level or full tank level

Notch: The opening in a weir or spillway for passage of water.

No-till agriculture: A method of planting crops by just (that involves no seedbed preparation) opening small areas in the soil for placing seed at the intended depth. There is generally no cultivation during crop production; instead, chemicals are used for vegetation control, aimed to reduce soil erosion.

No-tillage: Method of planting crops which does not involve seed bed preparation. The seed is deposited in slits or holes made in the soil. Weeds are controlled chemically. Also called zero tillage or slot planting.

NRSC: National remote sensing centre is one of the centres under Indian space research organisation (ISRO) department of space, Govt of India, mandated for collection, processing, promoting and marketing remote sensing data along with conducting research on application of these data.

Nuisance contaminant: Refers to constituents in water which are not normally harmful to health but may cause offensive taste, odor, color, corrosion, foaming, or staining.

Null hypothesis: Hypothesis of no differences the hypothesis that states there is no measurable difference between the observed information and measured data.

Nullah (nala): A normally dry water course, which runs only immediately after a heavy rain.

Nutrient cycling: The pathway of biochemical transformation of in cyclic manner nutrient substances from their occurrance in the physical environment to their incorporation in the living organisms and their return to the physical environment through the metabolic activity, death, and decay of organisms.

Nutrient: A chemical element required for the growth and development of an organism. Substance taken by a cell from its environment and used in catabolic or anabolic reactions. Major plant nutrients include nitrogen, phosphorus, carbon, oxygen, sulphur, and potassium.

Nutrient-deficiency symptoms: Visible changes in natural colour growth of leaves plants or any ports due to sufficient enemy of nutrient in soil and plant. symptoms are characteristic to each of the nutrient. The nature of the symptom varies from crop to crop and with degree of deficiency.

Nutrition: The sum of the processes by which an animal or plant absorbs or takes in and utilizes food substances.

Nutritional disorder: Any abnormality of plant caused by a deficiency of any essential element; or toxicity caused by a high level of any substance or ion in the soil; or any retarded growth due to a high osmotic pressure of the soil solution called nutritional disorder.

O

O horizon: Organic horizon in mineral soils.

Oa horizon (H layer): A layer occurring in mor humus consisting of well-decomposed organic matter of unrecognizable origin.

Observation well: Wells made for deliberate (up to a certain depth) observation of water table or piezometric level.

Observation: Record of the facts and information in a sequence of events exactly, during the research program.

Ochric horizon: Thin, light coloured horizon having low organic matter.

Odometer: A device to measures the distance travelled by a vehicle when attached to the wheel of any vehicle, such as carriage, cart bicycle, etc. It registers the number of revaluation of the wheel. Knowing the circumference of the wheel, the distance traversed may be obtained by multiplying the number of revolutions by the circumference of the wheel. It can be electronic, mechanical or combination of two.

Off stream use: Water withdrawn from a surface water source for uses such as irrigation, municipal and industrial water supply, steam electric power generation, etc.

Offsets: Lateral measurements from the base line to fix the positions of the different objects of interest with respect to base line. These are generally set at right angle on baseline. It can also be drawn with the help of a tape. There are two kinds of offsets:1) Perpendicular offsets, and 2) Oblique offsets.

Off-type: Plants or seeds significantly different from the variety in characteristics plant/seeds described by the breeder in any observable respect resulting from cross-pollination by other kinds or varieties, uncontrolled self-pollination during production of hybrid seed, or segregates from any of the above plants.

Ogee: Profile of overflow dam or spillway shaped like 'S'.

One-third atmosphere percentage: The percentage of water (by weight or volume) in a moist soil, subjected to, and is in equilibrium with, an applied pressure of 1/3 atmosphere. For coarse and medium textured soils, it is approximately numerically equal to moisture equivalent.

On-farm research and development: Agronomic and socio economic research studies conducted on the farms with farmer's active participation. The aim is to develop improved technologies and to devise ways to combine these technologies with farmer's knowledge and skill to efficiently utilize the available farm resources.

Open drain: Natural or constructed channel for conveying drainage water.

Open range: An extensive grazing area with unrestricted movement of livestock.

Open-formula mixed fertilizers: Refers to fertilizer mixtures whose composition and complete make-up are disclosed by manufacturers. Thus the fertilizer grade, the straight fertilizers and the filler used are disclosed on each bag.

Opportunity time: Time for which surface water is available for infiltration.

Optimum tillage: Combination of different tillage operations aimed at maximum crop growth.

Orchard bench terraces: These are narrow width terraces [about 1m] for individual trees are prepared in this type. These are also referred as intermittent terraces and step terraces.

Ore: Any mineral or solid material containing a precious or useful substance in a quantity and form that makes its extraction/mining profitable

Organic compound: Refers to carbon-based substance, including some petroleum products, solvents, pesticides, and halomethanes.

Organic matter (soil): The fraction of the soil that includes plant and animal residues at various stages of decomposition in soil, cells and tissues of soil organisms, substances synthesized by soil microbial activity. Plant leaves, stem, straw, husk, roots, stubbles or any remnants of crops or plant species and organic manures including farmyard manure are the cheap source of organic matter.

Organic phosphorus: Refers to phosphorus present as a constituent of organic compounds like glycerophosphoric acid, inositol phosphoric acid etc.

Organic soil: A soil containing a high percentage (greater than 20-30%) of organic matter throughout the solum.

Orientation (plane table survey): It is one of the essential operations in setting.table for plane table survey. Operation of keeping the table parallel at each of the succeeding station to the position it occupied at first station is called centring.

Orifices: Orifices are usually circular or rectangular opening in vertically bulkhead in open channels through which water flows. The edge of opening is sharp and often constructed of metal.

Orstein: An indurated layer in B-horizon of podzols, in which illuviated sesquioxides (predominantly iron) and organic matter constitute the cementing material.

Outer capillary water: It is that part of capillary water which is not very tightly held in the soil and moves readily from place to place. It is the most useful water for plants as it is very easily available.

Outfall: The point at which a pipe or channel discharges to a water body.

Outlet channel: A channel that carries water out or away from a reservoir, lake or other water body or waterway carrying water from terraces, tile lines or diversions etc.

Outlet gate: A gate designed to control the flow of water through a reservoir outlet in or around a dam.

Oven dry weight: Weight of soil after drying in an oven at 105 degree celsius until it looses no more water and final weight is recorded as oven dry weight. Equivalent moisture tension at this stage is 10,000 atmospheres.

Oven-dry soil: Soil is considered to be oven dry when it has reached equilibrium with the vapour pressure from an oven at 105°C and attains constant mass. The oven-dry condition corresponds to a relative humidity of approximately 0% or pF near 7.

Over head: Those general charges or expenses that cannot be associated directly to any specific part of the work. It is also fixed charges, establishment charges, administration charges, selling charges, and distribution charges, etc.

Over irrigation: The application of irrigation water in excess of quantity necessary for vegetation, resulting in loss of water through seepage and leaching.

Overfall: An abrupt change in elevation of stream channel; part of a weir or dam over which water flows.

Overstocked (forestry): A condition indicating higher tree population in a stand or forest area than normal.

Oxic horizon: Altered subsurface horizon having mixture of sesquioxides and 1:1 clays or/and quartz highly weathered and leached soil.

Oxisols: Soils having oxic horizons. They were formerly classified as latosols. Mostly found in tropical and subtropical climates. The subsurface horizons are high in clay and acid. The soils are productive but deficient in available P and micro-nutrients.

Oxygen demand: The demand of dissolved oxygen by decomposing or degrading food waste and dead plant or animal tissue in water. Chemical and biochemical oxygen demand (COD and BOD) are measures of the amount of oxygen consumed when a substance degrades.

P

P: Soil conservation practice factor in universal soil loss prediction equation (USLE).

Pan coefficient (kp): It is the ratio between reference evapotranspiration ETo and water loss by an open pan evaporimeter expressed as; k_p = ETo/E pan.

Pan evaporation: The quantity of water evaporated from an open pan evaporimeter, usually from standard USWB, class 'A' pan evaporimeter during a day.

Pans: Horizons or layers in soils that are strongly compacted, indurated or have high clay content.

Parallel lateral ditch system (Surface drainage): Similar to the field ditch sysyetm except deeper ditches that cannot be crossed with farm machinery. The main purpose is to control ground water table along with surface drainage. Farming must be practiced parallel to ditches.

Parallel field ditch system (Surface drainage): In this drainage system dead furrow run parallel along the field slope in raised plough lands. Channels are spaced farther apart with greater capacity. It is suitable for flat and poorly drained soils with numerous small depressions. Water moves only in one direction

Parent material: It is the unconsolidated and more or less chemically weathered mineral materials from which soil are developed. It is the regolith or at least its upper portion.

Parshall flume: A calibrated device for measuring the flow of water in open conduits that operates with a small drop in head. The loss of head for free flow limit is only about 25% of that weir. It is self cleaning and presence of sand or silt in the flowing water does not affect its operation or accuracy it allows accurate measurement even when partially submerged.

Part per million (ppm): It represents the quantity of a substance contained in a million parts of a mixture or solution in carrier such as air or water.

Partial correlation: Refers to the coefficients that measure the strength of the linear relationship between one dependent variable and one of several independent variables after controlling the effects of the other independent variables by holding them statistically constant.

Particle density: It is the weight of the soil solids (g) per unit volume (cc) of soil solids. It varies from 2.6 to 2.7 g/cc in most of the mineral soils with average of 2.65 g/cc. It is not affected by texture and structure of soil and it is static property.

Particle-size analysis: Determination of the various amounts of the different soil separates in a soil sample, usually by sedimentation, sieving, micrometry, or combinations of these methods.

Particulate matter: Matter comprised of very small, separate particles

Parts per billion: Number of unit of a substance per billion unit of water. Used to measure extremely small concentrations.

Pass: In digital filters, refers to the spatial frequency of data transmitted by the filter. High-pass filters transmit high-frequency data; low-pass filters transmit low-frequency data.

Passive absorption of water: The absorption of water by the roots without expenditure of metabolic energy as a result of forces originating in the leaves, such as transpiration pull.

Pasture improvement: Any practice meant for improving vegetation for grazing, such as contour furrowing, liming, fertilizer application, scattering of droppings, seeding, manuring or other method of management.

Pasture land: Land covered with grass or other herbaceous forage plants used for grazing animals.

Pasture management: Application of practices meant to encourage active growth of pasture plants for providing palatable feed of high nutritive value, while reducing weeds, or inferior grass spp.

Pasture renovation: Improvement of a pasture by tillage, seeding, fertilization and sometimes by addition of soil amendments.

Pasture: An area meant for the production of native or introduced forage, which is grazed.

Pathogen: Any disease-causing biological agent such as a bacterium, virus, or fungus.

Peak discharge: The highest stage or discharge attained in a flood. Synonym to flood peak, peak stage.

Peak flow: Refers to the maximum instantaneous discharge of a stream or river at a given location. It usually occurs at or near the time of maximum stage.

Peak or maximum supply (V max): Average daily supply requirement during the peak water-use period for a given crop or cropping pattern and climate.

Peak runoff rate: It is the maximum amount of flowing runoff per unit time.

Peak supply period (water): Water-use period for a given crop or cropping pattern during the month of period thereof of highest water requirements.

Peat soil: Soil containing more than 50% undecomposed or slightly decomposed organic matter.

Peaty and marshy soils: Soils are black, clayey, highly acidic (pH 3.5) soils that contain 10 to 40% organic matter, poorly drained, associated with high ground water table.

Ped: Unit of soil structure *i.e.* plate, prism, column, block, granule or crumb formed by natural processes. Arrangement of primary soil particle into aggregate.

Pediment: A gently sloping erosion surface of low relief, developed at the foot of a receding mountain.

Pedology: The science dealing with origin, formation and geographic distribution of the soil as a body in the nature. The study of the process through which rocks, sediments, and their constituent minerals are transformed into soils and their constituent minerals at or near the surface of the earth.

Pedon: A three-dimensional body of soil with lateral dimensions large enough to permit the study of horizon shapes and relations. Its area ranges from 1 to 10 m^2.

Peneplane: Earstwhile high, rugged area transformed by erosion into a low, gently rolling surface resembling a plane.

Perambulator: Device for rapid measurement of distance. It consist a single wheel provided with forks and a handle. It is wheeled along the line, the length of which is desired. The distance traversed is automatically registered on the dial.

Perched aquifer: A special type of unconfined aquifer created other than the main ground water body (usually above than main ground water body) due to impervious stratum of small area.

Perched water-table: The upper limit or surface of a small body of water above the main water-table. The water is retained in its elevated position by an impervious stratum and may form a limited source of water supply.

Percolation tank: A small size water storage structure also known as percolation pond, usually constructed across stream or drainage channel to collect runoff from stream during monsoon, store for considerable time and facilitate ground water recharge through percolation for longer period. Though primarily constructed for ground water recharge but can be used for multipurpose like irrigation and livestock.

Percolation: The down ward movement of excess water through saturated or nearly saturated soil due to the forces of gravity is known as percolation. Percolation occurs when water is under pressure or when the tension is smaller than about 1/3 atmosphere.

Perermanent wilting point: This is the lower limit of available moisture range for plant growth. The moisture content at which plant wilt and do not recover in humid environment. Below the wilting point extraction of moisture continues for some time but growth ceases completely. The force with which moisture is held by the soil at this point corresponds to 15 atmospheres.

Peripheral bunds: Bunds constructed along field boundaries without reference to contour. These bunds are called peripheral bunds. They serve as fences, and give protection from water and wind erosion in low rainfall areas.

or

Earthen embankment made around gully head and along sides to prevent flow of run-off water from upper area into the gully to check further erosion.

Permafrost: Permanently frozen material underlying the solum; a permanently frozen soil horizon.

Permanent agriculture: The design and maintenance of sustainable, ecologically favourable, energy efficient agricultural and horticultural systems. The concept includes not only agroforestry but the integration of organic farming principles and intermediate technology, the use of renewable resources and recycling, the exploitation of biodiversity, conservation and habitat protection, as well as social and institutional well-being. It can be applied to urban as well as rural environments.

Permanent crop land area: Land cultivated with crops that need not be replanted after each harvest, such as rubber, coffee, cocoa, including land under shurbs, fruit trees, nut trees and vines but excluding land under trees grown for food or timber.

Permanent cropping system: An agricultural system in which crop plants are grown continually on the same plots of land, either several crops in rotation or a single crop for several years.

Permanent grassland: Natural (mainly steppe areas) or agricultural soils with grass cover normally not ploughed.

Permanent gully control structure: It consist of reinforced concrete, concrete block, stone masonry, metal or earth and constructed where temporary structures are not sufficient.

Permanent pasture: Pasture of perennial or self-seeding annual plants maintained for several years for grazing.

Permanently absorbed water: Water which percolates deep beyond the root zone, finally reaching the zone of saturation where it becomes an increment to ground-water.

Permeability coefficient: The rate of flow of fluid through a unit cross section of a porous mass under a unit hydraulic gradient.

Permeability rate: The rate at which water moves through a soil under a standard pressure gradient, usually defined as amount of water traversing per sq cm of soil surface under a pressure gradient of one dyne per cm.

Permeability, soil: Relative ease with which gases, liquids and plant roots pass through a bulk mass of soil or a specified soil horizon.

Permeable spurs: These spurs are known as porous type as it allow water movement through it. It may be constructed alone with rows of wooden pole with brush wood in the gap or along with gabion depending on condition.

Permeameter: A device for measuring the permeability of soils or other materials.

Persistence: It is ability to withstand extremes of climatic, edaphic, and biotic stresses in nature. Resistance to degradation as measured by the period of time required for complete breakdown of a material. It depends on temperature, pH, soil type, light intensity, etc.

Pesticide: Refers to substance used for controlling, destroying, or repelling a specific pest. Fungicides, herbicides, insecticides, nematicides, rodenticides, defoliants, and plant growth regulators etc. comes under pesticide.

PET: Refers to potential evapotranspiration; the loss of moisture by direct evaporation and transpiration from vegetation; grown with unrestricted supply of water.

pF: It is the logrithm of height in cm of a water column that represents total stress with which water is held by a soil.

pH : The negative logarithm of the hydrogen ion concentration of a solution. The degree of acidity (or alkalinity) of a soil as determined by means of a glass quinhydrone or other suitable electrode or indicator at a specified moisture content or soil to water ratio and expressed in terms of the pH scale, from 0 to 14. pH 7 is neutral; <7 is acidic; and >7 is alkaline.

Phase, soil: A sub division of a soil taxon like soil series or other unit of classification based on variation of characteristics like topography, erosion, texture of the surface, content of stones, salinity etc. which affect the use and management of soil. These variations are not sufficient to differentiate the soil into different series. Phase of soil series is the major component of the mapping unit in detailed soil map.

Photo map: A mosaic map prepared from aerial photographs with physical and cultural features indicated on it.

Photodegradeable: Refers to capable of being degraded (decomposed) by a chemical reaction initiated by direct exposure to the sun's ultraviolet radiation.

Physical determinants: Physical factor (attributes of climate, water, and land) such as rainfall, topography, and hydrology that determine the performance of cropping patterns.

Physical environment: The climatic factors, the soil, and free water surrounding plants.

Physical weathering: Breakdown of rock or mineral particles into smaller particles by physical forces such as frost action, hitting by wind borne particles and by diurnal temperature variation, flowing water etc.

Physiological adaptation: The process of adaptation by which plant develop mechanism of resistance to parasites, greater ability to compete for nutrients, or ability to withstand desiccation.

Physiological drought: Non-availability of water to the plant due to unfavourable physiological factors, such as water logging, soil salinity, low temperature etc.

Physiological maturity: A developmental stage after which no further increase in dry matter occurs in the economic part. When a seed reaches its maximum dry weight. This usually occurs before harvest.

Pictogram: A form of graphical presentation of numerical data by drawing pictures of the particular object referring to the data.

Pie diagram: It consists of a circle cut into sectors, the areas of the sectors being proportional to the magnitudes of the component parts.

Piezometer: An open-ended tube placed vertically in the soil reaching to ground water for measurement of the hydrostatic pressure level of groundwater.

Piezometric surface: Imaginary surface to which water may rise above the aquifer in a well.

Piping: Loss of soil material through subsurface channels or 'pipes' created by seepage water. Sometime facilitated and accelerated by burrowing animal.

Pitting: Making shallow pits having suitable capacity and proper distribution for retention of rain water or snowmelt on pastures etc.

Plane surveying: A surveying method carried over area in which measurement and mapping is done simultaneously. It do not account curvature of earth. The degree of accuracy required in this type of surveying is completely low. Plane surveying is done on an area of less than 250 km^2.

Plane table surveying: Plane table is a graphical method of surveying in which the field works and the plotting is done simultaneously. It is particularly adopted in small area mapping. Plane table surveying is used for locating the field computation of area of field.

Planetary scale (Meteorology)**:** These systems have a diameter of 5000 to 10000 km and persist for several weeks. eg. Waves in the atmosphere circulation.

Plan: A scheme, program, or method worked out at sub-components level in some degree of elaborate detail for the accomplishment of an objective. A plan consists of diagram or list of steps with timing frame, specificity and resources.

Plant community: It is an assemblage of plants growing together under the same environmental conditions.

Plant succession: Natural development of plant communities of higher ecological order with passes

Plantation, forest: A tree stand established by sowing seed or planting seedlings.

Planting density: The rate at which seed or vegetative propagules are placed in a field or nursery planting.

Plasticity index (PI): Numerical difference between liquid limit (LL) and plastic limit (PL).

Plate like/Platy: Horizontally, layered, thin and flat like plates with horizontal dimensions greater than the vertical ones.

Playa: A shallow basin in a plane where run-off gathers after a rain and evaporates in due coarce.

Plough plant: Ploughing of field and planting the crop in the same operation simultaneously. Seed bed preparation is not done separately.

Plough sole placement: A method of fertilizer application in which fertilizer is placed in a continuous band in the bottom of the furrow. Ploughing cover fertilizer band in each furrow one after another.

Plough sole: A compacted layer at the bottom of the zone of ploughing. (Synonymous to plough pan)

Plough: an agricultural implement used to turn over the surface of the soil in order to achieve better physical condition for seed germination, plant growth, weed control etc.

Ploughing (tillage): mechanical working of agricultural soils by the plough to different depths creating land suitable for cultivation (10-15 cm: shallow, 20-30 cm deep).

Plow layer: The top 15-20 cm of soil normally plowed or disturbed with tillage operations. Normally rich in biological activity and plant nutrients.

Plow Pan (hard pan): A hard layer of soil at 15-20 cm depth developed through continuous plowing at the same depth. It reduces downward water loss during flooding and prevents penetration of roots. The layer has higher bulk density and lower pore space than soil immediately above or below it.

Plumb bob: A plumb-bob is a weight, usually conical with pointed tip towards bottom that is suspended from a string and used as a vertical reference line. It is also called plummet and most commonly used in construction for vertical line

Point row: A row which meets another row at an angle to suit ploughing of a field.

Point source contamination: The contamination of water from specific sources such as leaking underground storage tanks, landfills, industrial waste discharge points, or chemical mixing sites.

Point-of-use: water treatment system located at the tap which treats only water used from the tap.

Pollutant: Any physical, chemical and biological entity that negatively impacts the physical, chemical, or biological properties of the environment

Pollution: Presence of a contaminant higher than a certain limit in the environment (land, water, or air) and renders it unsuitable for a particular use.

Poorly graded: Refers to presence of non graded material a coarse grained soil or soil material consisting mainly of particles of nearly the same size. In poorly graded coarse soil large number of maesopores, less micro pores results lees effect of compaction due to similar size particle.

Pores (macro): Pore of diameter greater than 100 micron is known as macrospores. It helps maintain circulation of air.

Pores (meso): Pore size diameter ranges between 30 and 100 microns and helps in capillary water conduction or movement.

Pores (micro): Diameter of pores ranges from 3 to 30 microns these play important role in water retention (slow capillary flow).

Porosity: Refers to the volume other than solid volume in bulk soil. It is a measure of water-bearing capacity of soil. Pores can be expressed as $\frac{V - V_s}{V}$ where, V is bulk volume of soil and V_s is volume of soil solid.

Portal: The ground level entrance or opening to an under ground mine

Potable water (Drinking Water): Water that meets the prescribed standard and is safe to be used for drinking, cooking, dishwashing, or other domestic purposes. Water that is suitable for human consumption.

Potential (soil water): The amount of work that must be done per unit quantity of pure water in order to transport reversibly and isothermally an infinitesimal quantity of water from a pool of pure water at a specified elevation and atmospheric pressure to the soil water at the point under consideration. It includes matric, osmotic and gravitational potential.

Potential crop yield: Yield of a crop obtained at research stations under most ideal environment. Crop yield obtained under non limiting non stressed condition.

Potential difference: Work that must be done to move a body (unit mass, unit charge etc.) between specified points. In a field of force (gravitation, electric, magnetic etc.)

Potential evaporation: Evaporation from a large body of free water surface without any effect of addictive energy. It is primarily a function of evaporative demand of climate.

Potential Evapo-transpiration: It is the amount of water evaporated in a unit time from short uniform green crop growing actively and covering an extended surface and never short of water. It includes evaporation from soil as well as transpiration through vegetation.

Potential gravitational: A potential that is by virtue of elevation or vertical location. In content to soil water it is the amount of work that a unit quantity of water in an equilibrium soil-water (or plant-water) system at an arbitrary level is capable of doing when it moves to another equilibrium system identical in all respects except the elevation (reference level)

Potentially water-short area: An area of low natural runoff or where the watershed has a high level of allocation compared to natural supply.

PRA (Participatory Rural Appraisal): This is one of the techniques used for gathering information on community resources and needs for planning watershed development project. The technique ensures participation, incorporation of the knowledge and opinions of rural people in the planning and management of watershed project. Transect walks, maps, calendars, matrices, and diagrams using locally available materials are included in PRA.

Precious metal: a general term applied to expensive metals such as gold, silver, and platinum.

Precipitation interception: Stopping, interrupting and temporary retention of precipitation in any form by a vegetative canopy or residue is called precipitation interception. It helps reducing runoff in initial duration of rainfall.

Precipitation: Fall of any form of water (rain, dew, snow, hail etc.) on the earth called precipitation. Precipitation also refers deposition of solute in solution after reaching saturation (over saturation)

Preliminary estimate: This is a firsthand estimate to indicate financial involvement for the purpose of administrative sanction. Cost of major component of work including land is shown. It is supplemented by a brief report emphasising urgency of work and site plan. Estimate is prepared from practical knowledge.

Preparatory phase: Initial phase of watershed management planning in which information are collected through various extension tools like participatory rural appraisal, group meeting, schedules and questionnaire etc. in order to identify and prioritize problems for inclusion in detailed project report.

Preparatory tillage: Tillage operations carried out from the time of harvest of a crop to the sowing of the next crop are known as preparatory Tillage or Operations carried out in any cultivated land to prepare seedbed for sowing crops are preparatory tillage. These includes in sequence, plouging, clod crushing, leveling, discing, harrowing, manure mixing etc. Implements used are ploughs, clod crushers, disc ploughs disc harrow, bladed harrow etc. In context of climate change and environmental degradation, reducing preparatory tillage to a minimum essential is advocated.

Pressure head: It is pressure difference between point of reference and point of interest expressed in meters of water.

Primary drinking water standards: It is the enforceable standards which establish maximum contaminant levels for drinking water after considering health effects and the feasibility and cost of analysis and treatment of regulated contaminants.

Primary mineral: A mineral which has not altered chemically since deposition and crystallization from molten lava, *e.g.* Quarts, Feldspar.

Primary producer: Organism that adds biomass to the ecosystem by synthesizing organic molecules from carbon dioxide and simple inorganic nutrients.

Primary production: Production of organic compounds from atmospheric or aquatic carbon dioxide through photosynthesis or chemosynthesis. It is the production of chemical energy in organic compounds by living organism.

Primary productivity: This is the productivity of an ecosystem that measured in terms of biomass accumulation per unit area per unit time.

Primary soil particles: Sand, silt and clay are called primary soil particles. Individual soil particles are joined together into groups or clusters of various sizes and shapes by cementing agents.

Primary tillage: The ploughing operation that aims opening of the compacted soil with the help of different ploughs.

Primary wastewater treatment: The first stage of the wastewater-treatment process where mechanical methods, such as filters and scrapers, are used to remove pollutants.

Prism like: It is a type of soil structure in which aggregates are elongated like pillars or prism, often six sided, up to 15 cm dia. have vertical axis greater than horizontal prism like structures are commonly found in sub soil horizon of arid and semi-arid region soils.

Profile leveling: Process to determine the elevation of points at known distance apart along a given line. It is also called the longitudinal levelling or sectioning.

Profile, (soil): Vertical section of soil showing all horizons and extending into the parent material.

Protection forest: A forest area maintained primarily for soil and water conservation, rather than for wood or forage production.

Protection phase: This is the phase that takes care of the general health of the watershed and ensures normal functioning. The protection is against all factors which may be detrimental for watershed condition.

Psammophytes: Plants which prefer or tolerate fine to medium sand for their habitat.

Puertorican type terrace: This type of terrace is formed by establishing a mechanical or vegetative barrier across the land at suitable interval. Terrace is developed gradually over the years by pushing soil downhill and subsequent natural levelling. Terrace formation is accelerated by little excavation of soil during each ploughing.

Pyrolysis: chemical decomposition of a material by heat in the absence of oxygen.

Q

Quadrat: A sampling unit which has an area of definite size, which may be circular, rectangular or square in shape, usually one square meter.

Quadratic response: Refers to a responise where, the output goes on increasing up to a certain level of input and then starts decreasing when input is increased further. In such cases the response is said to be quadratic and is given by: $Y = a + bx + cx^2$.

Quadruple cropping: Growing of four crops a year in sequence on same piece of land.

Quantum yield: The quantum yield is a ratio of absorbed photons and photons used up in the chemical process. Quantum yield is usually dependent on temperature, pressure, and wavelength. The number of molecules of CO_2 reduced per molecule of quanta absorbed. A measure of how efficient an emission process is.

Quick sand: Sand which is unstable due to upward pressure of water. It is a non Newtonian fluid appears to be solid in unsaturated condition.

R

R horizon: Underlying consolidated bedrock in the soil profile, such as granite, basalt, sandstone, limestone etc. It is found below the C horizon.

R: Rainfall and runoff factor in universal soil loss equation (USLE)

Rabi (winter) crops: Crops which are grown during the winter season (October-November to March-April) with irrigation or on conserved soil moisture, *e.g.* wheat, barley, oat, chickpea, safflower etc.

Radiation: In context to the plane table survey a point is located on plane by drawing a ray from the plane table station to the point is called radiation. The method is suitable for the survey of the small areas which can be commanded from a single station.

Radiometric resolution: radiometric resolution is defined as the ability of a satellite sensor to record different levels of brightness/radiance. It refers to the effective bit-depth of the sensor (number of greyscale levels) and is typically expressed as 8-bit (0-255), 11-bit (0-2047), 12-bit (0-4095) or 16-bit (0-65,535).

Radon: Refers to colourless, odourless, tasteless, radioactive noble gs, with atomic number 86.

Rain shadow: A comparatively dry area on the leeward side of the high land which stands in the path of rain bearing clouds.

Rain water harvesting: It is an ancient technique of harvesting good quality rain water. Rain water is known for its purity. With scarcity of good quality water and increased cost of treated water, rain water harvesting is getting popular. There are several techniques to capture, store and use this free resource.

Rain: It is a form of liquid precipitation. When the falling water droplets are of size more than 0.5 mm, it is called rain.

Raindrop erosion: Soil splash caused by the impact of falling raindrops is known as raindrop erosion. It is also known as splash erosion.

Rainfall intensity: Rainfall intensity is defined as the rate of fall of precipitation, expressed in depth per time (mm/hr). I = P/T Where, I = Rainfall Intensity, mm/hr, P = Amount of rainfall, mm, T = duration of rainfall, hr

Rainfall simulator: It is a device which can reproduce, accurately and repeatedly, artificial rain which has precisely the same effect on the soil as natural rain. It is used for off season hydrological investigation.

Rainfed farming: Growing of field crops with rain water received during the crop season in areas with rainfall usually> 800 mm. Agriculture in these areas is complex, diverse and highly risk prone and marked by low productivity of crops.

Rainfed field: An unirrigated field surrounded by levees and depending on rainfall for moisture supply.

Rainfed lowland: Bunded fields where water depth does not exceed 50 cm for more than 10 consecutive days and the fields are inundated for at least part of the season. Such fields have no access to an irrigation system, but may have on-farm rainwater conservation facilities.

Rainfed wetland: Fields where rainfed rice is grown on puddle soil in fields bounded by dikes capable of ponding water to about 30 cm. Water depth seldom exceeds 30 cm. These area receive no irrigation and non-rice crops may be grown before or after the wetland rice.

Raingauge: Instrument for measuring the amount of water received through precipitation. Precipitation is expressed in terms of depth of water. The instrument used for measurement is also known as udometer, pluviometer or ombrometer..

Rainy day: A day (24 hours) having 2.5 mm or more of rainfall.

Rainy season: That period of the year in which monthly rainfall exceeds 10% of the monthly potential evapotranspiration (In India May-June to September-October). It is the period of the year witnessing most of the average annual rainfall.

Ramp: Inclined earthen passageway over and across earthen field bunds for carts, cattle and moving agricultural implements from field to field.

Ramser's formula: Based on field observation in semiarid climate with good infiltration soil, Ramser devised a formula for vertical interval between consecutive contour bund.

Random field ditch system: This surface drainage system is suitable for areas with scattered depressions and potholes. Depth of cut required is less than a meter. A relatively flat cross section of drains is laid to facilitate movement of farm machinery. These drains should be supplemented with land grading and smoothening in case of less permeable soil. Channel follows a rout of minimum cut and least interference with farming.

Random sample: A sample selected according to a chance mechanism such that every unit in the population has equal probability of being in the sample. These samples are obtained by using a random mechanism such as drawing of lots or using a table of random numbers.

Range condition class: One of a series of categories arbitrarily fixed for classifying condition of rangeland, such as excellent, good, fair, and poor.

Range condition trend: The direction in which range condition changes, either improving or degrading.

Range management: Application of principles and practices for improvement of range, by applying ecological principles and dealing with rangeland husbandry.

Range seeding: Propagation of adapted plant spp. in rangeland by means other than natural revegetation.

Rangeland: Open area, usually unfenced, used for grazing of cattle.

Ranging rod: A 7-8 foot long straight pole pointed at one end (metal point), painted alternately red/black and white in bands one foot wide and used by surveyors for locating points of reference. A straight rod used in surveying for making straight line

Ranging: The process of establishing intermediate point on a straight line between two end points is known as ranging

Raster format: A means of representing spatial data in the from of a rectangular grid of digital number, each rectangular grid has unique digital number representing theme value.

Rating curve: A graph showing output under specified series of conditions; a rating curve for flume indicates volume of flow per unit time at different stages or depths of flow.

Rating flume: An open conduit in a channel for measurement of flow and development of stage-discharge relationship. It is mainly used for calibration of flumes or other measuring devices.

Rational method: This is the most common method to predict the peak runoff rate. It is used to design the capacity of flow structure that must carry the peak runoff. Q_{peak} = CIA/36 = [0.0276x CIA] where, Q = peak runoff rate m^3/sec, C = runoff coefficient, I = rainfall intensity [cm/hr] for duration equal to time of concentration for a given recurrence interval and A = watershed area, [hectare].

Ratoon cropping: The cultivation of an additional crop from the regrowth of stubbles of previous main crop after its harvest, thereby avoiding reseeding or replanting such as in sugarcane, sorghum, rice, fodder grasses etc.

Ravine: A deep narrow gorge, network of gullies and extreme form of land degradation.

Receiving waters: Water bodies that receive runoff or wastewater discharges, such as rivers, streams, lakes, estuaries, and ground water.

Recession curve (hydraulics): Graphical representation of water depletion in stream channels, surface soil, and underground water etc. It is the specific part of the flood hydrograph after the crest where flow diminishes.

Recession phase (irrigation): The part of total irrigation time between the beginning of recession at the upper end and the disappearance of the water from the field surface. Time elapsed during this phase is known as recession time.

Recession time: Time interval between closure of water supply and disappearance of surface water in a specified length of run.

Recharge area: Refers to an area where precipitation is allowed infiltrated into soil and percolates downward to replenish an aquifer.

Recharge well: A well constructed for the purpose of introducing surface water into an underground aquifer. It accelerates the process of ground water recharge but quality of water must be ensured before putting it to aquifer though recharge well. Also known as injection well.

Recharge: Replenishment of ground-water storage from precipitation, infiltration from surface streams and other sources.

Reciprocal levelling: It is used to find accurate difference in elevation between two intervisible points, where it is not possible to set up the level midway between the two points.

Reclaimed wastewater: Treated wastewater that can be used for beneficial purposes, such as irrigating certain plants.

Reclamation of gullies: The process of putting gullies to productive uses such as agriculture, fuel-fodder reserve, sources of economic vegetation by adopting soil and water conservation measures.

Reclamation: The process of returning a site to its natural state that is lost or in the process of degradation by adopting principles and practices of conservation that prevents environmental impacts or threats to human health and safety

Recognition phase: It is the process during which, recognition of the problem, analysis of cause of the problem and its effect and development of alternative solutions of problem are determined. Information is obtained from different surveys like soil survey, land capability survey, agronomic survey, forest, engineering and socio economic survey, etc.

Reconnaissance: The preliminary inspection of the area based on visual observation is called reconnaissance. The surveyor inspects the area to be surveyed, and prepares index sketch or key plan.

Recording gauge: An automatic instrument for graphical record of water flow stage, rainfall, temperature etc. with respect to time.

Recreation forestry (India): It is the plantation of small blocks of forests close to urban centres for recreation and picnic corners etc. The practice is aimed at social development, and education in environmental matters.

Rectangular weirs: It takes its name from the shape of notch. They are used to measure comparatively large discharges.

Recyclables: Refers to materials that still have useful physical or chemical properties after serving their original purpose and that can be reused or remanufactured into additional products, thereby serving as substitutes for raw materials.

Recycled water: Water that is used more than one time before it passes back into the natural hydrologic system.

Recycling: The process by which materials otherwise destined for disposal are collected, reprocessed or remanufactured, and reused.

Red soils: The name is derived from the colour of the soil. These soils are well drained and derived from crystalline, metamorphic rocks, which consist of granites, gneisses and schist's. Formed *in situ* from the decomposed rock materials washed down to lower level by rain, light textured with porous and friable structure. They have neutral to acid reaction and are deficient in N, organic carbon, P_2O_5 and lime.

Reduced tillage: A tillage system in which primary tillage may be performed in conjunction with special planting procedures to reduce or eliminate secondary tillage operations. The objective is to reduce total tillage operation/soil disturbance.

Reference evapotranspiration (ET_O): ET_O can be defined as the rate of evapotranspiration of an extended surface of an 8 to 15 cm tall, green cover, actively growing completely shading the ground and not short of water.

Reforestation, re-afforestation: Systematic planting of trees, in the original forest area which had been cleared or burnt. It has potential to offset climate change effect through carbon sequestration.

Refractory: These are materials used to construct conventional combustion chambers in incinerators, as it can withstand sudden and high variations in temperature.

Regolith: Mantle of unconsolidated weathered rock and soil material on earth's surface. It refers to loose earth materials above solid rock.

Regosol: A soil without definite genetic horizons and developing from or on deep, unconsolidated soft mineral deposits like recent sand dunes, loess, glacial drift etc.

Rehabilitation: Treatment of land for making it productive in accordance with a land use plan without causing environmental deterioration. The treatments are planned with the aim of positive environmental externalities.

Relative net return (intercropping): It is the ratio between the monetary value of base and intercrop plus differential cost of cultivation under intercropping and monoculture of the base crop and monetary value of base crop in monoculture.

Relative yield total: It is the sum of two relative yields of crops under polyculture. Relative yield total (RYT) is used to evaluate production gain under intercropping system RYT = $P_1/M_1 + P_2/M_2$ where, P_1 and P_2 are the yields of two crops in polyculture, and M_1 and M_2 are the yields of each crop in a monoculture system.

Relay cropping: Refers to the seeding or planting of succeeding crop after flowering or before the harvest of the standing crop. It is analogous to a relay race where 1 crop hands over the land to the next crop in quick succession, *e.g.* sowing toria in standing crop of maize or lentil in standing crop of paddy.

Relief drain: Sub surface drain for removing water from the soil to lower the water table and reduce hydrostatic pressure. It is installed similar to the interceptor drain with design change for artificially lowering of the ground water. It can be constructed on surface to intercept surface water drainage

Relief pipe: It is a small size vertical riser, generally made of steel, extending from underground tile line to soil surface, serving to relieve excess water.

Relief well: It is a well or pit that is penetrating the water table or intersect oil or gas well in order to reduce hydrostatic pressure.

Remote sensing: Acquisition of physical data of an object without being in physical contact. Refers to activities of collecting information from a distance, *e.g.* the utilization at a distance (as from aircraft, spacecraft, or ship) of any device for measuring electromagnetic radiation, force fields, or acoustic energy.

Repelling type spur: Spurs constructed to point towards upstream at an angle of 5° to 10° to the line normal to the bank. Structural failure due to excessive scouring restricts its use.

Resection: The method of establishing the instrument stations only. After fixing the station, details are located either by radiation or intersection. The characteristic feature of resection is that the point plotted on plan is the station occupied by the plane table.

Reservoir area: The total surface of a reservoir measured in a horizontal plane at an elevation corresponding to the full supply level of the reservoir.

Reservoir capacity The total volume of water a reservoir is capable of holding when filled up to the full supply or normal water level. Storage derived from temporary flashboards, surcharge, or backwater curve is not included. Reservoir capacity usually is reported as of the date of construction of the dam.

Reservoir: A pond, lake, or basin, either natural or artificial, for the storage, regulation, and control of water.

During periods of low river flow, reservoirs can release additional flow if water is available.

Residential waste: The waste materials generated in single and multiple-family homes.

Residual material: Partly weathered unconsolidated mineral material accumulated in place *i.e.* at the site of rock after the rest is washed away.

Residue: Refers to materials remaining after processing, incineration, composting, or recycling normally disposed of in landfills.

Resolution/Resolving power: Capacity of sensor to resolve between closely placed object.

Resource recovery: Refers to the extraction and utilization of materials and energy from the waste stream.

Restoration phase: The phase during which selections of best solution to problems was identified and are applied to the land. Initially, treatments are applied to the critical areas and thereafter proper measures like biological and engineering measures are applied to all types of lands.

Restoration: The renewing or repairing of a natural system so that its functions and qualities are comparable to those of its original, unaltered state

Retarding basins: Depressions behind earthen dams in head water reaches of a stream which accumulate flood waters, for the control of floods.

Retards: A structure constructed parallel to the eroding bank and have some projection towards stream bank. Purpose of retards is to dissipate erosive force of water and to facilitate deposition of silt close to bank.

Retention: The amount of rainfall on a drainage area that does not go as run-off; difference between total rainfall and total run-off.

Retentivity profile, soil: Graph showing retaining capacity of a soil as a function of depth. Retaining capacity may be for water or any soil borne cations, substances etc.

Return flow: That part of a diverted flow that is not consumptively used and returned to its original source or another body of water. Drainage water from irrigated farmlands that re-enters the water system to be used further downstream.

Reuse: Refers to the use of a product, in its original form more than once for the same purpose such as bricks of old building, a softdrink bottle.

Reverse osmosis (RO): A water treatment process in which contaminants are removed by forcing water through a membrane having microscopic holes that allow water molecules to pass through, but not larger compounds. RO units do not remove all chemicals, and they generally discharge more than half of the total water as waste.

Revetment: Temporary or permanent facing of stone or other material along the edge of a stream channel for protection against erosive action of the stream.

Revised estimate: It is just like detailed estimate except inclusion of the component of work/rate that responsible for escalation of original sanctioned estimate. Sometimes there is chance of exceeding the cost of original sanctioned estimate during execution of work and that need a revised estimate to be prepared and submitted.

Rhizome: A horizontal underground stem throwing out roots and above ground shoots at the nodes.

Rhizosphere: The portion of the soil inhabited by the plant roots. It differs in biological activity and microbial composition from bulk soil.

Ridge planting: A method of planting crops on ridge formed by tillage operations.

Ridge terrace: A long, low ridge of earth with gently sloping sides and a shallow channel along the upper: side, to control erosion by diverting surface run-off across the slope instead of permitting it to flow uninterrupted down to slope.

Ridge tillage: The soil is left undisturbed from harvest to planting except for strips up to 1/3 of the row width. Planting is completed on the ridge and usually involves the removal of the top of the ridge. Planting is completed with sweeps, disk openers, coulters, or row cleaners. Residue is left on the surface between ridges. Weed control is accomplished with crop protection products (frequently banded) and/or cultivation. Ridges are rebuilt during row cultivation.

Rill erosion: It is sometime known as micro channel erosion. It is the removal of soil by running water with the formation of areas of small branching channels. There is no sharp time of demarcation where sheet erosion ends. It is regarded as a transition stage between sheet erosion and gully. Rill of small depth can be obliterated by ordinary tillage operation.

Rill: A narrow, very shallow, intermittent water course having steep sides resulting from accelerated erosion. A rill is generally a few centimeters deep and not wide enough to be an obstacle to farm machinery.

Riparian area: The area of water-loving vegetation beside a stream, river, lake, or pond. Riparian areas are critical in reducing the negative effects of various land-uses on adjacent waters.

Riparian land: Land situated along a river or any other water body.

Riparian outlet: A structure designed to pass water through a dam for the benefit of downstream water users or riparian users.

Riparian rights: The legal ability of a person owning or leasing land along a water body to use water and protect the quantity and quality of water in the water body.

Riparian: Pertaining to the banks of a river, stream, waterway, or other, typically, flowing body of water as well as to plant and animal communities along such bodies of water.

Riprap: Hand placed or dumped broken rock, cobbles or boulders or different types of concrete blocks, covering the water side of dams or levees exposed to wave action or current for erosion control.

Riser: Steep face of a bench terrace. It is generally stabilized by grasses.

River basin: An area of land drained to a river and its associated streams or tributaries. A large catchment of a river or source area of water.

River capture: It is the action of a river of acquiring the head streams of another river by expanding its own drainage area at the expense of the other. River piracy or beheading are synonyms for the term.

River training (torrent training): Process of channelizing flow of torrent to a reasonably narrow channel by means of constructing one or several type of mechanical structure on or along the bank. The main purpose is protecting the adjoining cultivated land.

River wash: Barren, alluvial land having coarse textured soils, exposed along the streams when the flow is low, and which may shift under normal high flow.

Rock-fill dam: A dam made of loose rock dumped in place, generally with the upstream part constructed of hand placed or derrick placed rock and faced with rolled earth or impervious concrete surface etc.

Rock fragments: Unattached pieces of rock 2 mm in diameter or larger that are strongly cemented or more resistant to rupture.

Rock land: Area containing shallow soil and rock out crops covering 25-90% of the land surface.

Rolling land: Land with moderately steep complex slopes intermediate between hilly and undulating topography.

Roof top rain water harvesting: It is a technique to capture rainwater falling on roof and store in reservoir underground or above ground. Here roof acts as catchment for water harvesting with high runoff coefficient

Rotation (forestry): Number of years for establishing trees to a specific maturity.

Rotation (grazing): System of grazing in which short periods of heavy grazing is followed by periods of rest for herbage recovery.

Rough broken land: Land having very steep slopes and intermittent drainage channels or gullies.

Roughness co-efficient (hydraulics): A coefficient proposed by Manning to indicated roughness effect of channel in discharge or velocity. It is an indication of the energy loss of flowing water.

Rubble drains: A somewhat equally substitute for tile drains is made by cutting narrow V shaped drains or rectangular in section, as for box drains, filling them up with rough stones large and small and then covering the whole up with soil level with surface field soil. Depth may be 90 cm.

Rubble land: Areas with more than 90% surface covered with stones and boulders. A miscellaneous land type.

Ruggedness number: A dimensionless number that expresses the geometric characteristics of a drainage system; It is the product of maximum basin relief and drainage density within the drainage basin.

Run: Length of gravity flow from point of release to end of area to. be watered.

Runoff coefficient: It is the ratio of peak run-off rate to rainfall intensity and is dimensionless. It is denoted by C. It depends on infiltration rate, surface cover, channel and surface storage and intensity of rainfall.

Runoff Cycle: It is that part of hydrological cycles which galls between the phase of precipitation and its subsequent discharge in the stream channels or direct return to the atmosphere through evaporation and evapotranspiration.

Runoff farming: It refers to the farming where harvested water is stored in the soil itself.

Runoff plots: Small areas of land from which surface flow may be measured. Used for comparing different vegetative or mechanical treatments for run-off and soil loss.

Runoff: It is that portion of the rainfall or applied water through irrigation which leaves a field either as surface or as subsurface flow as sheet flow or flow through rills, gullies and stream channels. Also includes ground water runoff and seepage.

S

S: It is the degree of slope factor for completing of soil loss using the universal soil loss equation (USLE).

Safe drinking water act (SDWA): An act established with a view to ensure safe drinking water. It directs for the establishment and enforcement of water quality standards to protect public health.

Safe velocity: The maximum velocity at which water may move in a channel or through a conduit without causing erosion or scour. Same as permissible velocity or non-eroding velocity.

Safe yield: It is the maximum rate at which water may be withdrawn from the ground water basin (aquifer), without deteriorations or degradation of the aquifer, depending upon the rate of recharge, change in quality of water and economics etc.

Saline and alkaline soils: Soils show white crustation of salts of Ca, Mg and Na on the surface, poorly drained and infertile.

Saline groundwater: Groundwater containing more than 4000 mg/l of total dissolved solids.

Saline soil: Refers to the soils containing sufficient neutral soluble salt to adversely affect the growth of most crop plants. The lower limit of electrical conductivity in the saturation extract of such soils is conventionally set at 4 dS m^{-1}(at 25°C), and has pH value of 8.5 and ESP 15%. Sensitive plants are affected at about half this salinity level and highly tolerant ones at about twice this salinity.

Saline water: Water with a total dissolved solids exceeding 4,000 milligrams per litre.

Salinity: Refers to the quality of water based on its salt content.

Salt marsh: These are low lying areas near sea frequently exposed to flooding in high tide and supporting salt tolerant vegetation. Also similar areas near saline springs or lakes, though not regularly flooded.

Saltation: Refers to the movement of soil particles due is wind or water involving skip or bounce along the land surface or channel bed.

Sample strip: Long narrow strip employed as a sampling unit in surveys.

Sand lens: Refers to a lenticular pocket of sand in sedimentary banded material.

Sand: Large fraction of the soil with very little surface area exposed (0.1 m^2/g specific area). These are fragments of quartz, insoluble; nutrients supplying ability are practically nil. Pore space are bigger (macro pores) which facilitates rapid movement of air and water.

Sand does not absorb water; do not exhibit properties swelling and shrinkages, stickiness and plasticity.

Sandy clay: A soil textural class that typically contains 35% or more of clay and 45% or more of sand.

Sandy loam: A soil textural class that typically contains 50% sand and less than 20% clay.

Sandy soil: A broad term for soils of the sand and loamy sand classes where more than 70% sand and less than 15% clay are present.

Sandy-clay loam: A soil textural class that typically contains 20-35% clay, less than 28% silt and 45% or more of sand.

Sanitary landfill: It is a solid waste disposal site where waste is spread in layers, compacted, and covered with soil or other cover materials each day to minimize pest, aesthetic, disease, air pollution, and water pollution problems.

Sapling: Refers to the young seedlings of forest trees or plantation crops having age of 6 months to about 1 year that are used as planting material.

Saturated soil: A soil having completely filled interspaces or void spaces with water to the extent to induce run-off.

Saturated zone: portion of the soil or rock profile in which all pores are filled with water.

Saturation line: It is line that separate saturated soil from unsaturated soil. For stability of dam it is essential that saturation line meet the base within dam section.

Saturation: Moisture content in the soil characterized by zero or positive pressure of the soil water. Under this condition water will flow from the soil matrix into an unlined auger hole.

Savanna (also savannah): Refers to grassland with scattered trees or tree clumps. It is generally a transitional type between forest and true grassland.

Scale (maps): A comparison of measurement on a map to measurement on the Earth usually represented by a fraction or ratio. Depending upon the fraction geographers call this application large scale because the scale fraction (*e.g.*, 1/20,000) is a larger number than broad area scales (*i.e.*, 1:200,000 is a relatively small number compared to 1/20,000).

Scalping: The process of removal of sod or any other vegetation in spots or strips.

Scavenger: Refers to any entity who illegally removes materials at any point in the solid waste management system.

Scour: To abrade and wear away such as a stream bed, diversion channel or terrace.

Scouring sluice: An outlet provided in a dam controlled by a gate, for ejecting silt, sand, gravel etc.

Scrap: Refers to discarded or rejected industrial waste material often suitable for recycling.

SCT (staggered contour trenches): In medium rainfall area, trenches are dug along the contour but in staggered manner. The length of trenches is kept 2-3 m and spacing may be 3-5 m depending upon runoff generating potential and size of trenches. There is less chance of breaching SCTs.

Sealing by compaction: Closure of macro as well as micro pore through compaction is required to reduce seepage loss from pond. In usual practice top 20-30 cm soil is loosed and compacted with several pass of sheep foot roller at suitable moisture condition.

Seasonal analysis: An analysis done in preparatory phase of watershed project in which, activity is analysed with respect to time (season) in a year. Agricultural activities like field preparation, sowing harvesting etc, social engagement like marriage, festival, religious tours etc are recorded with respect to time. The main aim is to identify suitable time for planned activities under watershed project.

Seasonal grazing: Grazing allowed in a specified season.

Second bottom: Refers to the first terrace above the normal flood plane of a river or stream.

Second growth, forest: Refers to natural forest growth after old stand has been cut, burnt or removed by any other means.

Secondary plant nutrients: These are the plant nutrients that are not applied directly to the soil as straight commercial fertilizers. (*e.g.* calcium, magnesium and sulphur) and are required in relatively less quantities as compared to primary nutrients for normal growth of plants.

Secondary productivity: The indirect computation of productivity of pasture or grassland, expressed in terms of animal gains or products such as milk, meat or wool instead of herbage yield, is called as secondary productivity. It is an indirect measurement of pasture productivity.

Secondary tillage: Refers to the shallow lighter mechanical manipulation of the soil after primary tillage, it includes the operations performed after ploughing, levelling, discing, harrowing etc. to create a good seed-bed for proper seeding or planting. It also provides additional soil pulverization, crop chemical mixing, soil surface levelling, and firming, and weed control.

Sediment concentration: The ratio of quantity (weight) of sediment in water sediment mixture (sampled) to the total volume of the mixture.

Sediment delivery ratio: It is the ratio of sediment delivered at a particular point to the gross erosion in the watershed above that point. There is no general equation to determine sediment delivery ratio, but there are factors that provide guidance such as drainage area, soil texture, and relief, type of sediment transport systems and areas of deposition.

Sediment discharge tap: There is a provision of tap at the bottom of storage tank flushing out deposited sediment in the tank.

Sediment load/sediment discharge: The quantity of sediment (suspended load and bed load) by volume or dry weight transported in unit time across a stream or channel cross-section.

Sediment production rate (SPR): Refers to the quantity of sediment produced in a watershed area. Annually and as expressed in terms of hectare metre of sediment per 100 sq. km area per year.

Sediment yield: It is gross erosion in a watershed excluding the sediment deposited enroute to the outlet of watershed.

Sediment: Refers to the eroded soil and rock material, and plant debris that has been transported from site of its origin through the agency of water, wind, ice or gravity and settled on another part of earth's surface either above or below sea level.

Sedimentary rock: It is the rock formed by lithification of mechanical, chemical or organic sediments with time, such as sand stone, limestone, conglomerates etc.

Sedimentation tanks: Tank for waste water treatment that allow settlement of solids while floating wastes are skimmed off and removed for disposal.

Sedimentation: It is the process involving deposition of sediment out of water.

Seed bed: The soil prepared by primary and secondary tillage to promote seed germination and seedling growth.

Seed tree: Refers to a superior tree or tree with desired characteristics left deliberately at the time of cutting to produce seed for reforestation.

Seedbed preparation: The process of bringing the soil to a condition suitable for germination of seeds & growth of crops, called as seedbed. It includes harrowing, leveling, compacting the soil, preparing irrigation layouts such as basins, borders, rides & furrows etc. and carried out by using hand tools or implements like harrow, rollers plank, rider etc.

Seepage consideration: It the process of bund construction, while designing the bund cross- section, the seepage through bunds due to accumulation of water behind it should be taken into account. The seepage rate changes with the head of water impounded, the side slopes of the bound and the permeability of the soil.

Seepage failure (dam): Failure of dam due to piping or sloughing as a result of passage of seepage water. It is common in poorly compacted dam.

Seepage: The slow movement of free or gravitational water through small cracks, pores, interstices, etc. in the surface of unsaturated material into or out of a body of surface or subsurface water.

Selective grazing: Refers to the tendency of animals for grazing certain plants as compared to others in a mixed population.

Self mulching soil: It is a soil well aggregated in the surface, so that it does not crust or seal due to impact of raindrops but serves as mulch on drying.

Self pruning: The process of removal of dead branches from live trees due to natural causes such as deficiency of food, light, insect attack, snow, ice etc.

Semi arid: Region or climate in cool as well as tropical areas, where dry land farming methods or irrigation is generally required for crop production. Upper limit of average annual precipitation in cool regions is 400 mm and in tropical regions 1000-1250 mm.

Semi confined aquifer: The term employs for aquifer that is completely saturated and bounded above by semiperveous layer.

Sensor: A device able to quantitatively and reversibly detect chemical species and produce an electrical signal that is measured by another part of the instrument.

Settling basin: An enlargement in a stream channel to permit settling of suspended debris from the water.

Settling pond (water quality): A natural or artificial water body used to collect wastewater in order to enable solids to settle of the bottom from it before it is released to the natural environment. The solid pollutants suspended in the water sink to the bottom of the lagoon and the liquid is allowed to overflow out of the pond.

Sewage disposal: The area and structures designed to contain facilities and treat sewage for their safe disposal.

Sewage farm: A farm which takes sewage, usually as sludge, from settlement tanks; the sewage is used as manure and the effluent is drawn off to irrigate the land. A farm with a sandy soil is preferred for sewage disposal since sand is porous and acts as a filtering material.

Sewage treatment plant: A unit designed to receive the wastewater from domestic sources and to remove materials that damage water quality and threaten public health and safety when discharged into receiving streams or bodies of water.

Sewage treatment: The processing of wastewater for the removal or reduction of contained solids or other undesirable constituents before releasing into streams of water.

Shaft horse power [SHP]: It is power required at pump shaft.

Sharp crested weir: A notch cut in a relatively thin plate and having a sharp edge on upstream side of the crest used for measuring water flow in such a way that over flowing sheet of water has the minimum surface contact with crest.

Sheet erosion: Refers to the process of removal of a fairly uniform layer of soil from the land surface by the action of rainfall and runoff.

Sheet flow: Storm run-off flowing in a thin layer over the ground surface.

Shelterbelt: A belt consisting of a continuation of trees and shrubs intended for protection of field crops from winds.

Shifting cultivation: A type of subsistence farming, consisting of clearing of the forest, drying, burning the dried material and raising a crop generally by dibbling seed with a hand tool. As soon as the fertility is lost by erosion, another patch of forest is cleared and the process is repeated. Also referred as jhuming. The practice is common in hilly regions.

Shoulder: Earthen embankment made on outer side of bench terrace for preventing run-off to the lower terrace.

Shrinkage limit (SL): Maximum water content at which a reduction in water does not cause reduction in volume of soil mass. It defines an arbitrary limit between solid and semisolid states.

Side slopes: Slope in one or both side of earthen and or permanent structure for geater stability against hydraulic pressure, seepage and erosion. It is conventionally expressed as ratio of horizontal to verticals unless it is specifically mentioned. A side slope of 2:1 indicates 2 part of horizontal for one part of verticals means 50 % slope.

Sigmoid growth curve: A graph meant to represent the growth pattern of a annual crop for a period of time. Sigmoid means S-shaped. The general pattern can be divided into three parts *viz.*(i) Period of initially small increase in size, followed by Period of rapid growth and then by a period during which the size of the crop increases slowly or not at all.

Significance level (statistics): A probability value that it is considered rare in the sampling distribution specified under the null hypothesis that one is willing to assert the operation of non chance factors. Common significance levels are 0.05 and 0.01.

Significance, test of: It is a statistical procedure designed to distinguish real treatment difference from that due to chance (*i.e.,* random variation). To distinguish differences due to sampling error from differences due to discrepancy between observations and hypothesis.

Significant difference: A statistical reality used to determine the differences among treatment comparisons; usually expressed to have a certain level of probability of being wrong due to chance.

Silt: These particles are intermediate in size to sand and clay. Because of adhering film of clay, they exhibit some plasticity, cohesions, adhesion and absorption and can hold more amount of water than sand but less than clay.

Siltation: In water body the process of deposition of silt or sediments that appear as suspended particles in water.

Silting: The process of deposition of water borne sediments in stream beds, lakes, reservoirs etc, due to reduction in velocity of water or by standing.

Silvopastoral system: A land use system in which forests are managed for the production of wood as well as for the production of fodder crops for rearing of domesticated animals. In this system, animals are kept and permitted to graze within the forest.

Simulation model: Any type of model that is described and investigated (usually with the aid of a computer) so as to imitate the essential features and behaviour of a real system.

Sinkhole: A depression in the Earth's surface caused by dissolving of underlying limestone, salt, or gypsum.

Site (ecology): A specific area defined by its biotic, climatic and soil factors in relation to its capacity to produce vegetation or particular climax vegetation.

Site index: A quantitative assessment of the productivity of the soil for forest growth under the existing or specified environment in terms of height in feet of the dominant forest vegetation taken at or calculated for an index age, generally 50 or 100 years.

Site specific nutrient management: It is sort of precision management of nutrient in which nutrients are applied after estimation of requirement of site instead of blanket dose. Sites are sampled and analysed for available nutrient. Balance is computed considering requirement of proposed cultivation accounting other losses and fertilizer/manure is applied as per requirement.

Skeletal soils: Soils having more than 35 percent (by volume) of fragments greater than 2 mm size.

Slip: Refers to the downward movement of a wet or saturated soil mass. It is a micro-landslide which produces micro relief in soils.

Slope (gradient) class: The description of an area or region in terms of the steepness of slopes.

Slope (gradient): Amount by which the surface of the earth deviates from horizontal, sometimes expressed in degrees, but more often as percent.

Slope characteristic: Refers to the characterization of slope based on surface characteristics. Slope is concave if steepness decreases in lower portion, it is convex if steepness increases in lower portion and uniform if steepness is uniform. Concave slope is less erodible than convex slope.

Sloping inwards bench terrace: These are bench terraces with inward slopes. In heavy rainfall areas, inward sloping bench terraces are more effective. It prevents accumulation of water and useful for crops susceptible to water logging also helps in safe disposal of excess water.

Sloping outwards bench terrace: Refers to outward sloping bench terraces. These are effective only in low rainfall areas with a permeable soil of medium depth at lower ends graded channels are provided for safe disposal of runoff.

Slough: Wet or marshy piece of land.

Sloughing: The term is borrowed from biological science where it infers the act of shedding or casting off dead tissue. In context of erosion it refers casting of soil material by stream bank. It takes place when bank is fully saturated. It develops minor slide and leaves relatively steep face saturated with water. Sloughing occurs due to saturation of stream bank by water by persistent high flood for long time

Sluice: These are the channels or conduit to drain off surplus water at high velocity or for passing debris. Also to allow a water flow at high velocity for ejecting debris.

Small farmer: A farmer with land holding less than 2 hectare.

Small watersheds: Watersheds where the overland flow is the main contributor to peak runoff/flow and channel characteristic do not affect the overland flow.

Snow surveys: Surveys conducted with a view to determine the depth and density of snow in order to determine water stored in a watershed for predicting runoff.

Social forestry: A scheme launched by Government of India to promote forestry practices to meet the basic and economic needs of the community. It includes farm forestry, extension forestry, reforestation of degraded land and recreation forestry through (*i*) mixed plantation on waste-lands and panchayat lands and (*ii*) reforestation of degraded forests and raising shelter belts.

Sod culture: A soil management system wherein the plants are grown in permanent grass without tillage.

Sod grass: These are stoloniferous or rhizomatous grass, which forms sod or turf.

Sod heating: Heat accumulation in tightly stacked sod; may reach lethal temperatures.

Sod planting: Planting of trees in killed sod without any tillage.

Sod production: Culture of turf to a quality and maturity that allows harvesting and transplanting.

Sod seeding: A practice of mechanically placing seed (legumes, small grains) directly into a grass sod.

Sod strength: Refers to the relative ability of sod to resist tearing during harvesting, handling, and transplanting.

Sod: Refers to the top few centimetres of soil permeated by and held together with grass roots or grass-legume roots.

Sod-bound: A term used to describe the poor productivity of grass sod due to lack of nitrogen.

Softening: Refers to the process of removal of hardness from water caused by calcium and magnesium minerals.

Soil adhesion: The sticking of soil to tillage tools or wheels.

Soil aeration: The exchange of air in soil with atmospheric air.

Soil aggregate: Unit of soil structure generally < 10 mm in diameter and formed by natural forces and substances derived from root exudates and microbial products which cement smaller particles into larger units.

Soil air: Air present in the soil pores. It is that volume of soil not occupied by solid or liquid.

Soil amendment: A substance added to the soil for the purpose of improving physical or chemical properties, enhancing soil productivity or promoting the growth of crops, excluding commercial fertilizers and organic manure. *e.g.* lime, gypsum, sawdust, or synthetic conditioner.

Soil analyst: A soil mapper responsible for soil mapping and coding of soil attribute data.

Soil application: Refers to the application of fertilizer or herbicides primarily to the soil surface rather than to vegetation.

Soil association: A group of defined and named taxonomic soil units used on reconnaissance soil maps, in which two or more taxonomic units (soil series) occurring together in a particular pattern are combined since they cannot be shown individually on the scale of the map. Sometimes it may not be necessary to delineate the soils separately.

Soil atmosphere: The composition of gases occupying the pore space in soil. Generally characterized as having a greater percentage of carbon dioxide and a lesser percentage of oxygen than the overlying air.

Soil classification: The systematic arrangement of soils into categories and classes on the basis of their characteristics. Broad groupings are made on the basis of general characteristics and subdivisions on the basis of more detailed differences in specific properties.

Soil complex: It is a mapping unit used in detailed soil surveys where two or more defined taxonomic units are very intimately inter-mixed geographically and it is undesirable or impracticable to separate them on the scale of the map. A more intimate mixing of smaller areas of individual taxonomic units than that described under soil association.

Soil conditioners: The materials which when added to soil helps to improve & maintain the physical condition of the soil, *e.g.* polyvinylites, polyacrylates, cellulose gums, lignin derivatives and silicates.

Soil conservation: An act of conserving soil by applying combination of all management and land use methods which safeguard the soil against depletion or deterioration by natural or by man-induced factors.

Soil conserving crops: Refers to crops that reduce or for event soil erosion and maintain or replenish organic matter.

Soil correlation: The process of defining, mapping, naming, and classifying soil in a soil survey area.

Soil creep: The process of slow mass movement of soil and soil material along comparatively steep slopes under the influence of gravity facilitated by moisture saturation and alternate freezing and thawing.

Soil degradation: It is a broad and diversified process resulting in loss of soil productivity brought about by various natural and man induced factors like erosion, water logging, soil compaction etc.

Soil depleting crops: Refers to crops that deplete soil organic matter and nutrients and deteriorate soil structure under the prevailing management.

Soil erodibility factor (K): The soil erodibiliy factor indicates the inherent susceptibility of a soil to erosion. It gives an indication of the soil loss estimated from a unit plot measuring 22 mm long with a 9% slope and continuous fallow culture.

Soil erosion: The process of detachment, transportation and deposition of soil particles from one place to another under influence of wind, water or gravity force. It is three phase phenomenon begging with the detachment of individual soil particles from the soil mass and their transport by erosive agents such as running water and wind and ends when energy to transport the particles is not available then third phase called deposition take place.

Soil fertility: The nutrient supplying capacity of the soil to plants for normal growth in adequate amount & in a balanced proportion to normal plants in adequate amounts and in a balanced proportion to produce crops of economic value and maintain the health of the soil for future use.

Soil granule: A cluster of soil partic1es acting as a unit in soil structure.

Soil loss tolerance: It is the maximum average annual soil loss (tonnes per ha) that may be permitted for a particular soil.

Soil management: Sum total of tillage operations, cropping practices, application of lime, fertilizers etc. and any other treatments made to the soil for production of plants.

Soil map delineation: It is an area delineated on a map to represent a definite tract of land (a Soil Landscape) about which information is to be communicated. For a tract to be definite, distinct from its neighbors the tract must have discernible consistency in attributes i) that are important, and ii) that can be conceptualized, defined, and named. Assigned to the delineation, usually through symbols, the names and definitions impart the meaning of the tract it represents.

Soil map unit: A combination of kinds of soil, or miscellaneous land types that can be shown at the scale of mapping for the defined purpose and objectives of a particular soil survey.

Soil map: Map showing distribution of soil types or other mapping units in relation to important physical and cultural features of the earth's surface.

Soil microbiology: The science that deals with micro organisms, its population, classification, its role in transformations

Soil moisture characterstic curve (moisture retentive curve): A curve showing the relationship between the amount of water remaining in the soil at equilibrium as a function of matric suction. '

Soil moisture constant: The moisture water contents under certain standard conditions of pressure & temperature are referred as soil moisture constants. Under field conditions, water content of soil is always changing constantly with time and depth of soil and is not static or constant.

Soil moisture deficit: The amount of water required to be added to bring the soil moisture status to the field capacity.

Soil moisture stress: Sum of soil water tension and osmotic pressure to which water must be subjected, to be in equilibrium with soil water; also called soil water potential expressed in atmosphere or bar.

Soil moisture tension: Force at which water is held by the soil or negative pressure or suction that must be applied to bring water in a porous cup into static equilibrium with the water in soil. Soil-moisture tension does not include osmotic pressure and also referred to as matric potential expressed in atmospheres or mm of mercenary.

Soil moisture: Refers to the quantity of water contained in the soil, expressed as a percentage of weight of water per unit weight of dry soil or the percentage of volume of water per unit volume of bulk soil.

Soil monolith: It is a vertical section obtained from a soil profile and mounted for preservation and study.

Soil organic matter: The organic fraction of the soil that includes plant and animal residues of various stages of decomposition, cells and tissues of soil organisms, and substances synthesized by the soil population.

Soil permeability: The characteristics or state of a soil or any horizon in the soil profile relating to the transmission of water or air to all parts of the mass.

Soil pH: A measure of the degree of acidity or alkalinity of a soil. A pH of 7.0 is neutral; below 7.0 is acidic, and above 7.0 is alkaline.

Soil physics: Soil physics is a branch of soil science that study physical properties of soil in relation to various soil functions. Texture, bulk density, soil structure, permeability etc. are important.

Soil porosity: The proportion of soil occupied by water and air is termed as porosity. The amount of pore space depends upon the arrangement of solid particles, organic matter content, granulation and aggregation (texture), depth of the soil, cultivation and cropping pattern. The pore spaces are of two types, Macro or non-capillary (more than 0.06 mm) and Micro or capillary pores (less than 0.06 mm)

Soil productivity: The capacity of the soil, to produce a specified plant or sequence of plants under a specified system of management under normal climatic conditions. It emphasizes the capacity of the soil to produce crops and is expressed in terms of yield in relation to the input of production factors.

Soil profile: Vertical section of soil horizons from upper layer to the parent material (C horizon), showing the arrangement (configuration) of soil horizons typical for single soil types and used as a basis for soil classification.

Soil quality: Refers to the capacity of soil to function as a vital living system to sustain biological productivity, maintain the quality of the environment, and promote plant, animal, and human health.

Soil reaction: The acid or alkaline reaction of a soil expressed in terms of pH units, generally in the range of 4.5 to 9.5 pH.

Soil saving dam: A dam of earth or other material constructed across a gully or other water stream to impound silt and surface run-off and to control erosion.

Soil science: The branch of agricultural science dealing with the study of soil as a natural resource on the surface of the earth, including pedology (soil genesis, classification and mapping) its physical, chemical and biological properties and fertility of soil in relation to their management for successful crop production.

Soil separates: Soil mineral particles smaller than 2 mm in equivalent diameter. These are the individual soil particles after standard dispersion treatment recognized by the International Society of Soil Science are (a) coarse sand, 2.0 to 0.2 mm (b) fine sand, 0.2 to 0.02 mm (c) silt, 0.02 to 0.002 mm and (d) clays, 0.002 mm diameter.

Soil series: A conceptualized clears of soils (polyhedrons) with horizons similar in differentiating characteristics and arrangement in the profile, excepting for surface texture. A basic unit of soil classification. The soil series serve as a major vehicle to transfer soil information and research knowledge from one soil area to another.

Soil specific gravity (As): Ratio of the weight of oven dried soil to its volume also called bulk density expressed in g/cm^3.

Soil structure: The arrangement of primary soil particles into secondary particles (aggregates or pedo) into certain pattern in the soil mass, called as soil structure. Soil structure influences the soil properties through its effect on the amount and size of pore spaces, water holding capacity, availability of plant nutrients and growth of micro-organisms. Soil structure types are plate-like, prism like, block like (blocky) and spheroidal.

Soil survey: A systematic study of soil involving examination, description, classification and mapping of soils in an area. Surveys are categorized as detailed and reconnaissance in accordance with kind and intensity of field examinations.

Soil texture: It refers to the relative proportions of soils separates *i.e.* sand, silt and clay (< 2mm) in soil. It is permanent or static property of soil. A soil is described as a coarse, medium or fine textured depending on the predominent particle size.

Soil tilth: Refers to the physical condition of the soil as a result of tillage operation that influences crop emergence, establishment, growth and development. A soil is said to be in good tilth when it is soft, friable & properly aerated.

Soil type: Sub-division of a soil series depending on texture surface soil. The term is now obsolete, and it is considered as a kind of phase. It is not a part of the present soil classification system.

Soil variant: Refers to soil having properties sufficiently different from other known soils, but covering a very small geographical area that designating a new soil series is not justified.

Soil water potential (capillary): The amount of energy required per unit quantity of pure water in order to transport reversibly and isothermally an infinitesimal quantity of water, identical in composition to the soil water, from a pool at the elevation and the external gas pressure at the point under consideration to the soil water.

Soil: Defined as a dynamic natural body of unconsolidated mineral and organic material on the surface of the earth developed as a result of pedogenic processes during and after weathering of rocks, consisting of minerals and organic constituents, possessing definite chemical, physical, mineralogical and biological properties having variable depth over surface of the earth and serves as natural medium for growth of land plants.

Solid waste management: Refers to storage, collection, transportation, treatment, utilization, processing, and final disposal of solid waste or resource recovery, and facilities necessary for such activities.

Solubility: The quantity of a substance that will dissolve in a given volume of another substance, typically water.

Soluble: Capable of being dissolved easily.

Solum: It is the upper part of the soil profile above the parent material, in which processes of soil formation take place. In mature soils they include A and B horizons.

Solvent: Liquid capable of dissolving another substance.

Spacing of contour bund: Bund spacing is expressed as the vertical or the horizontal distance between corresponding points on two adjacent bunds.

Spatial resolution: The size of pixel of an image representing the size of the surface area being measured on the ground. It is the power of resolving closely spaced object on the ground in satellite imageries. Pixel size and hence spatial resolution is determined by the sensors' instantaneous field of view.

Specific retention (ground water): Defined as the ratio of volume of water a material can retain after drainage by gravity to the total volume. It is a property of unconfined aquifer.

Specific yield (ground water): It is a measure of water yielding capacity of aquifer and is defined as the ratio of the water tha an unconfined aquifer will release from storage under gravity per unit surface area of an aquifer per unit decline in water table to the total volume. Water that can be obtained frm saturated material is expressed by specific yield.

Spectral distance: A decision rule for image classification that assigns pixels to a cluster based on the minimum difference in spectral values to other pixels.

Spectral enhancement: Modifying pixel values in an image to enhance certain feature over others.

Spectral resolution: The wavelength interval size (discreet segment of the Electromagnetic Spectrum) and number of intervals in which response are recorded by satellite. More the number of band and narrower the band means higher spectral resolution. Hyper spectral satellite has very high spectral resolution.

Spectral response pattern: Degree to which an object reflects incident electromagnetic energy in different regions of the electromagnetic spectrum.

Spheroidal: The aggregates are rounded or like a sphere. All the axes are approximately of the same dimensions, with curved or irregular faces, not more than 1 cm dia.

Spillways: A chute, weir, conduit, tunnel, channel, or other structure designed to permit discharges or escape of excess water. The primary purpose of a spillway is to discharge flood flows safely past a dam, but they may also be used to release water for other purposes. A spillway may be gated (controlled) or not. Gates are used to regulate the level of the reservoir above the spillway crest.

Spillway capacity: The maximum flow a spillway is capable of discharging when the reservoir is at its highest water surface elevation.

Splash erosion: Process of water erosion by which soil particles are spattered by the impact of raindrops on wet soil. These spattered particles mayor may not be transported by run-off. It is the initial stage of erosion. It is also called rain drop erosion.

Split application: Application of chemical or fertilizer divided into two or more parts and applied at given intervals.

Split-plot design: An experimental design that can be used only for factorial experiments. A lay-out in which one set of treatments is assigned to large plots called main plots into which a replicate is divided and another set of treatments to subdivisions of the main plots called subplots is termed a split-plot design. The precision of the measurement of effects related to the main plot factors is sacrificed to improve that of the subplot factors.

Spodosols: Soils belong to forests with low content of bases, having coarse texture (sandy). Found in humid climates where temperatures are low. The subsurface horizons have accumulation of org. matter and sesquioxide.

Spoil bank: It is a pile of soil, subsoil or rock material excavated from a drainage ditch or pond etc.

Spoil: Soil or rock material dug out from a canal, ditch etc.

Spot planting (forestry): It is planting in restricted open areas among established tree stands.

Spreader (hydraulics): It is a device to ensure uniform distribution of water from a channel.

Spreader strip: It is a relatively permanent contour strip of variable width under erosion resisting vegetation where run-off from upper land can slow down and fan out.

Sprinkler or overhead irrigation: This method consists of application of water to soil in the form of spray, somewhat as rain. In sprinkler irrigation, water is conveyed under pressure through pipes to the area to be irrigated where it is passed out through sprinklers; the system comprises four main parts *viz.* Power generator, Pump, Pipeline and, Sprinkler. It is particularly useful for sandy soils because they absorb water fast. This method is suitable for areas having uneven topography and where erosion hazards are great.

Spurs: Spurs are structure constructed at an angle extending from bank towards the stream for deflecting the current away from the bank and direct to flow centrally. It is usually constructed in series for river training.

Square foot method: It is a technique in range surveys for the determination of average density and composition of vegetation by estimating each species of herbage in square feet of coverage in systematically located plots.

Stabilized grade: It is the grade or slope of a channel at which neither erosion nor deposition takes place.

Staff gauge: It is a graduated scale mounted on a plank, wall or pier etc. from where water level could be read.

Stage: It is the water surface elevation above a datum line.

Standard deviation: The measure of variability expressed in mathematical terms of how much an observation differs from the mean of set of observations. A measure of dispersion of variable around the general mean and is a calculated as square root of sum of the squares of the deviation of each observation from the mean dividing by the number of observations.

Standard error: The measure of the average chance departure of a statistic from its expected value. It is sometimes known as the standard deviation of the means. The standard deviation of the sampling distribution of a statistic.

Static discharge head: It is vertical distance from the center line of the pump to discharge water level.

Static suction head: It is vertical distance from center of pump to free level of water to be pumped.

Static water level: Refers to the water level in a well before pumping.

Station: Refers to a point whose elevation is to be determined. It may be noted that it is a point where the staff is held not the point where the level is set up.

Steady flow: Refers to a continuous flow of water which remains constant with time at a specified cross section in a channel.

Stilling basin: It is an open structure constructed at the foot of a spillway, chute, overfall etc. to reduce the energy of descending stream.

Stocking: It is the degree to which an area is effectively covered, with living trees.

Stolon: It is a horizontal stem of a plant growing along the soil surface and striking root at the nodes.

Stony land: It is an area, usually covered with stones to an extent of 15-90 percent, where the use of agricultural machinery is impractical. A miscellaneous land type.

Storage curve (hydraulics): It is a graphical expression of stage or level of water and the volume of water at that stage in a pond, reservoir etc.

Storativity/storage coefficient: It is a storage property of confined aquifer defined as volume of water aquifer releases from or takes into storage per unit surface area of the aquifer per unit change in the component of hydraulic head normal to the surface.

Storm: It is a meteorological disturbance of the atmosphere such as windstorm, sandstorm, rainstorm or thunderstorm etc.

Stream bank erosion: Wearing away of embankments along a stream due to the scouring of material from the side and bottom of a stream or water channel and the cutting of bank by running water. It is mainly due to removal of vegetation, over grazing or cultivation on the area near to the streams banks.

Stream density: It is the number of streams per unit area.

Stream gauging: Refers to the quantitative determination of stream flow at a particular location using weirs, gauges, current meters etc.

Stream load: Refers to the quantity of solid and dissolved substances carried by water flow in a stream.

Stream order: It is a measure of the degree of stream branching. A first-order stream has no branch, a second-order stream is a tributary formed by two or more first-order streams and in general, an nth order stream is a tributary formed by two or more streams of $(n-1)^{th}$ order and streams of lower order.

Strip cropping: Refers to the cultivation of crops in a systematic arrangement of strips or bands that provide vegetative barriers to wind erosion and water erosion. It is practiced by growing erosion resisting and erosion permitting crops in alternate strips running perpendicular to the slope of the land or to the direction of prevailing winds for the purpose of reducing erosion.

Strip grazing: Restricting feeding of animals to an area of forage to be consumed in a short period of time usually a day. It is also called ration grazing.

Strip intercropping: Growing two or more crops simultaneously in strips wide enough to permit independent cultivation but narrow enough for the crop to interact agronomically.

Strip plot design: An experimental design suitable for experiments involving two different sets of treatments can be tried in large plot with one set of plots superimposed over the other set at right angles. A block may be divided into' strips in one direction to be allotted to 1 set of treatments and into another set of strips to be allotted to the second set of treatments, this design is used when two sets of treatments needs larger plots.

Structural design: Structural engineering is a field of engineering dealing with the analysis and design of structures that support or resist loads. Structural engineering is usually considered a specialty within civil engineering, but it can also be studied in its own right.[

Structures temporary: Mechanical structures to control erosion, which are not of permanent type, such as wooden check dams, brushwood check dams, random rubble check dams etc.

Stubble mulch: Refers to the stubble of crops left in place on the land as a surface cover during fallow for protection against erosion and for conserving moisture by favouring infiltration and reducing evaporation and the growing of a succeeding crop.

Stubble: Basal portion of crop plants left in the field after harvest of the top portion.

Sub surface or under ground drainage: A type of drainage system to remove excess soil water. It percolates water in to themselves, just like open drains. Underground drains may be classified as: Tile or pipe drain, Box drains, Rubble (coarse stones or gravels filled) drains and Mole drains.

Sub watershed: It is a watershed sub division of unspecified size forming a convenient natural unit for management.

Subcritical flow: It is the flow at velocities which are less than critical.

Sub-irrigation: Refers to the application of irrigation water below the land surface by either raising the water table near or within the root zone of the crops, or by burying perforated or porous pipes that supply water inside the root zone. Also sub-surface irrigation.

Subsidiary or the tie stations: Subsidiary or the tie stations are the point selected on the main survey lines, where it is necessary to locate the interior detail such as fences, hedges, building etc.

Subsistence farming: It is farming enterprise involving growing of crops and, where appropriate, keeping animals so as to provide food (cereals, pulses, vegetable and fruits), shelter materials, and possibly other products (fibres, medicinals) which provides food and commodities just sufficient for the farming family, and there are no surplus to sell.

Subsoiling: It is the tillage of sub-surface soil, without inversion, for breaking up any dense or hard layer in order to ensure better water percolation and root growth.

Subsurface drainage system: It is a artificial drainage system includes underground ditches and buried darins within soil profile to collect and convey excess ground water to a gravity or pumped outlet.

Subsurface irrigation: Irrigation of crops by applying water below surface of the ground through pipes.

Subsurface layer: Any surface soil horizon (A, E, AB, or EB) below the surface layer.

Subsurface runoff: The portion of unfiltered water which penetrated to shallow depth travels laterally and is intercepted by channels. That part of rainfall which first leaches into the soil and moves laterally without joining the water table, to the stream, rivers or ocean is known as sub-surface runoff. It is usually referred as inter-flow.

Subsurface tillage: The tillage of soil with special equipment without inversion of surface residual mulch.

Succession: The progressive development of vegetation towards climax types.

Sum of squares: The sum or addition of the squares of the differences between the mean of a set of observations and individual observations. Deviation from the mean squared and summed.

Sump: An excavation for the purpose of catching or storing liquids.

Superfluous water: It includes gravitational water (excess of field capacity). This water is also unavailable to the use of plants because it is lost due to deep percolation. The presence of superfluous water in soil for longer period is harmful to plant growth.

Supervised classification: It is digital image processing in which image classification using software is done in strict supervision of an individual who decide how to ascertain feature class. Prior collected information is generally used in assigning feature. Normally a vector layer containing training points or polygons of well known feature are used for deciding class of unknown pixel.

Supplemental irrigation: Refers to the application of irrigation water to the crops in regions where normal rainfall ordinarily supplies most of the moisture. It is provided to ensure or increase crop production, when crop is facing moisture stress due to dry spells.

Supplementary estimate: First detail estimate of the additional work. Due to some development during execution, some additional work is to be done. Abstract of cost should mention both original estimate and total amount including the cost of additional work

Surcharge storage: The quantity of water stored between highest flood levels to normal water level is called surcharge storage. It is a temporary storage.

Surface creep: It is a way of transportation of eroded particles by moving water, in which larger size particles move through rolling and sliding along the stream bed maintaining continuous contact with bed.

Surface detention: The amount of water on the land surface in transit towords stream channels is called detention storage/surface detention.

Surface drainage: Removal of the excess water form soil surface is called surface drainage. It consist of open ditches that are laid out by eye judgment, leading from one wet spot to another and finally into a nala or river. This is often called natural system.

Surface irrigation: Water is applied directly to the soil from channel located at upper ridge of the field. Proper land preparation, adequate control of water is necessary for uniform distribution of water.

Surface profile (hydraulics): It is the longitudinal profile of water surface of a stream flowing in an open channel. Same as hydraulic grade line.

Surface runoff: The movement of water over ground surface into the channels when rainfall intensity is greater than infiltration rate. The loss of water through runoff is the largest and is almost damaging because it causes soil erosion. The rate of loss of water through run-off depends upon the soil type, intensity of precipitation or quantity of irrigation water.

Surface storage: It is the sum of detention storage and channel storage *i.e.* the total water from a watershed enroute to an outlet.

Surface tension: The attraction of molecules to each other on a liquid air interface surface.

Surface water: Refers to water that is present on the Earth's surface, such as in a stream, river, lake, or reservoir.

Surplusing arrangement: Construction of outlet in contour bunds to drain excess water in order to avoid breaching and damage to crop is called surplusing arrangement. It is constructed at lowest places and also called waste weirs.

Surveying: It is the art of determining the relative positions of different object on the surface of the earth by measuring the horizontal distance between them and by preparing a map to any suitable scale. Thus, in this process, the measurements are taken only in the horizontal plane.

Suspended load: Stream load moving in suspension and consisting of particles having such density or size as to permit movement far above and for long distance out of contact with stream bed. The particles are held in suspension by upward components of turbulent currents contributing to turbidity.

Suspended sediment: Very fine soii particles that remain in suspension in water for a considerable period of time due to the upward components of turbulence and currents.

Suspended solids: These are organic and inorganic particles, such as solids from wastewater, sand, and clay that are suspended and carried in water.

Suspended-sediment concentration: The ratio of the mass of dry sediment in a water-sediment mixture to the volume of the water-sediment mixture.

Suspended-sediment discharge: The quantity of suspended sediment passing through point of observation in unit time. It is multiplication of water discharge by the suspended-sediment concentration.

Suspension: The term refers to a heterogeneous fluid containing solid particles that are sufficiently large for sedimentation but small enough to remain in flowing water for considerable period of time with little turbulence. In hydrology it is process of transportation of fine particle.

Sustainability: The balancing of opportunities for growth with the need to protect the environment. It reflects a vision of a vibrant economy and a healthy environment with a view to manage renewable resources (*e.g.* water, timber, fish, and wildlife), so that their status, condition, or use is maintained over time. Regarding non-renewable resources (*e.g.* coal, oil, gas, and minerals), sustainability involves the development of resources in a responsible manner.

Sustainable agriculture: Sustainable agriculture involves judicious use and management of resources for agriculture to satisfy changing human needs while maintaining or enhancing the quality of the environment and conserving natural resources for generations to come.

Sustainable development: The management and conservation of the natural base, and the orientation of technological and institutional change, in such a manner as to ensure the attainment and continued fulfillment of human needs for present and future generations. It conserves land, water, plant and animal genetic resources, is environmentally non-degrading, technically appropriate, economically feasible and socially acceptable manner.

Sustainable land use: Land use that achieves production sufficient to meet the needs of present and future populations while conserving or enhancing the land resources on which that production depends.

Swamp: An area which remains saturated with water for most of the year, without any deep submergence. Such an area is usually characterized by hydrophytes.

Swath (satellite): The width of surface on the earth which is imaged during a single pass of satellite referred to as the satellite swath.

Swath: The width of the area covered by a sprayer making one sweep or one trip across the field or other treated area.

Swathing: The cutting or pulling of a crop into a windrow to dry and/or to facilitate harvest.

Synoptic scale (Meteorology): These systems have a diameter of few thousand km. and life time of about 5 days eg. Tropical storm, cyclones.

Systems approach: Refers to the study of a system as an entity made up of all its components and their interrelationships, together with relationships between the system and its environment.

T

Table top bench terrace: This type of bench terrace is suitable for areas receiving medium rainfall which is evenly distributed and which have highly permeable and deep soils. In paddy fields it may be used for slopes as mild as 1% and used where irrigation facilities are available

Tail water (hydraulics): Water in a river or channel immediately downstream of a structure; irrigation water that reaches the end of a crop field.

Tail water recovery: The collection of tail water for re-use for irrigation.

Tank silt: It consists of large proportion of finer soil particles of silt and clay and organic matter carried by run-off water from the surrounding soil to the tanks during heavy rains.

Target area: Large priority development area in a country for which improved cropping system technologies are developed through on-farm cropping systems research conducted at sites in the area.

Temperate zone: Either of the two latitudinal zones on the earth's surface which lie between 23° 27' and 66°27' N and S.

Temperature inversion: The abnormal reversal of temperature in the troposphere caused by meteorological conditions.

Temperature: The degree of hotness of coldness of a body or environment.

Temporal resolution: The amount of time (*i.e.* days) that passes between imagery collection periods. Usually it is revisit time of specific sensor of satellite. It may differ for different sensor for same satellite due to different swath.

Temporary pasture: A pasture grazed for a short period only, usually not more than 1 crop season.

Temporary structure (hydrology): Are the structure designed for short effective life usually less than five to ten year. There is little risk associated with failure of these structures. Design criteria considers short term return period of rainfall.

Temporary wilting: A temporary condition of the plant due to loss of water which would recover from wilted condition during the night without addition of any water.

Tensiometer: Tensiometer is also called irrometers since they are used in irrigation scheduling. Tensionmeters provide a direct measure of tenacity (soil-water matric potential) with which water is held by soil. It consist of 7.5 cm porous ceramic or clay cup, a protective metallic tube, a vacuum gauge and a hollow metallic tube holding all parts together. It is used in scheduling of irrigation.

Terminal velocity (rainfall): It is the velocity attained by a rain drop after falling from a height of 10.5 m or more. It varies from 4.5 metre per second for 1 mm drop to 9.0 metre per second for 5 mm drop.

Terrace interval: It is the horizontal or vertical distance between corresponding points on two adjacent terraces.

Terrace outlet channel: A channel, usually vegetated, into which run-off from one or more terraces is conveyed.

Terrace: An earthen embankment or a combination of embankment and channel constructed across the land slope in order to divert run-off and control erosion. Alignment of terraces may be parallel or non-parallel and the terrace gradient may be level, uniform or variable. The terrace cross-section may be narrow base, broad base, bench, back slope etc. Outlets may be vegetated waterways, tile outlets or their combinations. Terrace made with live hedge is called Puertorico or California terrace.

Terracing: The process of construction of an embankment or ridge of earth across a slope to control runoff and minimize soil erosion. It reduces the length of the hill side slope, thereby reducing sheet and rill erosion and prevents formation of gullies.

Textural classes: All soils have all the three soil separates in varying proportions. Based on their proportions, the soils can be grouped into textural classes and are named according to the soil separates which is predominant in them.

Textural triangle: A classification of earth materials with equivalent particle diameters less than 2.0 mm based solely on particle-size distribution.

Texture, soil: The relative proportions of sand, silt, and clay particles in a mass of soil. The basic textural classes, in order of increasing proportion of fine particles, are sand, loamy sand, sandy loam, loam, silt loam, silt, sandy clay loam, clay loam, silty clay loam, sandy clay, silty clay, and clay. The sand, loamy sand, and sandy loam classes may be further divided by specifying "coarse," "fine," or "very fine."

Thedolite: Thedolite is a high precision instrument for measuring angles in the horizontal as well as in vertical planes and mainly used for surveying. A modern theodolite consists of a movable telescope mounted within two perpendicular axes - the horizontal and the vertical axis. By means of reading of upper and lower stadia distance of an object can be measured. By using central cross hair reading, thedolite can be used for leveling just like IOP or dumpy level. It is most suitable for topographic survey in hilly region.

Theissen method of average rainfall evaluation: It is a method of determining average rainfall over a watershed by dividing the area around the rain gauges installed in the watershed into polygons, adding up the products of theissen constants for the' polygons and rainfall recorded by the respective rain gauges, and dividing by the number of rainfall stations in the watershed.

Thematic data: Qualitative and categorical raster data, usually map or land cover classes such as pasture, urban areas, standing water, etc.

Thematic map: A map designed to demonstrate particular features or concepts.

Thematic mapper (TM): A cross-track scanner deployed on Landsat that records seven bands of data from the visible through the thermal IR regions.

Thermograph: Apparatus used to give a continuous record as a graphical chart of temperature with time. A self-recording thermometer.

Thermo-hygrograph: A hybrid instrument resulting from the combination of a hygrograph and thermograph. It furnishes on the same chart simultaneously a continuous recording of atmospheric temperature and humidity

Thinning (Forestry): Cutting of immature tree stands in order to provide space for development of the remaining trees into exploitable size.

Threshold velocity: The minimum velocity at which wind start moving sand or other soil material.

Tidal swamps: Low elevation coastal area affected by tidal flooding.

Tight soil: A compact, relatively impervious and tenacious soil or sub-soil.

Tile drain: Drainage of land by a series of tile drains laid out at specified depth, spacing and grade. It consists of digging a narrow trench, placing short section of tiles at the bottom and covering the tiles with earth. The loose joints between two sections of the tiles serve as a place where drainage water may enter into the drainage system. Water moves by gravity into the joints between tiles and through tile walls.

Tillage depth: It is the vertical distance from the initial soil surface to a specific point of penetration of the tillage implement.

Tillage practices: Refers to the mechanical manipulation of soil to provide a favorable environment for good germination of seed and crop growth, to control the weeds, to maintain infiltration capacity and soil aeration. Tillage practice protects and maintains a strong soil structure to fight against erosion.

Tillage: Tillage is the physical manipulation of soil with tools & implements for loosening the surface crust & bringing about conditions favorable for the germination of seeds and the growth of crops.

Tilth : The physical condition of soil in terms of its ease of tillage, fitness as a seedbed and lack of impedence to seedling emergence and root penetration.

Time of concentration: The time required by runoff water to flow from the remotest point in a watershed to the outlet.

Toe drain: Interceptor drain constructed near the toe of a structure.

Toe wall: Wall constructed at the downstream end of a structure.

Toe: Lower terminal edge of a structure.

Top down approach: an approach to a problem begins at the highest conceptual level and works down to the details. It is an autocratic and hierarchal style of decision making in which strategies and plan are first conceived by few top level officer and disseminated down ward on which lower level are bound to act on the decision. It is simple and fast in decision making but ensures poor participation and ignores expertise of lower level.

Topoclimatology: Study of local climate as affected by slope and other surface characteristics.

Topographic inversion: An optical illusion that may occur on images with extensive shades. Ridges appear to be valleys, and valleys appear to be ridges. The illusion is corrected by orienting the image so that the shadows trend from the top margin of the image to the bottom.

Topographic levelling: Process of obtaining necessary data for producing topographic map showing the relief or undulation etc. of an area including natural or artificial feature *e.g.* streams, gullies, road, culverts, fences and building.

Topographic map: Map that displays topography through the use of elevation contour lines. Base elevation on these maps is usually sea-level.

Topographic profile: A two-dimensional diagram that describes the landscape in vertical cross-section.

Topographic reversal: A geomorphic phenomenon in which topographic lows coincide with structural highs and vice versa. Valleys are eroded on crests of anticlines to cause topographic lows, and synclines form ridge, or topographic highs.

Topographical survey: To determine natural features of a country such as valleys, rivers and artificial features such as road, railways, etc.

Topography: A description of the features of a place, or a landscape, especially the rise and fall of the land. On a map it is usually indicated by contour lines.

Topology: Method of determining spatial relationships in vector data models (tells computer what is inside or outside a polygon or which nodes are connected by arcs). Turns vector nodes, arcs, and polygons into intelligent maps.

Toposequence: A sequence of related soils that differs from each other, primarily because of topography as a soil formation factor.

Total discharge head: It is sum of static discharge head, friction and exit loses in discharge piping plus the velocity head and pressure head at the point of discharge.

Total dissolved solids (TDS): Refers to the concentration of all substances dissolved in water (solids remaining after evaporation of a water sample).

Total suction head: It is vertical distance from the center line of the pump to free level of the liquid to be pumped minus, all friction loses in suction pipe and fitting plus any pressure head existing on the suction supply.

Toxic substance (Toxicant): Refers to the substances that are harmful to plant or animal life, either immediately (acute toxicity) or over a long time period (chronic toxicity).

Training sites: These are sites of known feature for which spectral response is observed and used for training software for classification of image. Spatial information of these sites is collected before image processing using GPS or Toposheet of any referenced map and information is used for supervised classification of image. Some of the training site of prominent feature class like, deep waterbody, large patch of particular crop, dense forest etc, may be collected at intermediate steps for image processing.

Transect: A sample cross-section of an area for recording, mapping or studying vegetation. The transect may be a series of plots, a belt or strip or a line, depending on the purpose of study.

Transmissivity: Refers to the rate at which water passes through a unit width of an aquifer.

Transpiration losses: The process by which water in the form of water vapour leaves the plant body and enters the atmosphere. It involves continuous movement of water from the soil into roots, through the stem and cut through the leaves to the atmosphere.

Transplant (forestry): A seedling that has been transplanted in the nursery once or more frequently.

Transportation (soil): The movement of detached soil material over the land surface or through air by the agency of water, wind or gravity.

Transverse drainage: A method of drainage where the drains are placed in a direction more or less at right angles to the direction of the steepest slope of the land to be drained.

Trap efficiency: The capability of a pond or other reservoir to trap sediment.

Trapezoidal: Earthen embankment made with trapezoidal cross- section with wide base, narrow top and side slopes.

Traversing: This method is similar to that of compass or transit traversing. It is used for running survey lines between stations which have been previously fixed by other methods of surveying to locate the topographical details. It is also suitable for the survey of roads, rivers etc.

Tree cropping: A cropping system concept using tree crops as the basis of an agricultural system. It results in replacement of grain crops with tree crops, consisting of an upper tree storey of one or more types of forage trees, at ground level permanent pasture and one or more types of domestic animals that feed on the pasture or on tree products are maintained.

Trench drain: A trench backfilled to the surface with a coarse material, such as sand, gravel, or crushed rock, for the purpose of removing excess surface water rapidly.

Trenching: A method of soil and water conservation, in which trenches of different types (continuous contour or staggered) are prepared depending upon the quantity of runoff.

Triangulation: The lines of survey form a network of triangles. (It is the systems of surveying in which the area is divided into simple geometrical figures and the work is carried out by taking its measurements.)

Tributary: Secondary or branch of a stream or channel which contributes flow to the main or primary channel.

Trickle irrigation: The process of supplying water to plants using equipment that drips small quantities at a slow rate. Water is usually applied at positions determined by the location of the nozzles although, in some systems (for example, 'seep hose'), it comes from all along the feeder line. Can be above ground or subsurface.

Trigonometric levelling: It is the process of leveling in which the elevations of points are computed from the vertical angles and horizontal distance measured in the field.

Triple cropping: Growing three crops a year in sequence from same piece of land.

Truncated soil profile: Soil profile that has been deprived of part or all of A horizon and sometimes the B horizon by accelerated erosion or by mechanical means, leaving only C horizon. Comparison with a virgin profile in the area would indicate the degree of truncation.

t-test: A statistical test criterion in comparing two samples of data believed to be normally distributed.

Tuff: Volcanic ash more or less stratified and in different states of consolidation.

Turbidity: The amount of solid particles that are suspended in water and that cause light rays shining through the water to scatter. Thus, turbidity makes the water cloudy or even opaque in extreme cases. Turbidity is measured in nephelometric turbidity units (NTU). High turbidity makes water appear unclear or cloudy and is harmful to organisms such as fish.

Turbulence: A state of fluid flow in which instantaneous velocities exhibit irregular and apparently random fluctuations.

Turbulent velocity (hydraulics): It is the velocity above which water flow is always turbulent and below which it may be turbulent or laminar depending upon circumstances.

Type, forest: A descriptive term indicating forest stands of similar composition and development based on ecological factors.

U

Udic: A soil moisture regime that is neither dry for as long as 90 cumulative days nor for as long as 60 consecutive days in the 90 days following the summer solstice at periods.

Ultisols: These are strongly acid, normally forest soils with low content of bases extensively weathered soils of tropical and subtropical climates, respond to good management practices, have clay of 1:1 type and give good crop production with adequate fertilization. They are usually moist, but during the warm season of the year some are dry, part of the time.

Unavailable soil water: Water below the hygroscopic co-efficient above 31 atmospheric suction is held so tenaciously that is unavailable to plants. It includes whole of the hygroscopic water plus a part of inner capillary water being below the wilting point. Types of water are not available to the plants are a)

Hygroscopic water, b) Fraction of inner capillary, c) Water vapour

Unconfined aquifer (Water table): Aquifer that is not restricted by impervious layers of rock whose upper boundary is the water table.

Unconfined groundwater: Groundwater that is not restricted by impervious layers of rock.

Undergrazing: An intensity of grazing in which the quantity of available forage under a grazing system is not used to best advantage.

Underground run-off (seepage): Water flowing after infiltration into the soil towards water channels or streams etc.

Undergrowth (forestry): Seedlings, shoots and saplings etc. growing under a stand of trees.

Undermining: Process of impinging and eroding stream bank by stream current during normal period of flow is called undermining. When continued for long period it results in under cutting of bank and destabilization or collapse of overhanging soil mass. Wider and deeper flow with frequent wave generation accelerates undermining.

Understory: Portion of trees in a forest area below the upper crown cover. Also under wood.

Undifferentiated soil group-(mapping unit): Two or more soil or land types which may be mapped as one unit, as their differences do not influence soil management or are not relevant to the purpose of soil survey.

Uniform flow: A state of steady flow when the mean velocity and cross-sectional area are the same at different sections of a reach.

Universal soil loss equation (USLE): An equation used to estimate soil loss under different conditions of rainfall, soil, slope (degree and length), cropping management and conservation practices, propounded by Wischmeier and Smith. A=RKLSCP Where, A: Average annual soil loss in tons per acre per year or tonnes per ha per year, R-Rainfall factor (Energy x Intensity), K - Soil erodibility factor, being equal to soil loss in tonnes per ha per year per unit of erosion index (rainfall factor), L-Length of slope factor, S-Degree of slope factor, C- Cropping management factor, P-Conservation practice factor.

Unsaturated zone: Refers to the portion of the soil profile which contains both air and water. Water in this zone cannot enter a well.

Unsupervised classification: It is a digital image processing in which classification of satellite imageries is done by software without supervision or interference of user. Classes are made based on spectral value. Unsupervised classification requires less input information from the analyst because clustering does not require training data. It is important to understand the spectral characteristics of the terrain to be able to assign specific feature class to label clusters.

Upland (geology): Land at a higher elevation, in general, than the alluvial plain or stream terrace; land above the lowlands along streams.

Upland field: A land lying above the flood plain, a land area with no levees or dikes surrounding it to impound water; sowing is by direct seeding.

Uplift (hydraulics): Upward pressure exerted by water on the base of a structure.

Upper and lower moisture plastic limits: The upper limit is that moisture content at which the soil will barely flow under an applied force. The lower plastic limit is that moisture content at which the soil can be rolled out into wire.

Urea [$CO(NH_2)_2$]: A synthetic nitrogenous fertilizer, crystalline or made into granules or prills for fertilizer use and containing 46% nitrogen.

V

V- Notch Weir: The 90° V notch weirs are commonly used to measure small and medium size streams. The advantage of V- notch weir is its ability to measure small flows accurately.

Validation: Refers to the process of assessing the quality of the data products derived from the system outputs by independent means/agency.

Valley cross section: Vertical and horizontal outline of a valley normal to the direction of water flow.

Vapour: A substance in the gas state that is below its critical temperature but still suspended in air. It is possible for a vapor to be liquefied by increased pressure. Vapors are usually not visible.

Vapour form: The water is present in gaseous form in the soil atmosphere but it is not directly used by plants and is therefore, not important for plants unlike other forms of water.

Vapour pressure: The pressure exerted against the walls of the container and the surface of the water by the water-vapour molecules.

Variable: A quantity capable of assuming different numerical values. Data or some characteristics that show variability. The characteristic may be numerical (quantitative) or non-numerical (qualitative).

Variance: A statistical measure of the dispersion of observation values in a data set. The variance of a sample is the sum of the square of each value in the data set subtracted from the mean divided by one less than the total number of observations in the data set.

Vector: A carrier, typically an insect or rodent, capable of transmitting a disease.

Vegetation type: A plant community possessing distinguishable characteristics.

Vegetative spurs: A type of permeable spurs made of live branches of tree. Live braches of the tree are properly arranged and secured to the bed and bank of stream.

Velocity head: It is the pressure expressed in meters of water required to create the velocity of flow. $H_v = V^2/2g$. Where, H_v = velocity head in m, V = velocity of water through the pipe m/sec. and g = Acceleration due to gravity, m/sec.

Venturi flume: A calibrated flume with a contracted throat section, which produces a differential head related to discharge.

Vermicompost: Compost produced by the digestion and discharge of refuse and other organic wastes by earthworms.

Vertical angle: Angle between two intersecting lines in a vertical plane, one of the two lines is commonly taken as horizontal in surveying.

Vertical Interval = Term used to express vertical distance between two consecutive conservation structures usually laid along the contour. In case of bund VI is calculated as $VI = 0.3\left(\frac{\text{Per cent slope}}{3} + 2\right)$

Vertical line: It is a line normal to the level surface through that point *e.g.* a plumb line.

Vertical mulching: Incorporation of vegetative materials in standing or vertical position in suitably spaced 25-30 cm deep trenches in agricultural fields for interception of run- off and moisture conservation in dry land farming areas with low rainfall. About 8-10 cm of the mulch protrudes above the trenches.

Vertical plane: It is a plane containing a vertical line.

Vertical revolution in agriculture: Maximizing production per unit land area per unit of time using intensive cropping systems, high production inputs and improved management practices.

Vertisols: Clayey soils (>30% clay) characterised by high shrink-swell potential, having wide, deep cracks when dry. Most of the soils have clear dry and wet periods in the year. Good for crop production with fine texture which are plastic and sticky when wet and hard when dry. Difficult to manage due to very little time for their proper preparation by tilling good for the production of cotton, millet, sorghum, wheat, paddy, etc.

Virgin forest: Mature or over mature forest, uninterfered by human activity.

Virgin material: Refers to raw materials which have never been processed in a manufacturing system, usually requiring more energy to produce than when substituted for by recyclable materials.

Void ratio: The ratio of the volume of soil pore (or void) space to the solid-particle volume.

Void space: The space between the particles in a bulk of stored grain, usually expressed as per cent of total volume.

Volatilization: Refers to the conversion of substance to gaseous form.

Volumetric water content: The soil-water content expressed as the volume of water per unit bulk volume of soil.

W

Wage: The money paid periodically to the labours for the work done in the field.

Waste stream: A stream carrying total waste generated by all contributors (households, industry, government) in a particular area.

Waste: Any solid or liquid material, product, or combination of them that is intended to be treated or disposed of or that is intended to be stored and then treated or disposed. This does not include recyclables.

Wasteland: A miscellaneous land type which is not capable of producing materials or services of value.

Wastewater lagoon: A wastewater treatment plant that consists of one or more designed and constructed surface impoundments used for biological and physical treatment of wastewater, but does not include such a plant where it uses mechanical aeration.

Wastewater treatment: Any of the mechanical or chemical processes used to modify the quality of waste water in order to make it more compatible or acceptable to man and his environment.

Wastewater: A combination of liquid and water-carried pollutants from homes, businesses, industries, or farms; a mixture of water and dissolved or suspended solids.

Wastewater-treatment return flow: Water returned to the environment by wastewater-treatment facilities.

Water application efficiency: Water application efficiency is the measure of efficiency with which water delivered to the field is stored in the root zone. Water application efficiency = Water stored in the root X 100/Water delivered to the field.

Water application rate: The rate in cm depth or ha-cm/hr that irrigation water is applied to fields.

Water balance: The hydrological balance between rainfall plus irrigation to that of changes in soil moisture, evaporation, percolation and run-off. A procedure whereby water inputs and outputs are accounted for a given soil leaving a balance called the storage.

Water body: Any location where water flows or is present, whether or not the flow or the presence of water is continuous, intermittent, or occurs only during a flood. This includes, but is not limited to, wetlands and aquifers.

Water compaction: Water furnished by destruction of pore space owing to compaction of sediments.

Water conservation: Physical control, protection, management and use of water resources for optimum benefits for different segments of national economy like agriculture, grazing, forests, industry etc.

Water consumption: The complete removal of water from some type of source, like groundwater, for some use by humans. This water is not returned to the source. Compare with water withdrawal.

Water content: Water contained in a material expressed as the mass of water per unit mass of oven-dry material.

Water control: To control the amount and depth of water in the rice field during the required time necessary for crop growth.

Water conveyance efficiency: It is the proportion of water delivered to the irrigated field from the total water diverted from the source. It estimates the conveyance losses. It is expressed as $E_c = W_f \text{ X } 100/W_s$. Where, E_c = Water conveyance efficiency (percent), W_f = Water delivered at the field, W_s = Water delivered at the source.

Water culture: An experimental means of determining the mineral nutrient requirement of a plant; the plant is grown with its roots dipping in solution of known composition.

Water cushion: Pool of water meant for absorbing impact of water flowing from an over fall structure.

Water cycle: The process by which water is transpired and evaporated from the land and water, condensed in the clouds, and precipitated out onto the earth once again to replenish the water in the bodies of water on the earth.

Water deficit: Refers to the shortage of water or inadequate water supply. The amount of water needed to return the soil-moisture status to the field capacity (FC).

Water distribution efficiency: Water distribution efficiency is defined as the percentage of difference from unity of the ratio between the average numerical deviations from the average depth stored during the irrigation. It indicates uniformity in distribution of water over the entire root zone. Water distribution efficiency = {1-Y/d} X 100 Where, d = Average depth of precipitation along the run off during irrigation and Y = Average numerical deviation from –d.

Water harvesting catchment: It is the area for collecting and storing precipitation. Basic components of the catchment consist of an apron to collect water, a conveyance system and a storage basin.

Water harvesting: The capture and use of runoff from rainfall and other precipitation Conservation of rain water under unirrigated condition, by collecting run-off of precipitation in order to supplement soil moisture in an adjacent area. (eg: the collection of rainwater in cisterns)

Water holding capacity: The weight of water held by a given quantity of absolutely dry soil when saturated. Of a soil, the amount of water that it is capable of holding, between field capacity and permanent wilting point.

Water in motion: Refers to water flowing in rivers, canal, pipelines, field channels. it is expressed in rate of flow such as liters per second, liters per hour, cubic meters per second, hectare centimeter per hr and hectare – meter per day.

Water management plan: A document developed under the Water Act that provides broad guidance regarding water conservation and management, sets clear and strategic directions regarding how water should be managed, or results in specified actions.

Water meter: A device that measures the quantity of water used at a house, business, factory, etc.

Water penetration: Depth to which irrigation water or rain water penetrates the soil before its movement becomes negligible.

Water pollution: Addition of objectionable materials in water in quantities sufficient to adversely affect its quality.

Water potential: The free-energy status of water. The capability of soil water to do work compared with free-water. The water potential at the surface of free-water is taken as zero.

Water productivity: The amount of water that is required to produce a unit of any good, service, or societal value.

Water quality indicators: Constituents or characteristics of water that can be measured to determine its suitability for use.

Water quality standard: The allowable contaminant concentration in a water supply that is enforceable under environmental control laws set by government. Water quality standards are site-specific. For example, the quality of an industrial effluent that is emptied into a body of water must maintain a certain standard so that it does not significantly change the receiving water body's quality.

Water quality: The chemical, microbiological, and physical characteristics of water. It refers to the characteristics of a water supply that will influence its suitability for a specific use, like for irrigation of crops; usually the emphasis is placed on the chemical and physical characteristics of the water.

Water regimes: Regime means level; different levels of water (standing or flooding) depth applied in irrigation experiments. Such as 2.5, 5, 7.5, 10 cm etc. standing water to saturation or field capacity (FC) to rice crop etc.

Water requirement of crops: It is that quantity of water regardless of its source, required by a crop in a given period of time for its maturity, and it includes losses due to ET plus the unavoidable losses during application of irrigation water and water required for special operations such as land preparation, puddling, leaching etc. and is expressed in depth for given time. Water requirement (WR) is therefore, demand and the supply would consist of contribution from irrigation, effective rainfall and soil profile contribution including that from shallow water tables (S). WR = IR + ER + S

Water retention curve: Graph showing soil-water content as a function of increasingly negative soil water potential.

Water retention: A property of soil that results from the attraction of the soil matrix for water.

Water reuse: Any beneficial use of the treated *wastewater* directed to a specific purpose other than the general release to the surface or subsurface environments.

Water short area: A region where natural conditions or development pressures limit the availability of surface water and ground water for future sustainable development and protection of the aquatic environment.

Water spreading: The practice of diverting small portions of flood waters by diversion ditches and dykes on range lands and spreading them in a free manner.

Water stable aggregate: A soil aggregate which is stable under the beating action of ram drops or during agitation for wet sieve analysis.

Water storage efficiency: This parameter estimates whether the amount of water necessary for the crop is stored in the root zone or not. It is expressed as the percentage of water needed in the root zone prior to irrigation to that stored in the root zone during irrigation. Water storage efficiency = Water stored in the root zone X 100/Water needed in the root zone.

Water table perched: Surface of a local zone of saturation perched above the main body of ground water on account of the presence of an impermeable stratum like clay, separated from the ground-water by an unsaturated zone.

Water table: The upper surface of the zone of saturation is called the water table. At the water table, the water in the pores of the aquifer is at atmospheric pressure. The hydraulic pressure at any level within a water table aquifer is equal to the depth from the water table to the point and is referred to as the hydraulic head.

Water use efficiency (WUE): Water use efficiency is defined as yield of marketable crop produced per unit of water used in evapotranspiration. WUE = Y/ET Where, WUE = Water use efficiency (kg/ha/mm of water), Y = marketable yield (kg/ha), ET= Evapotranspiration (mm).

Water use ratio: The ratio of the weight of water actually transpired by a crop during its growing season to the weight of dry matter produced.

Water use: Water that is used for a specific purpose by an activity or organism, either in the place it is found or by withdrawing it.

Water withdrawal: The removal of water from some type of source, like groundwater.

Water yield: It is the total annual run-off volume from an area.

Water: Water is a molecule consisting of two hydrogen atom and one oxygen atom (H_2O). Water covers three-fourths of the Earth's surface, 60-70% of the world's weight, regenerates and redistributes through evaporation and other atmospheric processes.

Watercourse: The bed and shore of a river, stream, lake, creek, lagoon, swamp, marsh or other natural body of water, or a canal, ditch, reservoir or other artificial surface feature made by humans, whether it contains or conveys water continuously or intermittently.

Waterlogged: Saturated with water.

Watershed (Drainage Basin): An area of land and water that drains runoff to a stream or other surface water body.

Watershed approach: An integrated approach that focuses efforts within a watershed, taking into consideration both ground and surface water flow. This approach recognizes and plans for the interaction of land, water, plants, animals, and people. Focusing efforts at the watershed level gives the local watershed community a comprehensive understanding of local management needs and encourages locally led management decisions.

Watershed area: Land and water within the confines of a drainage divide.

Watershed based farming system: It involves the optimum utilization of the catchment precipitation through improved water, soil and crop management directly through infiltration of monsoon rainfall after run-off collection and storage or after deep percolation recovery from well for the improvement and stabilization of agriculture on the watershed.

Watershed degradation: A marked deterioration in the hydrological behaviour of a river system which reduces the potential of land and water by causing a water flow of inferior quality, quantity and timing.

Watershed lag: Time interval between centre of mass of effective rainfall and peak of hydrograph.

Watershed management planning: (Watershed management plan) A comprehensive, multi-resource management planning process involving all stakeholders within the watershed, who, together as a group, cooperatively work toward identifying the watershed's resource issues and concerns as well as develop and implement a watershed plan with solutions that are environmentally, socially and economically sustainable.

Watershed management: Utilization, regulation and treatment of land and water resources of a watershed to meet specified objectives of protection and conservation of water and aquatic ecosystems, including their associated riparian area. Watershed management plans require water and land use managers to work together to ensure healthy watersheds.

Watershed planning: Formulation of a plan for the use and treatment of land and water resources of a watershed.

Watershed protection and flood prevention: Land treatment or soil conservation practices including structural measures for improvement of infiltration and reduction of erosion as well as floods in a watershed.

Watershed treatment: Include all practices applied to the land that are effective in reducing flood runoff, controlling erosion, and increasing the amount of surface storage, rate of infiltration and water holding capacity of the soil.

Watershed: The total area from which a single river collects surface water runoff; the catchment or drainage area of a river system. It is the area above a given point on a stream that contributes water to the flow at that point. Catchment basin and drainage basin are synonymous with it.

Waterway: A natural or constructed channel for the flow of water.

Weathering: A soil forming process involving the disintegration or decomposition of rocks and minerals through physical and chemical processes due to exposure to surface temperatures and pressure, air, water, wind and biological activity.

Weep holes (engineering): Openings left in retaining walls, linings, aprons etc. to facilitate drainage and reduce hydrostatic pressure on these structures.

Weir (engineering): Device for measurement or regulation of water flow.

Weir crest: Bottom of weir notch.

Weir notch (engineering): Opening in weir for passage of water.

Weir pond: Portion of channel immediately upstream from the weir.

Weir scale or gauge: The scale fastened on the side of weir pond to measure the head on weir crest.

Weir: A structure in a water body over which water flows, and whose prime purpose is to raise the water level, usually to divert water into a watercourse. Weirs are used to measure the flow of runoff; an irrigation channel or discharge of a well or channel outlet at the source.

Well (water): An artificial excavation put down by any method for the purposes of withdrawing water from the underground aquifers.

Wet bulb temperature: Temperature recorded on a thermometer whose bulb is surrounded by a wet muslin bag, thus lowering the temperature by loss of latent heat through evaporation degree Celsius.

Wet density: Ratio of the wet mass of soil to the bulk volume of soil.

Wetland: Refers to land that is saturated with water or submerged, at least during most of the growing season; wetlands generally include swamps, marshes and bogs

Wetted perimeter: Length of contact between a liquid and its containing conduit, measured perpendicular to the direction of flow.

Whole farm analysis: A methodology designed to identify optimal solution through incorporation of farmers' objectives, farming systems, and resources to arrive at improved cropping and livestock patterns and management practices for overall farming systems performance.

Whole farm approach: An essential characteristic of farming systems research and development in which whole farm is considered as a unit to identify problems, opportunities, and interrelationships, to design and conduct experiments, and to evaluate results.

Wild flooding: Water is released at high points in the field Water distribution is uncontrolled.

Wilting point: Water content of a soil when indicator plants growing in that soil wilt and fail to recover when placed in a humid chamber. It is soil-moisture condition at which the release of water to the plant roots is reduced to levels to counterbalance the transpiration losses. On an oven-dry basis it is the moisture content of soil at which plants wilt and fail to recover their turgidity when placed in a dark humid atmosphere. It is also called wilting coefficient or permanent wilting point. It is approximately equal to soil moisture content at 15-bar tension.

Wind break (shelter belts): A strip of trees or shrubs or crop plants serving to reduce the force of wind and provide a protective shelter against wind.

Wind erosion equation: An equation connecting wind erosion to various parameters E = f (IKCLV), Where E = average annual soil loss in tons per acre by wind, I = soil erodibility, K = soil ridge roughness, C = climatic factor, L=unsheltered distance across the field in the direction of wind erosion and V = vegetative cover.

Wind erosion: The detachment, transportation, and deposition of soil by the action of wind.

Wind strip cropping: Growing of crops in narrow strips perpendicular to the direction of prevailing winds.

Wind vane: A mechanical device used to measure the direction of wind flow.

Wind: Air in motion is referred as wind, is best expressed in km/hr. It is measured by anemometer.

Windbreak: A barrier of trees or trees and shrubs or other vegetation grown adjacent to a farm and perpendicular or nearly so to prevailing wind direction in order to protect the crops homesteads etc. from hot or cold winds and wind erosion.

Windward: Upwind side or side directly influenced to the direction that the wind blows from.

Wing wall: Side walls of a structure which serve to prevent sloughing of banks and direct and confine over fall.

Wok phase: It is a phase in watershed management in which most of the developmental work especially engineering and construction work is executed in watershed.

Woodland: Any land used for growing trees and includes forest plantations, shelterbelts, and windbreaks. Hedgerows having forest trees and shrubs, wooded stream banks etc.

X

Xeric: A soil moisture regime typical of Mediterranean climates having moist cool winters and warm dry summers. Irrigation or summer fallow is generally essential for crop production.

Xeriscaping: A method of landscaping that uses plants that are well adapted to the local area and are drought-resistant.

Xerophyte: Plant that can survive long periods of moisture deficiency.

Xylem: The woody portion of the conducting tissue in the plant specialized for the conduction of water and minerals. The supporting and water-conducting tissue of vascular plants; plant tissue consisting primarily of tracheids and vessels; woody tissue.

Y

Yellow podzolic soils: Soils with light to medium textured A_1 horizon over a pale A_2 horizon.

Yield components (yield attributes): The factors that contribute to grain yield. These are the components which finally make up or control yield of any crop, for example in cereal grain weight/grain, grain number/ear, ear number/plant and plant number/unit area.

Yield maximization: Agronomic practices adapted to get the highest possible crop production per unit area per unit time without considering the cost of input used for production or net return

Yield potential: Full production capability of a crop. The maximum grain yield of a given variety in a given environment without constraints involving water, nutrients, competition, pests, diseases, or climatic conditions.

Yield stability: The maintenance of yield at desired level over a period of time. Its index is measured by inverse of coefficient of variation, regression between yield and environmental index and disaster level estimated by probability of system.

Yield sustained: Continual annual or periodic yield from plants in an area through management practices which help to maintain productive capacity of the land.

Yield trials: Trials in which the main objective is to determine and compare the yields of a cultivar against a check.

Z

Zaid: A relatively short duration crop cultivated during April-June in between the two main seasons Rabi and Kharif.

Zero plane displacement: An empirically determined constant introduced into the logarithmic velocity profile to extend its applicability to very rough surfaces or to take in to account the displacement of a profile above a dense crop.

Zero tillage (no-till): Growing crops without cultivation of the soil, the extreme in conservation tillage is no-till (zero tillage) wherein the new crop is planted in the residue of the previous crop without any prior soil tillage or seed-bed preparation and is usually possible when all weeds are controlled by the use of herbicides.

Zingg bench terrace: Type of bench terrace suited for moisture conservation in dry land agriculture. It has an earthen embankment and. a part of the terrace interval immediately above the embankment is bench levelled. Run-off from the sloping area is collected and absorbed on the levelled area.

Zonal soil: A soil type that is defined largely on the basis of climatic belts, where the influence of such factors as parent material is less evident than the influence of climatic development processes.

Zone: An area or belt characterised by similar flora or fauna.

Zoned embankment: In this type of dam a highly impervious core (along central line) extends from above the waterline to an impermeable structure in foundation.

Appendices

List of ICAR Institutes

Deemed Universities - 4

1. Indian Agricultural Research Institute, New Delhi
2. National Dairy Research Institute, Karnal
3. Indian Veterinary Research Institute, Izatnagar
4. Central Institute on Fisheries Education, Mumbai

Institutions - 45

1. Central Rice Research Institute, Cuttack
2. Vivekananda Parvatiya Krishi Anusandhan Sansthan, Almora
3. Indian Institute of Pulses Research, Kanpur
4. Central Tobacco Research Institute, Rajahmundry
5. Indian Institute of Sugarcane Research, Lucknow
6. Sugarcane Breeding Institute, Coimbatore
7. Central Institute of Cotton Research, Nagpur
8. Central Research Institute for Jute and Allied Fibres, Barrackpore
9. Indian Grassland and Fodder Research Institute, Jhansi
10. Indian Institute of Horticultural Research, Bangalore
11. Central Institute of Sub Tropical Horticulture, Lucknow
12. Central Institute of Temperate Horticulture, Srinagar

13. Central Institute of Arid Horticulture, Bikaner
14. Indian Institute of Vegetable Research, Varanasi
15. Central Potato Research Institute, Shimla
16. Central Tuber Crops Research Institute, Trivandrum
17. Central Plantation Crops Research Institute, Kasargod
18. Central Agricultural Research Institute, Port Blair
19. Indian Institute of Spices Research, Calicut
20. Central Soil and Water Conservation Research & Training Institute, Dehradun
21. Indian Institute of Soil Sciences, Bhopal
22. Central Soil Salinity Research Institute, Karnal
23. ICAR Research Complex for Eastern Region including Centre of Makhana, Patna
24. Central Research Institute of Dryland Agriculture, Hyderabad
25. Central Arid Zone Research Institute, Jodhpur
26. ICAR Research Complex Goa
27. ICAR Research Complex for NEH Region, Barapani
28. National Institue of Abiotic Stress Management, Malegaon, Maharashtra
29. Central Institute of Agricultural Engineering, Bhopal
30. Central Institute on Post harvest Engineering and Technology, Ludhiana

31. Indian Institute of Natural Resins and Gums, Ranchi
32. Central Institute of Research on Cotton Technology, Mumbai
33. National Institute of Research on Jute & Allied Fibre Technology, Kolkata
34. Indian Agricultural Statistical Research Institute, New Delhi
35. Central Sheep and Wool Research Institute, Avikanagar, Rajasthan
36. Central Institute for Research on Goats, Makhdoom
37. Central Institute for Research on Buffaloes, Hissar
38. National Institute of Animal Nutrition and Physiology, Bangalore
39. Central Avian Research Institute, Izatnagar
40. Central Marine Fisheries Research Institute, Kochi
41. Central Institute Brackishwater Aquaculture, Chennai
42. Central Inland Fisheries Research Institute, Barrackpore
43. Central Institute of Fisheries Technology, Cochin
44. Central Institute of Freshwater Aquaculture, Bhubneshwar
45. National Academy of Agricultural Research & Management, Hyderabad

National Research Centres - 17

1. National Research Centre on Plant Biotechnology, New Delhi

2. National Centre for Integrated Pest Management, New Delhi
3. National Research Centre for Litchi, Muzaffarpur
4. National Research Centre for Citrus, Nagpur
5. National Research Centre for Grapes, Pune
6. National Research Centre for Banana, Trichi
7 National Research Centre Seed Spices, Ajmer
8. National Research Centre for Pomegranate, Solapur
9. National Research Centre on Orchids, Pakyong, Sikkim
10. National Research Centre Agroforestry, Jhansi
11. National Research Centre on Camel, Bikaner
12. National Research Centre on Equines, Hisar
13. National Research Centre on Meat, Hyderabad
14. National Research Centre on Pig, Guwahati
15. National Research Centre on Yak, West Kemang
16. National Research Centre on Mithun, Medziphema, Nagaland
17. National Centre for Agril. Economics & Policy Research, New Delhi

National Bureaux - 6

1. National Bureau of Plant Genetics Resources, New Delhi
2. National Bureau of Agriculturally Important Micro-organisms, Mau, Pradesh

3. National Bureau of Agriculturally Important Insects, Bangalore
4. National Bureau of Soil Survey and Land Use Planning, Nagpur
5. National Bureau of Animal Genetic Resources, Karnal
6. National Bureau of Fish Genetic Resources, Lucknow

Directorates/Project Directorates - 25

1. Directorate of Maize Research, New Delhi.
2. Directorate of Rice Research, Hyderabad
3. Directorate of Wheat Research, Karnal
4. Directorate of Oilseed Research, Hyderabad
5. Directorate of Seed Research, Mau
6. Directorate of Sorghum Research, Hyderabad
7. Directorate of Groundnut Research, Junagarh
8. Directorate of Soybean Research, Indore
9. Directorate of Rapeseed & Mustard Research, Bharatpur
10. Directorate of Mushroom Research, Solan
11. Directorate on Onion and Garlic Research, Pune
12. Directorate of Cashew Research, Puttur
13. Directorate of Oil Palm Research, Pedavegi, West Godawari
14. Directorate of Medicinal and Aromatic Plants Research, Anand

15. Directorate of Floriculture Research, Pusa, New Delhi
16. Project Directorate for Farming Systems Research, Modipuram
17. Directorate of Water Management Research, Bhubaneshwar
18. Directorate of Weed Science Research, Jabalpur
19. Project Directorate on Cattle, Meerut
20. Project Directorate on Foot & Mouth Disease, Mukteshwar
21. Project Directorate on Poultry, Hyderabad
22. Project Directorate on Animal Disease Monitoring and Surveillance, Hebbal, Bangalore
23. Directorate of Information & Publication in Agriculture (DIPA), New Delhi
24. Directorate of Cold Water Fisheries Research, Bhimtal, Nainital
25. Directorate of Research on Women in Agriculture, Bhubaneshwar

All India Coordinated Research Projects - 61

1. AICRP on Pesticides Residues, New Delhi
2. AICRP on Nematodes, New Delhi
3. AICRP on Maize, New Delhi
4. AICRP Rice, Hyderabad
5. AICRP on Chickpea, Kanpur
6. AICRP on MULLARP, Kanpur
7. AICRP on Pigeon Pea, Kanpur
8. AICRP on Arid Legumes, Jodhpur

9. AICRP on Wheat & Barley Improvement Project, Karnal
10. AICRP Sorghum, Hyderabad
11. AICRP on Pearl Millets, Jodhpur
12. AICRP on Small Millets, Bangalore
13. AICRP on Sugarcane, Lucknow
14. AICRP on Cotton, Coimbatore
15. AICRP on Groundnut, Junagarh
16. AICRP on Soybean, Indore
17. AICRP on Rapeseed & Mustard, Bharatpur
18. AICRP on Sunflower, Safflower, Castor, Hyderabad
19. AICRP on Linseed, Kanpur
20. AICRP on Sesame and Niger, Jabalpur
21. AICRP on Biological Control, Bangalore
22. AICRP on Honey Bee Research & Training, Hisar
23. AICRP -NSP(Crops), Mau
24. AICRP on Forage Crops, Jhansi
25. AICRP Tropical Fruits, Bangalore
26. AICRP Sub Tropical Fruits, Lucknow
27. AICRP Arid Zone Fruits, Bikaner
28. AICRP Mushroom, Solan
29. AICRP Vegetables including NSP vegetable, Varanasi
30. AICRP Potato, Shimla
31. AICRP Tuber Crops, Thiruvananthapuram
32. AICRP Palms, Kasaragod

33. AICRP Cashew, Puttur
34. AICRP Spices, Calicut
35. AICRP on Medicinal and Aromatic Plants including Betelvine, Anand
36. AICRP on Floriculture, New Delhi
37. AICRP in Micro Secondary & Pollutant Elements in Soils and Plants, Bhopal
38. AICRP on Soil Test with Crop Response, Bhopal
39. AICRP on Long Term Fertilizer Experiments, Bhopal
40. AICRP on Salt Affected Soils & Use of Saline Water in Agriculture, Karnal
41. AICRP on Water Management Research, Bhubaneshwar
42. AICRP on Ground Water Utilisation, Bhubaneshwar
43. AICRP Dryland Agriculture, Hyderabad
44. AICRP on Agrometeorology, Hyderabad including Network on Impact adaptation & Vulnerability of Indian Agri. to Climate Change
45. AICRP Integrated Farming System Research, Modipuram including Network Organic Farming
46. AICRP Weed Control, Jabalpur
47. AICRP on Agroforestry, Jhansi
48. AICRP on FIM, Bhopal
49. All India Coordinated Research Project on Ergonomics and Safety in Agriculture

50. AICRP on Renewable Sources of Energy for Ag.and Agro Based Indus.,Bhopal
51. AICRP on Utilization of Animal Energy (UAE), Bhopal
52. AICRP on Application of Plastic in Agriculture, Ludhiana
53. AICRP on PHT, Ludhiana
54. AICRP on Goat Improvement, Mathura
55. AICRP- Improvement of Feed Sources & Nutrient Utilisation for raising animal production, Bangalore
56. AICRP on Cattle Research, Meerut
57. AICRP on Poultry, Hyderabad
58. AICRP-Pig, Izzatnagar
59. AICRP Foot and Mouth Disease, Mukteshwar
60. AICRP ADMAS, Bangalore
61. AICRP on Home Science, Bhubaneshwar

Network Projects - 17

1. All India Coordinated Research Network on Underutilized Crops, New Delhi
2. All India Network Project on Tobacco, Rajahmundry
3. Network Project on White Grubs & Other Soil Arthropods, Durgapura
4. Network on Agricultural Acarology, Bangalore
5. Network on Economic Ornithology, Hyderabad
6. All India Network Project on Rodent Control, Jodhpur

7. All India Network Project on Jute and Allied Fibres, Barrackpore
8. Network project on Improvement of Onion & Garlic, Pune
9. Network Bio-fertilizers, Bhopal
10. Network Project on Harvest & Post Harvest and Value Addition to Natural Resins & Gums, Ranchi
11. Network project on Animal Genetic Resources, Karnal
12. Network Project on R&D Support for Process Upgradation of Indigenous Milk products for industrial application Karnal
13. Network Programme on Sheep Improvement, Avikanagar
14. Network Project on Buffaloes Improvement, Hisar
15. Network on Gastro Intestinal Parasitism, Izatnagar
16. Network on Haemorrhagic Septicaemia, Izatnagar
17. Network Programme Blue Tongue Disease, Izatnagar

Other Projects - 10

1. Technology Mission on Cotton (CICR, Nagpur)
2. Technology Mission on Jute (CRIJAF, Barrackpore)
3. Continuation, Strengthening and Establishment of Krishi Vigyan Kendras
4. Strengthening & Development of Higher Agricultural Education in India, New Delhi
5. Central Agricultutral University, Imphal

6. Strengthening and Modernization of ICAR Headquarters
7. Intellectual Property Management & Transfer/ Commercialisation of Agricultural Technology (Upscaling of existing component IPR HQ)
8. Indo US Knowledge Initiative
9. National Agricultural Innovative Project, New Delhi
10. National Fund for Basic and Strategic Research, New Delhi

Krishi Vigyan Kendras	**No.of KVKs**
Zone I – 62 KVKs	
1. Delhi	1
2. Haryana	18
3. Himachal Pradesh	12
4. Jammu and Kashmir	14
5. Punjab	17
Zone II – 77 KVKs	
1. A & N Islands	1
2. Bihar	38
3. Jharkhand	21
4. West Bengal	17
Zone III – 70 KVKs	
1. Assam	20
2. Arunachal Pradesh	12

3. Manipur	9
4. Meghalaya	5
5. Mizoram	8
6. Nagaland	8
7. Sikkim	4
8. Tripura	4
Zone IV – 79 KVKs	
1. Uttar Pradesh	66
2. Uttaranchal	13
Zone V – 55 KVKs	
1. Andhra Pradesh	22
2. Maharashtra	33
Zone VI - 57 KVKs	
1. Rajasthan	32
2. Gujarat	25
Zone VII – 93 KVKs	
1. Chattisgarh	16
2. Madhya Pradesh	47
3. Orissa	30
Zone VII – 76 KVKs	
1. Karnataka	27
2. Tamil Nadu	30
3. Kerala	14
4. Goa	2
5. Pondicherry	2
6. Lakshadweep	1

AGRICULTURAL UNIVERSITIES IN INDIA

Sl.No.	*Name, E-mail & Website*	*Address*
1.	**Acharya NG Ranga Agricultural University** **Website:** http://www.angrau.net **E-mail:** angrau_vc@yahoo.com, raghuvardhanreddy_s@rediffmail.com	Adminstrative Office, Rajendra Nagar, Hyderabad-500030, Andhra Pradesh
2.	**Anand Agricultural University** **Website:** http://www.aau.in **E-mail:** vc@aau.in, vc_aau@yahoo.com	Anand 388110, Gujarat
3.	**Assam Agricultural University** **Website:** http://www.aau.ac.in **E-mail:** vc@aau.ac.in, ssb@aau.ac.in	Jorhat 785013, Assam
4.	**Bidhan Chandra Krishi Viswavidyalaya** **Website:** http://www.bckv.edu.in **E-mail:** vcbckv@vsnl.net	Mohanpur, Nadia-741252, West Bengal
5.	**Birsa Agricultural University** **Website:** http://www.baujharkhand.org **E-mail:** vc_bau@rediffmail.com	Kanke, Ranchi-834006, Jharkhand

Sl.No.	Name, E-mail & Website	Address
6.	**Central Agricultural University** **E-mail:** snpuri04@yahoo.co.in, snpuri@rediffmail.com	P.O. Box 23, Imphal-795004, Manipur
7.	**Chandra Shekar Azad University of Agriculture & Technology** **Website:** http://www.csauk.ac.in **E-mail:** vc@csauk.ac.in, surivkgreatmaster@yahoo.com	Kanpur-208002, Uttar Pradesh
8.	**Chaudhary Charan Singh Haryana Agricultural University** **E-mail:** vc@hau.ernet.in	Hisar-125004, Haryana
9.	**CSK Himachal Pradesh Krishi Vishvavidyalaya** **Website:** http://www.hillagric.ernet.in **E-mail:** vc@hillagric.ernet.in	Palampur-176062, Himachal Pradesh
10.	**Dr Balasaheb Sawant Konkan Krishi Vidyapeeth** **Website:** www.dbskkv.org **E-mail:** vcbskkv@yahoo.co.in	Dapoli Distt, Ratnagiri - 415 712, Maharashtra

Sl.No.	Name, E-mail & Website	Address
11.	**Dr Panjabrao Deshmukh Krishi Vidyapeeth** **Website:** http://www.pdkv.mah.nic.in **E-mail:** vc@pdkv.mah.nic.in	Krishinagar, Akola-444104, Maharashtra
12.	**Dr Yashwant Singh Parmar Univ of Horticulture & Forestry** **Website:** http://www.yspuniversity.ac.in **E-mail:** vc@yspuniversity.ac.in, vcuhf@yahoo.com	Solan, Nauni-173230, Himachal Pradesh
13.	**Govind Ballabh Pant University of Agriculture & Technology** **Website:** http://www.gbpuat.ac.in **E-mail:** pl_gautam@yahoo.com, vc@gbpuat.ernet.in	Pantnagar-263145, Distt Udham Singh, Nagar, Uttaranchal
14.	**Guru Angad Dev Veterinary and Animal Science University**	Ludhiana - 141004, Punjab
15.	**Indira Gandhi Krishi Vishwavidyalaya** **Website:** www.igau.edu.in **E-mail:** hazracr@yahoo.co.in	Krishak Nagar, Raipur-492012, Chhattisgarh

Sl.No.	Name, E-mail & Website	Address
16.	**Jawaharlal Nehru Krishi Viswavidyalaya** **Website:** http://www.jnkvv.nic.in	Jabalpur-482004, Madhya Pradesh
17.	**Junagadh Agricultural University** **Website:** http://www.jau.in **E-mail:** vc@jau.in	Junagadh-362001, Gujarat
18.	**Kerala Agricultural University** **Website:** http://www.kau.edu **E-mail:** vckau@sancharnet.in	Vellanikara, Trichur 680656, Kerala
19.	**Maharana Pratap Univ. of Agriculture & Technology** **Website:** http://www.mpuat.ac.in **E-mail:** vc@mpuat.ac.in, vcmpuat@yahoo.co.in	Udaipur, Rajasthan 313001
20.	**Maharashtra Animal Science & Fishery University** **Website:** http://www.mafsu.in **E-mail:** atsherikar@hotmail.com, mafsul@hotmail.com	Seminary Hills, Nagpur-440006, Maharashtra

Sl.No.	Name, E-mail & Website	Address
21.	**Mahatma Phule Krishi Vidyapeeth** **Website:** http://mpkv.mah.nic.in **E-mail:** vc.mpkv@nic.in	Rahuri-413722, Maharashtra
22.	**Marathwada Agricultural University** **Website:** http://www.mkv2.mah.nic.in **E-mail:** vcmau@rediffmail.com, vc@mkv2.g8.net	Parbhani-431402, Maharashtra
23.	**Narendra Deva University of Agriculture & Technology** **E-mail:** nduat@up.nic.in, smilyas@sify.com	Kumarganj, Faizabad -224229, Uttar Pradesh
24.	**Navsari Agricultural University** **Website:** http://www.nau.in **E-mail:** vc_2004@yahoo.co.in	Navsari-396450 Gujarat
25.	**Orissa Univ. of Agriculture & Technology** **Website:** http://www.ouat.ac.in **E-mail:** vcouat@indiatimes.com, bsenapati1942@yahoo.com	Bhubaneshwar-751003, Orissa

Sl.No.	Name, E-mail & Website	Address
26.	**Punjab Agricultural University** **Website:** http://www.pau.edu **E-mail:** vcpau@pau.edu	Ludhiana-141004, Punjab
27.	**Rajasthan Agricultural University** **Website:** http://www.raubikaner.org **E-mail:** vcrau@raubikaner.org	Bikaner-334006,Rajasthan
28.	**Rajendra Agricultural University** **Website:** http://www.pusavarsity.org.in **E-mail:** : vcrau@sify.com	Pusa, Samastipur 848125, Bihar
29.	**Sardarkrushinagar-Dantiwada Agricultural University** **Website:** http://www.sdau.edu.in **E-mail:** vc@sdau.edu.in	Sardar Krushinagar, Distt Banaskantha, Gujarat-385506
30.	**Sardar Ballabh Bhai Patel Univ. of Agriculture & Technology** **Website:** http://www.svbpuniversitymerut.org **E-mail:** yadav_mp@hotmail.com	Modipuram, Meerut - 250110, Uttar Pradesh

Sl.No.	Name, E-mail & Website	Address
31.	**Sher-E-Kashmir Univ of Agricultural Sciences & Technology**	Railway Road, Jammu 180012, J&K
32.	**Sher-E-Kashmir Univ of Agricultural Sciences & Technology of Kashmir** **Website:** http://www.skuastkashmir.ac.in **E-mail:** anwar_alam@jk.nic.in, vcskuastk@jk.nic.in	Shalimar Campus, Shrinagar-191121, Jammu & Kashmir
33.	**Sri Venkateswara Veterinary University**	Administration Office, Regional Library Building, Tirupati-517502
34.	**Tamil Nadu Agricultural University** **Website:** http://www.tnau.ac.in **E-mail:** vc@tnau.ac.in	Coimbatore-641003, Tamil Nadu
35.	**Tamil Nadu Veterinary & Animal Science University** **Website:** http://www.tanuvas.tn.nic.in **E-mail:** vctanuvas@vsnl.com	Chennai-600051, Tamilnadu

Sl.No.	Name, E-mail & Website	Address
36.	**University of Agricultural Sciences, Bangalore** **Website:** http://uasbng.kar.nic.in **E-mail:** mnsheelavantar@yahoo.co.in, uas-vc@uasblr.kar.nic.in	GKVK,Bangalore-560065, Karnataka
37.	**University of Agricultural Sciences, Dharwad** **Website:** http://www.uasd.edu **E-mail:** jhkulkarni@yahoo.co.in	Dharwad-580005, Karnataka
38.	**UP Pandit Deen Dayal Upadhaya Pashu Chikitsa Vigyan Vishwa Vidhyalaya evam Go Anusandhan Sansthan** **Website:** http://www.upvetuniv.edu.in **E-mail:** mlmadan@hotmail.com	Mathura-281001, Uttar Pradesh
39.	**Uttar Banga Krishi Viswavidyalaya**	P.O. Pundibari, Dist. Coach Bihar-736165,West Bengal
40.	**West Bengal University of Animal & Fishery Sciences** **E-mail:** wbuafs@wb.nic.in	68 KB Sarani, Kolkata-700037, West Bengal

Sl.No.	Name, E-mail & Website	Address
41.	**Karnataka Veterinary, Animal and Fisheries Sciences University** **Website:** http://www.kvafsu.kar.nic.in http://www.kvafsu.edu.in **E-mail:** vckvafsu@yahoo.co.in dekvafsub@yahoo.com	Nandinagar, PB No 6, Bidar-585401, Karnataka
42.	**University of Agricultural Sciences** **Website:** http://www.uasraichur.edu.in **E-mail:** souasr09@redifffmail.com vcuasraichur10@rediffmail.com	Lingasugur Road, Raichur – 58 Karnataka
43.	**University of Horticultural Sciences** **Website:** http://www.bagalkot.nic.in	Sector No 60 Navanagar Bagalkot 587102 Karnataka
44.	**Andhra Pradesh Horticultural University** **Website:** http://www.aphu.edu.in **E-mail:** vcaphu@gmail.com	DCC Bank Buildings, PB No 7 Tadepalligudem 534101 West Godavari District, Andhra Pradesh

Sl.No.	*Name, E-mail & Website*	*Address*
45.	**Rajmata Vijayraje Sciendia Krishi Vishwa Vidyalaya** **Website:** http://www.rvskvv.nic.in **E-mail:** vcrvskvv@gmail.com	Race Cource Road, Gwalior 474002 Madhya Pradesh

ACRONYMS

International

AARRO- Afro-Asian Rural Reconstruction Organization

ACIAR- Australian Centre for International Agricultural Research

AFRC- Agricultural Food Research C~uncil, UK

AGRIS- International Information System for Agricultural Sciences and Technology

ARC- Africa Rice Center Cotonou, Benin

AVRDC- Asian Vegetable Research and Development Centre, Taiwan.

CAB (I)- Commonwealth Agricultural Bureaux (International since 1986)

CFTC- Commonwealth Fund for Technical Co-operation

CGIAR- Consultative Group of International Agricultural Research, Washington (USA)

CIAT- Centro Internacional de Agricultura Tropical (International Center for Tropical Agriculture) Coli-Columbia (South America)

CIDA- Canadian International Development Agency, Cubac

CIFOR - Center for International Forestry Research, Indonesia

CIMMYT- Centro International de Mejorimiento de Maizy Trigo (International Centre for the Improvement of Maize and Wheat), Mexico

CIP- Centro International de la Papa (Intemational Potato Centre), Peru (South America)

ENSA- Ecole National Superieur Agronomique

ESCAP- Economic and Social Commission for Asia and Pacific

FAO- Food and Agricultural Organization of the United Nations, Rome (Italy)

IARC(s)- International Agricultural Research Centre (s)

IBGE- Institute Brasiliero de Geografia e Estadistica (Brazil)

IBPGR- International Board for Plant Genetic resources, Rome, Italy.

IBRD- International Bank for Reconstruction and Development (The World Bank), Washington, D.C. (U.S.A.).

IBSNAT- International Benchmark Soils Network for Agrotechnology Transfer, Hawai

ICARDA- International Center for Agricultural Research in the Dry Areas, Aleppo, Syria

ICIMOD- International Center for Integrated Mountain Development, Nepal

ICIPE- International Center for Insect Physiology and Ecology, Kenya.

ICITV- Institute de la Carte Internationale du Tpis vegetable

ICRAF- International Council for Research in Agroforestry, Nairobi, Kenya

ICRISAT- International Crops Research Institute for the Semi-Arid Tropics, Patancheru, A.P. (India)

ICSU- International Council of Scientific Unions

IDRC- International Development Research Centre, Canada

IFAD- International Fund for Agricultural Development, Cubac, Rome

IFDC- International Fertilizer Development Centre, Muscale Shoals, Alabama (USA)

IFPRI- International Food Policy Research Institute, Washington DC (USA)

IIASA- International Institute for Applied Systems Analysis, Luxemberg, Vienna, Austria

IIMI- Internatinal Irrigation Management Institute, Digana Village, Srilanka.

IITA- International Institute of Tropical Agriculture Ibadan, Oyo State, Nigeria

IJO- International Jute Organization

ILCA- International Livestock Centre for Africa, Addis Ababa, Ethiopia.

ILRAD- International Laboratory for Research on Animal Diseases, Nairobi, Kenya.

ILRI - International Livestock Research Institute Nairobi, Kenya

INRA- Institute Nacionale de la Recherche agronomique

INSFFER- International Network on Soil Fertility and Fertilizer Evaluation on Rice (IRRI)

IRDC- International Research and Development Council

IRRI- International Rice Research Institute, Manila, Philippines

IRTP- International Rice Testing Programme

ISNAR- International Service for National Agricultural, Research, The Hauge, Netherland.

ISRIC- International Soils Reference and Information Centre, Netherlands

ISSS- International Society of Soil Science

IUFRO- International Union of Forest Research Organizations

IWMI - International Water Management Institute Battaramulla, Sri Lanka.

LRDC- Land Resources Development Centre (UK)

SAARC- South Asian Association for Regional Co-operation

SAREC- Swedish Agency for Research Co-operation with Developing Countries

SIDA- Swedish International Development Agency

TPRI- Tropical Pesticides Research Institute, Arusha, Tanzania

UNDP- United Nations Development Proogramme

UNEP- United Nations Environment Programme

UNESCO- United Nations Educational, Scientific and Cultural Organization

UNFPA- United Nations Fund for population Activities

USAID- United States Agency for International Development

USNO- United Nations Sudana-Sahelian Office

WARDA- West African Rice Development Association, Monrovia, Liberia

WINROCK- Winrock International Institute for Agricultural Development, Canada

WMO- World Meteorological Organizatio, Geneva (Switzerland)

National

ARIC- Agricultural Research Information Centre

ATIC- Agricultural Technology Information Centre

BARC- Bhabha Atomic Reseaarch Centre, Trombay, Bombay

CARI- Central Avian Research Institute, Izatnagar, Uttar Pradesh 243 122

CARIANGI- Central Agricultural Research Institute for Andaman and Nocobar Groups of Islands, Port Blair, Andamans and Nicobar 744 101

CAZRI- Central Arid Zone Research Institute, Jodhpur, Rajasthan 342 003

CFTRI- Central Food Technological Research Institute, Mysore

CHES- Central Horticulture Experiment Station

CIAE- Central Institute of Agricultural Engineering, Bhopal, Madhya Pradesh 462 003

CIBA- Central Institute of Brackishwater Aquaculture, Madras, Tamil Naduu 500 028

CICFRI- Central Inland Capture Fisheries Research Institute, Barrackpore, West Bengal 743 101

CICR- Central Institute for Cotton Research, Nagpur, Maharashtra 440 001

CIFA- Central Institute of Freshwater Aquaculture, Bhubaneshwar, Orissa 751 002

CIFE- Central Institute of Fisheries Education, Bombay, Maharashtra 400 061

CIFRI- Central Inland Fisheries Research Institute

CIFT- Central Institute of Fisheries Technology, Willingdon Island, Cochin, Kerala 682 029

CIPET- Central Institute of Post-harvest Engineering and Technology, PAU, Ludhiana, Punjab 141004

CIHNP- Central Institute of Hoticulture for Northern Plains, B 217 Indira Nagar, Lucknow, Uttar Pradesh 226 016

CIMAP- Central Institute of Medicinal and Aromatic plants, Lucknow

CIRB- Central Institute for Ressearch on Buffaloes, Hisar, Haryana 125 001

CIRG- Central Institute for Research on Goats, Makhdoom, Farah, Uttar Pradesh 281122

CMFRI- Central Marine Fisheries Research Institute, Cochin, Kerala 682 018

CPCRI- Central Plantation Crops Research Institute, Kasargod, Kerala 671124

CPPTI- Central Plant Protection Training Institute,Hyderabad

CPRI- Central Potato Research Institute, Shimla, Himachal Pradesh 171 001

CRIDA- Central Research Institute for Dryland Agriculture, Hyderabad, Andhra Pradesh 500 659

CRIJAF- Central Research Institute for Jute and Allied Fibres, Barrackpore, West Bengal 743 101

CRRI- Central Rice Research Institute, Cuttack, Orissa 753 006

CSIR- Council of Scientific and Industrial Research, New Delhi.

CSSRI- Central Soil Salinity Research Institute, Karnal, Haryana 132 001

CSWCRTI- Central Soil and Water Conservation Research and Training mstitute, Dehradun, UK.

CSWRI- Central Sheep and Wool Research Institute, Avikanagar, Rajasthan 304 501

CTCRI- Central Tuber Crops Research mstitute, Trivandrum, Kerala 695 017

CTRI- Central Tobacco Research Institute, Rajahmundary, Andhra Pradesh 533 105

CTRL- Cotton Technological Research Laboratory, Matunga, Bombay, Maharashtra 400 019

DARE- Department of Agricultural Research and Education, New Delhi

FRI- Forest Research mstitute, Dehradun, U.K.

IARI- Indian Agricultural Ressearch Institute, New Delhi 110012

IASRI- Indian Agricultural Statistics Research Institute, New Delhi 100012

ICAR- Indian Council of Agricultural Research, New Delhi 110 001

IGFRI- Indian Grassland and Fodder Research Institute, Jhansi, Uttar Pradesh 284 003

IIAER- Indian Institute of Agricultural Economics Research

IIHR- Indian Institute of Horticultural Research, Bangalore, Kamataka 560 080

IIPR- Indian Institute of Pulses Research, Kalyanpur, Kanpur 208 024, Uttar Pradesh

IISR- Indian Institute of Sugarcane Research, Lucknow, Uttar Pradesh 226 002

IISS- Indian Institute of Soil Science, Bhopal, Madhya Pradesh 462 011

ILRI- Indian Lac Research Institute, Namkum, Ranchi, Bihar 834 010

ISI- Indian Statistical Institute, Culcutta.

IVRI- Indian Veterinary Research Institute, Izatnagar, Uttar Pradesh 243 122

JARI- Jute Agricultural Research Institute, Barrackpore, West Bengal743101

JTRL- Jute Technological Research Laboratory, Calcutta, West Bengal 700 040

KVK- Krishi Vigyan Kendra

LLP- Lab-to-Land Programme

MANAGE- National Institute of Agricultural Extension Management, Hyderabad

NAIP- National Agricultural Innovation project.

NATP- National Agricultural Technology project.

NBAGR- National Bureau of Animal Genetic Resources, Karnal, Haryana 132001

NBFGR- National Bureau of Fish Genetic Resources, Shivanagar, Allahabad, Uttar Pradesh 211 006

NBPGR- National Bureau of Plant Genetic Resources, New Delhi 110 012

NAARM- National Academy of Agricultural Research Management, Hyderabad, Andhra Pradesh 500 030

NABARD- National Bank for Agriculture and Rural Development

NAFED- National Agricultural Co-operative and Marketing Federation of India

NARP- National Agricultural Research Project

NBRI- National Botanical Research Institute, Lucknow, Uttar Pradesh

NBSS & LUP- National Bureau of Soil Survey and Land Use Planning, Nagpur, Maharashtra 440 006

NDRI- National Dairy Research Institute, Kamal, Haryana 132 001

NIAG- National Institute of Animal Genetics, Kamal Haryana 132 001,

PRII- Potash Research Institute of India, Gurgaon, Haryana

SBI- Sugarcane Breeding Institute, Coimbatore, TamilNadu 641 007

VPKAS- Vivekananda Parvatiya Krishi Anusandhan Shala, Almora, Uttar Pradesh 262 601

List of Important Publications of ICAR

Sl.No.	Title	Authors
1.	Acid Soils of India	I C Mahapatra, S C Mandal, C Mishra, G N Mitra and N Panda (Technical Editors)
2.	Advances in Kodo Millet Research	H S Yadava & A K Jain
3.	Advances in Pulse Production Technology	M L Jeswani and B Baldev
4.	Agricultural Entomology and Pest Control	S Pradhan
5.	Agril. Biotechnology in the ICAR Research Institutes	
6.	Commercial Fibre Crops and their Utilisation	Bhairab Chandra Mitra
7.	Cottonseed and its Utilization	S N Pandey
8.	Drainage Engineering	A K Bhattacharya
9.	50 Years of Crops Science Research in India	
10.	Forestry for People	S A Shah
11.	Farm Machinery Principles and Application	Surendra Singh

Sl.No.	*Title*	*Authors*
12.	Farm Machinery Maintenance and Management	Surendra Singh and S R Verma
13.	Housing and Space Management	S Renuka, Mahalakshmi V Reddy
14.	Irrigation of Field Crops	S S Parihar and B S Sandhu
15.	Odyssey of Sandal Wood Tree	S P Raychaudhuri
16.	Pearl millet and its Improvement	Khem Singh Gill
17.	Plant Genetic Resources in Indian Perspective: Theory and Practices	B P Singh and Umesh Srivastava
18.	Potential Appl. of Agroforestry Systems from Indian Subcontinent to the Analogous Ecozones of Africa	G B Singh
19.	Rising Atmospheric Carbon Dioxide and Crops	D C Uprety and V R Reddy
20.	Rust Resistance in Varieties of Wheat and Barley in India	L M Joshi and Sheodhan Singh
21.	Handbook of Agriculture	
22.	Soil and Water Conservation Research in India	V V Dhruva Narayana

Sl.No.	Title	Authors
23.	Technologies for Commercialization and Adoption	
24.	Textbook of Community Nutrition	Salil Sehgal & Rita S Raghuvanshi (Technical Editors)
25.	Textbook of Drainage Engineering	Ranbir Kumar and Joginder Singh (Technical Editors)
26.	Textbook of Family Approach in Extension Programme Management	Sunita Roy, Tej Verma and Pushpa Gupta (Technical Editors)
27.	Textbook of Fundamentals of Clothing Construction	Labanya Mazumdar and R Vatsala (Technical Editors)
28.	Textbook of Mycology	A K Sarbhoy
29.	Textbook of Textiles & Clothing	R Vatsala
30.	Textbook of Soil Science	R K Mehra
31.	Tobacco	N C Gopalachari
32.	Alternate Sources of Energy	N S Rathore, A N Mathur & S Kothari

Sl.No.	Title	Authors
	HORTICULTURE	
1.	CACTI Botany Culture and Uses	Supriya Kumar Bhattacharjee
2.	Citrus Fruits	S P Ghosh
3.	Exploitation of Hybrid Vigour in Vegetables	Harbhajan Singh, Vishnu Swarup & Brijendra Singh
4.	Genetics and Breeding of Vegetable	K V Petter & T Pradeep
5.	Gladiolus	A Mukhopadhyay
6.	Handbook of Rock Gardening on the Hills	P Kachroo & Priya Zarabi
7.	Minor Spices and Condiments Crop Management and Post-Harvest Technology	J S Pruthi
8.	Handbook of Horticulture (Under Revision)	
9.	Orchids	S K Mukherjee
10.	Ornamental Horticulture in India	K L Chadha & B Choudhury
11.	Pineapple	K L Chadha, B M C Reddy & S D Shikhamany

Sl.No.	Title	Authors
12.	Pineapple Leaf Fibres	S N Pandey
13.	Producing Seeds of Biennial Vegetables in Temperate Regions	T S Verma & S C Sharma
14.	Safed Musli	Satyabrata Maiti & K A Geetha
15.	The Grape in India	R M Pandey & S N Pandey
16.	The Rose in India	B P Pal
17.	The Strawberry	V P Sharma & R R Sharma
18.	Textbook of Temperate Fruits	T R Chadha
19.	Vegetables for the Tropical Region	Prem Nath, Sundhari Velayudhan & D P Singh
20.	Indoor Gardening	Vishnu Swarup
21.	Preservation of Fruits and Vegetables	Girdhari Lal, G S Siddappa & G L Tandon

Sl.No.	Title	Authors
	ANIMAL SCIENCE & FISHERIES	
1.	Aquahouse- New Dimension of Sustainable Aquaculturer	Rina Chakarabarti & Jai Gopal Sharma
2.	Animal Genetic Resources of India	A E Nivsarkar, P K Vij & M S Tantia
3.	Angora Rabbit	J M Mahajan
4.	Atlas of the Buffalo Anatomy	H P Singh & K S Roy
5.	Bluetongue	Gaya Prasad Minakshi & Yashpal Singh Malik
6.	Chronic Bovine Haematuria	H C joshi, Mahesh Kumar & D S T Rao
7.	Convenience Chicken Products–Simple Technologies for Small Scale Entrepreneurs	N kondaiah, A S R Anjaneyullu & B Panda
8.	Convenience Products from Fish	T K Srinivasan Gopal, C N Ravishak, A C joseaph & K G Ramachandran

Sl.No.	Title	Authors
9.	Environmental Pollution and Effects of Lead and Fluoride on Animal Health	D Swarup & S K Dwivedi
10.	Epidemiology, Diagnosis and Management of Zoonoses	K G Narayan
11.	Feeding of Poultry	B Panda, V R Reddy, V R Sadagopan & A K Shrivastav
12.	Fresh Water Fish Culture	V R P Sinha & V Ramchandran
13.	Genetic Concepts in Animal Breeding	H K B Parekh & P N Srivastava
14.	Handbook of Animal Husbandary	
15.	Indian Dairy Co-Operatives	Rattan Sagar Khanna
16.	Makhana	R K Mishra, Vidyanath Jha & P V Dehadrai
17.	Mithun	S C Gupta, Neelam Gupta & A E Nivsarkar
18.	Ovarian Biology in Buffaloes and Cattle	S S Guraya

Sl.No.	Title	Authors
19.	Poultry Production	R P Sharma, R N Chattargee, S V Bama Rao & S P Sharma
20.	Protozoa and Protozoan Diseases of Domestic Livestock	B B Bhatia & H L Shah
21.	Psyllidae of the Indian Subcontinent	R N Matur
22.	Report of the Working Party on Sardine and Mackerel Resources	
23.	Rinderpest	R P Bansal & B Rattan
24.	Stock Assessment of Tropical Marine Fishes	E Vivekanandan
25.	Principles of Animal Nutrition and Nutrient Dynamics	S P Arora & Harjit Kaur
26.	Swine Production	D P Sharda
27.	Reproductive Disorders in Indian Livestock	A Ramamohan Rao
28.	Techniques in Diagnostic Virology	R P Bansal

Sl.No.	Title	Authors
29.	Textbook of Clinical Veterinary Medicine	M C Sharma, Mahesh Kumar & R D Sharma
30.	Textbook of Fish Genetics and Biotechnology	P V G K Reddy, S Ayyappan, D M Thampy & Gopal Krishna
31.	Textbook of Fish Processing Technology	K Gopalkumar (Technical Editor)
32.	Textbook of Veterinary Protozoology	B B Bhatia
33.	Trypanosomes and Trypanosomiases of Indian Livestock	B Gill
34.	Veterinary and Medical Mycology	Mahendra Pal
35.	Veterinary Helminthology	Kr Suresh Singh
36.	Yak Production	A E Nivsarkar, S C Gupta & Neelam Gupta
37.	Text Book of Oyster Biology and Culture in India	K N Narasimham & V Kripa
38.	Handbook of Fisheries and Aquaculture	

ICAR Awards

Sardar Patel Outstanding ICAR Institution Award: Three awards of Rupees 5 lakh each to two ICAR Institutes and one State Agricultural University (SAU) is awarded annually for the best performance in agricultural research, extension and education.

Choudhary Devi Lal Outstanding All-India Coordinated Research Project Award: To recognize outstanding performance of an All-India Coordinated Research Project(AICRP) and its cooperating centres in terms of linkages, research output and its impact, and to promote a sense of partnership pride and belonging in the minds of the co-operators, the ICAR has instituted this annual award of Rupees 1 lakh.

Rafi Ahmed Kidwai Award: Awarded since 1956 for research work in agriculture, animal husbandry and allied sciences. Nine awards of Rupees 3 lakh each are given once on two years.

Fakhruddin Ali Ahmed Award for Tribal Areas: It encourages 'Agricultural Research in Tribal Areas'. Since 1977, the award of Rupees 50,000 is being given once in two years for outstanding research work done for the improvement of tribal farming systems.

Hari Om Ashram Trust Award: Instituted in 1972, recognizes published original research, fundamental or applied, in crop science, horticulture, resource management and animal science. The award carries 4 prizes of the value of Rupees 40,000 each and are awarded once in two years.

Jawaharlal Nehru Award: Distributed since 1969 among young scientists for excellence in Postgraduate Agricultural Research submitted for their doctorate degree as an incentive for high-quality fundamental or applied research among the post-graduate students in India. There are eighteen awards with a cash prize of Rupees 20,000 each with a Gold Medal given annually.

Vasantrao Naik Award: It has been started in 1994 for distribution annually based on published work of a scientist or an extension worker suggesting reforms in Water Conservation and Dryland Farming. This is an annual award of Rupees one lakh.

Lal Bahadur Shastri Young Scientist Award: This award has been instituted to promote high-quality research efforts in selected areas of agriculture and allied sciences and to provide recognition and incentives to promising young scientists for original research work. This is awarded once in two years. Each award consists of sanction of the proposed research scheme and a cash prize of Rupees 25,000.

Bharat Ratna Dr. C Subramaniam Outstanding Teacher Award: To provide incentive and encouragement for good teaching and to recognize outstanding teachers in the field of agriculture, eight national awards of Rupees 50,000 (enhanced from Rs. 25,000) each are given once in two years. This award was instituted in 1994-95.

Punjab Rao Deshmukh Woman Agricultural Scientist Award: An annual award, instituted in 1995 to encourage the woman scientists. Women-scientists working at the Institutions under the ICAR system, including State Agricultural Universities are eligible for this award. Two awards of Rupees 50,000 each are given to individual woman scientist.

Chaudhary Charan Singh Award for Excellence in Journalism in Agricultural Research and Development: In recognition of outstanding contributions in Journalism in Agriculture Research and Development in the Country, the ICAR has instituted an annual award of Rupees 1 lakh for the first time during year 2000. The award is given to an individual for his/ her significant contribution in writing/ analyzing/ reporting for promotion of Indian agriculture.

N.G. Ranga Farmer Award for Diversified Agriculture: In recognition of outstanding contributions in diversified agricultural activities, ICAR has instituted this annual award in the name of Prof. N. G. Ranga for the first time in 2001. The award is given to an individual practising new entrepreneurship/ enterprise/ management strategies for additional information to existing one in the field of diversified agriculture in India which will result in generating additional income to individual farmer/ farming community. This award carries Rupees 1 lakh.

Jagjivan Ram Kisan Puruskar: ICAR has instituted this annual award of Rupees 1 lakh to recognize the outstanding contribution and distinguished farming attributes of individual farmer in the area of Agricultural Productivity and Allied Activities.

Swamy Sahajanand Saraswati Extension Scientist / Worker Award: ICAR Instituted it in 1995 to be given away to the outstanding Extension Scientists/ Workers from the ICAR-SAU-NGO/ State Government Research Extension Network for their innovative research in developing extension education programmes, adopting extension methodologies and creating impact of the program on the farming community, especially to the downtrodden. Four awards of R. 25,000 along with a citation and a plaque are given away once in two years.

ICAR Award for Outstanding Multidisciplinary Team Research in Agriculture and Allied Sciences: To provide recognition to outstanding interdisciplinary team research in agriculture and allied sciences to promote the culture of interdisciplinary team effort in the solution of inherently interdisciplinary problem. Nine awards of Rupees 1 lakh each are given away to a team of scientists (normally restricted to eight members) once in two years.

National Krishi Vigyan Kendra Award ICAR: In order to recognize outstanding institutional performance by Krishi Vigyan Kendras, which have run for a minimum period of five years, three awards of Rupees 1,00,000 each are given away every year.

Dr. Rajendra Prasad Puruskar for Technical Books in Hindi in the Field of Agriculture and Allied Sciences: To provide incentive and recognition to the Indian writers/authors to write standard Hindi work in agriculture and allied sciences. Eight awards of Rupees 50,000 each are given to an individual as well as team of authors once in two years.

Important Books on Watershed Management

Crop Management under Rainfed and Irrigated Conditions By S.S. Singh. Kalyani Publishers, Ludhiana.

Cropping System Research By R.S. Dixit, Kalyani Publisher.

Cropping System, Theory and Practice By B.N. Chatterjee, S.I Maiti and B.K. Mandal. Oxford & IBH pub. Pvt. Ltd., New Delhi, Bombay, Calcutta.

Crops and Weather By S. Venkataraman and A. Krishnan, I.C.A.R., New Delhi.

Desertification and its Control By I.C.A.R., New Delhi.

Ecology and Environment By P.D. Sharma, Rastogi pub., Shivaji Road, Meerut-250002..

General Climatology By Howard J. Critchfield, Prentice Hall of India, Pvt. Ltd., New Delhi.

Handbook of Agriculture By I.C.A.R., New Delhi.

Introduction to Agrometeorology By H.S. Mavi. Oxford & IBH publishhing Co. Pvt. Ltd., New Delhi.

Irrigation of Field Crops-Principles and practices By 5.5. Prihar and B.S. Sandhu I.C.A.R., New Delhi.

Irrigation principles and Practices By Vaughn E. Hansen; Orson W. Israelsen & Glen E. Stringham. John Wiley & Sons, New York.

Irrigation-Theory and Practice By A.M. Michael. Vikas pub. House Pvt. Ltd., New Delhi-110014.

Manual of Soil and Water Conservation Practices in India. CSWCR&TI (ICAR), Dehradun. Gil, N. (1985).

Manures and Fertilizers By K.S, Yawalkar; J.P. Agarwal and S. Bokde. Agri-Horticultural pub. House, Nagpur-440010, India.

Modem Techniques of Raising Field Crops By Chhidda Singh. Oxford & IBH pub. Co. Pvt. Ltd., New Delhi.

Natural Resource Management for Agricultural Production in India. ISSS, New Delhi. J.S.P. Yadav, G.B. Singh (2000).

Physiological Aspects of Dryland Farming By U.S. Gupta. Oxford & IBH pub. Co. Pvt. Ltd., New Delhi.

Principles & practices of Agronomy By S.S. Singh. Kalyani publishers, New Delhi & Ludhiana.

Principles of Agronomy By S. Sankaran and V.T. Subbiahmudaliar. The Bangalore Printing & Pub. Co. Ltd., Bangalore-560018.

Principles of Agronomy. Kalyani Publisher, New Delhi. S.R. Reddy (2004).

Principles of Agroonomy By T. Yellamanda Reddy & G.H. Sankara Reddy. Kalyani publishers, Ludhiana (India).

Principles of Plant Nutrition By K. Mengel and E.A. Kirk by. International Potash Institute, Bern, Switzerland.

Soil and Water Conservation Research in India By V.V. Dhruva Narayana. I.C.A.R., New Delhi.

Soil and Water Conservation Research in India. ICAR, New Delhi. Dhruva Narayan, V.V. (1993).

Soil and Water Conservation Research. ICAR, New Delhi. Tejwani, K.G., Gupta, S.K. and Mathur, H.N. (1975).

Soil Erosion and Conservation, by RPC Morgan. John Wiley & Sons, Inc New York, US.

Soil Fertility and Fertilizers By Samuel L. Tisdale; Werner L. Nelson & James D. Beaton. Macmillan publishing Co., 866, Third Avenue, New York-10022.

Technologies for wasteland Development By I.P. Abrol & V.V.Dhurva Narayana. I.C.A.R., New Delhi.

Text book of Soil Science By T.D. Biswas and S.K. Mukherjee. Tata McGraw-Hill pub. Co. Ltd. New Delhi.

The Nature and Properties of Soils By Nyle C. Brady. Macmillan publishing Co., New York. & Collier Macmillan publishers, London.

Water Harvesting and Recycling: Indian Experience. CSWCRTI, Dehradun, India. J.S. Samra, V.N Sharda & A.K. Sikka (1996).

Watershed Management for Drought Mitigation. ICAR, New Delhi. Dhruvanarayan, V.V., Singh, R.P., Bhardwaj, S.P., Sarma, S.B., Sikka, A.K., Vitta, K.P.R. and Das, S.K. (1987).

Watershed Management for Sustainable Agriculture. Agrobios, Jodhpur (India). Khan M.A. (2002).

UNITS

Conversion from One Unit to Another more Commonly Used Unit

Distance/length	
Angstrom Unit	10^{-10}meter (10^{-8}cm)
Angstrom Unit	0.1 nanometer
nanometer	10^{-9}meter (10^{-7}cm)
Inch	25.4 millimeter
Foot	0.305 meter
Micron	10^{-6} meter
mile	1.61 kilometer
millimeter	10^{-3} meter
decimeter	10^{-1} meter
Area	
acre	4.05×10^{3} square meter (m^2)
acre	0.405 hectare
acre	4.05×10^{-3} square kilometer
hectare	10^{4} square meter (m^2)
square feet	9.29×10^{-2} square meter
square inch	645 square millimeter (6.45 square centimeter)
square mile	2.59 square kilometer
square kilometer	100 hectare
square kilometer	247 acre
Volume	
Cubic feet	0.028 cubic meter (m^3)
Cubic feet	28 liter (lit)

cubic inch	16.4 cubic centimeter (cm^3)
cubic inch	1.64×10^{-5} cubic meter (m^3)
cubic meter	1000 liter
hectare – meter	10^4 cubic meter (10^7 liter)
hectare -centimeter	100 cubic meter (10^5 liter)
gallon	3.78 liter
quart (liquid)	0.946 liter
ounce (fluid)	2.96×10^{-2} liter
pint (liquid)	0.473 liter
Weight/mass	
ounce	28.4 gram
pound	454 gram
quintal (metric)	10^2 kilogram(kg)
tonne (metric)	10^3 kilogram (kg)
ton (2000 Ib)	907 kilogram (kg)
milligram	10^{-6} kilogram (kg)
centigram	10^{-5} kilogram (kg)
Rate	
gallon per acre	9.35 liter per hectare
pound per acre	1.12 kilogram per hectare
pound per acre	1.12×10^{-3} mega gram per hectare (Mg ha^{-1})
pound per bushel	12.87 kilogram per cubic meter (kg m^{-3})
ton (2000 Ib) per acre	2.24 mega gram per hectare,
Density	
pound per cubic foot	16.02 kilogram per cubic meter (kg m^{-3})

pound per cubic inch	2.77×10^4 kilogram per cubic meter (kg m^{-3})
gram per cubic centimeter	megagram per cubic meter (Mg m^{-3})
	1000 kilogram per cubic meter (kg m^{-3})
	tonne (metric) per cubic meter (t m^{-3})
Pressure/Force	
atmosphere	0.101 megapascal (MPa)
bar	0.1 megapascal (MPa)
bar	0.98692 atmosphere
millibar	100 pascal
dyne	10^{-5} newton (N)
dyne per square centimeter (poise)	0.1 pascal
pound per square foot	47.9 pascal (Pa)
pound per square inch	6.90×10^3 pascal
pascal	Newton per square meter (N m^{-2})
torr	133.32 Newton per square meter (N m^{-2})
one centimeter of water (4°C)	98.06 pascal
one centimeter of mercury (0°C)	1333 pascal
Energy/radiation	
British thermal unit	1.054×10^3 joule
Calorie	4.19 joule

Larngley (Calorie per square centimeter)	4.19 × 10^4 Joules per square meter (J m^{-2})
Curie	3.7 × 10^{10} Becquerel (Bq)
erg	10^{-7} joule
foot-pound	1.36 joule
gauss	10^{-4} tesla (T)
watt	0.2389 calorie per second (cal s^{-1})
horsepower	745.7 watts
horsepower	178.1 calorie per second
Crop Yield	
quintal per hectare	100 kilogram per hectare
gram per square meter	10 kilogram per hectare
metric tonne per hectare	10 quintal per hectare
metric tonne per hectare	892.2 pound per hectare
quintal per acre	0.247 tonne per hectare
Flow	
cubic centimeter per second	0.06 liter per minute
cubic centimeter per second	0.01585 gallon per minute
liter per second	15.85 gallon per minute
cubic foot per minute	0.4719 liter per second
cubic meter per second	1000 liter per second
Others (commonly used)	
degree (angle)	0.01746 radian (rad)
radian	57.27 (degree)

micromole (H_2O) per square centimeter second (transpiration)	180 milligram (H_2O) per square meter second (mg $m^{-2}s^{-1}$)
gram per square decimeter hour (transpiration)	27.8 milligram per square meter second, mg m^{-2} s^{-2}
mile per hour	0.477 meter per second (ms^{-1})
milligram per square decimeter hour (apparent photo-synthesis)	0.0278 milligram per square meter second (mg m^{-2} s^{-1})
milligram per square centimeter second (Transpiration)	10000 milligram per square meter second (mg m^{-2} s^{-1})
millimhos per centimeter	0.1 siemen per meter (sm^{-1})
	desi siemen per meter(dsm^{-1})
rad	0.01 Gy
roentgen	2.58×10^{-4} C (coulomb) kg
square centimeter/gram	0.1 square meter per kilogram
square millimeter/gram	10^{-3} square meter per kilogram
part per million	milligram per koligram (mg kg^{-1})
	10^{-3}millileter per liter
	Milligram per liter
temperature (°F-32) × 5/9	temperature°C
temperature (°C + 273)	temperature K

Some of the Common Parameters and their Unit and Symbol

Parameters	*Unit*	*Symbol*
Area	Square meter	m^2
	Hectare	ha
Specific surface area of soil	Square centimeter per gram	$cm^2\ g^{-1}$
	Square meter per kiligran	$m^2\ g^{-1}$
Bulk density	Gram per cubic centimeter	$g\ cm^{-3}$
	Megagram per cubic meter	$Mg\ m^{-3}$
Electrical conductivity	Deci siemen per meter	dsm^{-1}
Hydraulic conductivuty	Centimeter per hour	$cm\ hr^{-1}$
Infiltration	Meter per day	$m\ day^{-1}$
	Centimeter per hour	$cm\ hr^{-1}$
Concentration	Mol per liter	$mol\ L^{-1}$
	Part Per million	ppm
	Milligram per liter	$mg\ L^{-1}$
	Milliliter per liter	$ml\ L^{-1}$

Parameters	Unit	Symbol
Nutrient concentration	Millimol per kiligram	$m\ mol\ kg^{-1}$
	Gram per kilogram	$g\ kg^{-1}$
Stomatal resistance	Second per meter	$s\ m^{-1}$
Water content	Gram per gram	$g\ g^{-1}$
	Cubic meter per cubic meter	$m^3\ m^{-3}$
Elongation rate (plant)	Millimeter per second	$mm\ s^{-1}$
Thermal conductivity	Joule per meter per second per centigrade	$J\ m^{-1}\ s^{-1}\ {}^{\circ}c^{-1}$
Radiation	Watt per meter square	$w\ m^{-2}$
Wind speed	Meter per second	$m\ s^{-1}$
Vapour flux density	Gram per square meter per second	$g\ m^{-2}\ s^{-1}$
Heat capacity (mass)	Joule per gram per centigrade	$J\ g^{-1}\ {}^{\circ}c^{-1}$
Heat capacity (volume)	Joule per cubic meter per degree centigrade	$J\ m^{-3}\ {}^{\circ}c^{-1}$
Vapour diffusion coefficient	Square meter per second	$m^2\ s^{-1}$
Heat flux density	Watt per square meter	$w\ m^{-2}$

Parameters	Unit	Symbol
Thermal diffusivity	Square meter per second	$m^2\ s^{-1}$
Ion uptake	Mol per kilogram (dry plant tissue) per second	$mol\ kg^{-1}s^{-1}$
Photosynthetic rate	Micromol per square meter per second	$\mu\ mol\ m^{-2}\ s^{-1}$
Plant growth rate	Gram per square meter per day	$g\ m^{-2}\ day^{-1}$
Leaf Area Index (LAI)	Square meter per square meter	$m^2\ m^{-2}$
Cation exchange capacity	Centimol of proton per kilogram	$c\ mol + kg^{-1}$